Books by William Cahn

THE STORY OF PITNEY-BOWES

THE LAUGH MAKERS:
A PICTORIAL HISTORY OF AMERICAN COMEDIANS

EINSTEIN: A PICTORIAL BIOGRAPHY

HAROLD LLOYD'S WORLD OF COMEDY

GOOD NIGHT, MRS. CALABASH:
THE SECRET OF JIMMY DURANTE

THE STORY OF WRITING
(*with Rhoda Cahn*)

LET US DO
YOUR BAKING

Uneeda Biscuit

NATIONAL BISCUIT
COMPANY

Out of
the Cracker Barrel

THE NABISCO STORY
FROM ANIMAL CRACKERS TO ZUZUS

BY

William Cahn

SIMON AND SCHUSTER
New York

This book was commissioned by
the National Biscuit Company.

First Printing

SBN 671-20360-6
Library of Congress Catalog Card Number: 71-84118
Designed by Edith Fowler
Manufactured in the United States of America

Dedicated to
cookie-eating children around the world,
may their numbers increase

FERMENTED CRACKERS.

	Price.
Extra Tea, Hand Packed	$7\frac{1}{2}$
Tea	$7\frac{1}{4}$
Fancy Tea	$7\frac{1}{4}$
Gilt Edge Butter	$6\frac{3}{4}$
Phœnix "	$6\frac{3}{4}$
Star "	$6\frac{1}{4}$
Sponge "	$5\frac{3}{4}$
Wafer "	$6\frac{3}{4}$
Boston, large	$8\frac{1}{4}$

SWEET CRACKERS AND SNAPS.

	Pri
Lemon Biscuit	
Lemon Creams	
Wine Crackers	
Imperial Biscuits	1
Nic-Nac or Cornhills	1
Dominoes	1
Brilliants	1
Oat Meal Crackers	
Sugar "	

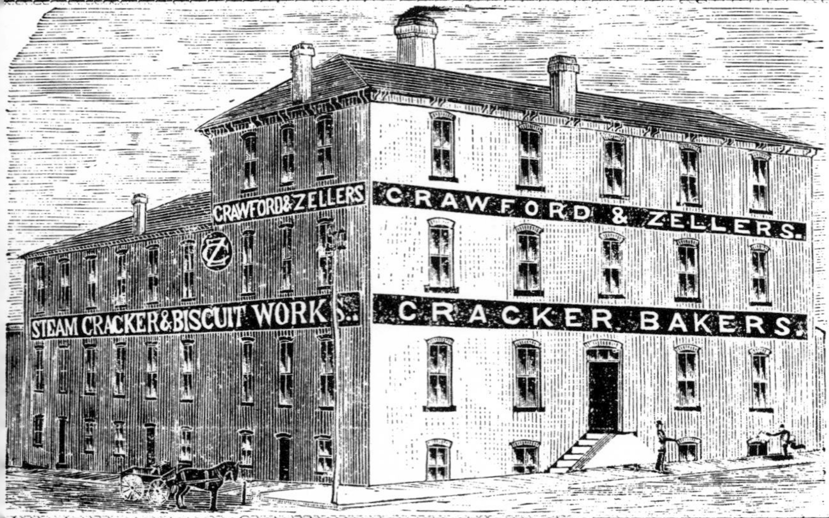
CRAWFORD&ZELLERS
CZ
STEAM CRACKER&BISCUIT WORKS.
CRAWFORD & ZELLERS.
CRACKER BAKERS.

	Price.
Our own make, warranted strictly pure, Mixed and Stick Candy	
Buck Wheat Flour	
Buck Wheat Flour, Self-raising	
Pancake Flour, "	

OYSTER CRACKERS.

	Price.
Monitor	$7\frac{1}{2}$
Extra Pic-Nic	7
Extra Farina	7
Pearl Oyster	$6\frac{3}{4}$
Pearl Oyster, crimped	$6\frac{3}{4}$
Pic-Nic	$6\frac{3}{4}$
Farina	$6\frac{3}{4}$
Oyster	$6\frac{3}{4}$
XXX Oyster	$5\frac{3}{4}$
XX Oyster	$5\frac{1}{2}$
XXX Farina	$5\frac{3}{4}$
XX Farina	$5\frac{1}{2}$
Gilt Edge Oyster	$6\frac{3}{4}$
Cracker Meal, bulk	7
Cracker Meal, 1 lb. pkgs	$8\frac{1}{2}$

FINE JUMBLES AND CAKES.

	Pri
Assorted Jumbles	1
Lemon "	1
Strawberry "	1
Cocoanut "	1
Letters	1
Menagerie	1
Cracknells	1
Almond Macaroons	4
Cocoanut Macaroons	4
Fruit Biscuit, plain	1
Fruit Biscuit, iced	1
Lemon Drops	1

Contents

Introduction

THE NEXT TIME you pick up a gingersnap, saltine, graham cracker or sugar wafer, pause a moment.

You are holding the descendant of a long line of pioneer ancestors who helped feed the crews who sailed our ships, sustained our frontiersmen, and provided nourishment for a growing country.

The men who made those early biscuits toiled at hot ovens, long-handled peels in their hands. For decades small local cracker bakers had received their flour from the mill in wooden barrels. They often economized by using the same barrels for shipping crackers to stores in their area.

Over the years the cracker barrel, along with the general store, became an American institution and a symbol of enterprise, democracy, hospitality. Families were nourished from it. Gossip was exchanged over it. The cat slept in it.

It was Adolphus W. Green, father of the Uneeda Biscuit and one of the founders of the National Biscuit Company, who finally took the cracker out of the barrel. He also stripped the symbol of its sentimentality and exposed it as an unsanitary hangover from frontier days.

Speaking for his young company, Green announced, "We propose to get business by selling better goods . . . Instead of broken, soggy crackers in bulk, stored in old barrels and boxes, we are to supply fresh, whole crackers in triple-wrapped packages."

In 1899 these were revolutionary ideas. Green put them into action with fierce determination. The National Biscuit Company embarked on a packaging and promotional upheaval which led to the creation of "brand names" and opened the way for modern supermarkets.

Fortune magazine claimed that the National Biscuit Company "did almost as much as the introduction of canned foods before it, and the invention of the electric refrigerator after it to change the techniques of modern merchandising."

Today the National Biscuit Company operates some sixty-eight plants: twenty-nine in the United States, ten in Canada and twenty-nine overseas.

About eight out of ten families in the United States consume one or more of National Biscuit's approximately 300 products. Lorna Doone, Oreo, Ritz, Barnum's Animal Crackers, ZuZu and scores more have become household words.

Practically every grocery store in the country is a customer.

The story of how this was accomplished is a piece of industrial Americana worth knowing. It began in New England many years ago . . .

Out of

the Cracker Barrel

The Passion
of Adolphus W. Green

THERE WAS something about John Henry Green, who arrived in Boston in 1822 from northern Ireland, that attracted Jane Ryan. It certainly was not his money, because he did not have any. Perhaps it was the fact that Green, a bootmaker by trade, had respect for learning.

Jane Ryan was a determined young woman who had contempt for superstition and reverence for books. She had a sharp tongue, and she used it to distinguish herself from her uneducated neighbors, many of whom were suspicious of learning even to the point of boycotting schools.

In 1825 Jane and John were married. Eleven children were born to them. The last, Adolphus Williamson, arrived one cold night in January 1843.

The infant grew into a lanky, curly-haired, dour-faced boy whose passion for books and learning delighted his mother.

Down the street from John Green's bootmaking shop was the home of Wendell Phillips, son of the first mayor of Boston and powerful foe of slavery. Another neighbor was Theodore Parker, famous crusading clergyman. No one in Boston had a greater passion for learning than Parker or was more impatient with ignorance or more confident of the correctness of his views. The Parker home with its enormous library, one of the largest in Boston, was open to all.

When Dolph Green was thirteen years old, the famous abolition-

◀ *The youthful Adolphus W. Green*

ist John Brown visited Parker's home and successfully pleaded at an all-night session with Parker and five other Massachusetts men for funds to carry forward his struggle against slavery. Soon the nation would be at war over this issue. In the days ahead Parker was to work in his library with a Bible at one hand and a gun at the other.

The era was crowded with such hardheaded, independent-minded advocates of many points of view jostling each other for supremacy. But though the city teemed with ideas from waterfront to Common, it was formal schooling, Mrs. Green thought, that the children needed most. John Green had died, and Jane ran a boardinghouse to support her family. Somehow she managed to have them all get to school. When Dolph was only five years old, he trudged half a dozen blocks to primary school on Franklin Street, just opposite the Holy Cross Roman Catholic Cathedral, where the family attended church. This huge edifice was built just after the turn of the century as the result of a popular subscription whose first contributor was John Adams, President of the United States.

At thirteen Dolph was tall, serious-minded, with a devotion to hard work that was to become almost a mania in future years. He won the coveted Franklin Medal Scholarship Award given annually since 1792 in Boston schools.

Adolphus showed such promise that his mother felt that he should continue his studies. She arranged for him to attend the famous Boston Latin School, located on Warren Avenue not far from where they lived. The boys at Boston Latin had an advantage in getting into Harvard, which was just across the Charles River in Cambridge.

Dolph did well at Boston Latin, earned a prize at "declamation," and was admitted to Harvard at the age of sixteen "without conditions," which meant that he had passed all his entrance examinations satisfactorily.

When Green entered Harvard in July 1859, there were only five hundred undergraduates in the entire college. Students were required to study Greek, Hebrew, Latin and Shakespeare. The influence of the famous Swiss scientist Louis Agassiz was still potent throughout the college, as was that of his Darwinian opponent, Asa Gray.

Green did well at Harvard. "Hard work is the only thing that I do not get tired of," he wrote.

It was a dramatic year in the history of the country. Green had not been at college twelve months before he read of John Brown's insurrection at Harpers Ferry. A year later Lincoln was elected

President. In April 1861 Fort Sumter was fired upon and the war began. Some undergraduates volunteered in the Union forces, but most continued their studies.

In July 1863 Adolphus Williamson Green graduated with a bachelor's degree. He stood twenty-sixth in a class of a hundred and twenty students. His mother and most of his sisters and brothers were present to celebrate the occasion.

Typically, Adolphus had his future well planned. "I shall teach school for two or three years," he said, "then I shall probably study law."

Although Harvard had a famous law school, it was customary for many aspiring lawyers—especially if they lacked wealthy parents —to prepare for the bar by reading under the guidance of an established lawyer or law firm. But well-known firms had waiting lists of applicants, and it was not always easy for a young man to obtain the necessary introductions.

Green's plan was to move to New York as soon as he could obtain a position that would sustain him. So, after a year of teaching school at Groton, Massachusetts, he accepted a job as assistant librarian of the Mercantile Library Association of the City of New York. The association was founded in 1820 by a group of prominent merchants, primarily for their clerks, "to promote the spirit of useful inquiry" and "to facilitate mutual intercourse among its members."

There was an obvious need for such educational facilities. Thousands of poor, uneducated immigrants from nations abroad were arriving at Boston and New York. Jobs were hard to find, and lack of education was a demoralizing handicap. The association sought to encourage independent reading and study.

Twenty-two-year-old Adolphus W. Green was glad to be in New York where museums, the theater and books were plentiful. He lived with an older sister, Mary Jane, at her home on 23rd Street, at the time considered far uptown. He was quiet, studious, ate little, often skipping meals when absorbed in reading.

The library comprised more than forty thousand volumes shelved in a large elliptically shaped chamber, which extended through two floors of the building. While the public library system had started earlier, it had not expanded rapidly. The Mercantile Library Association therefore performed a unique service in supplying books for those who, like Green himself, had a passion for learning.

Among the eight thousand members of the association who supported the library were such famous figures as Henry J. Raymond, founder of *The New York Times*; Horace Greeley, editor of *The New York Tribune*; Charles Francis Adams; and William Cullen Bryant.

Green did his work well. Eight months later he was promoted to the position of head librarian. But Green had not lost sight of his initial desire to study law. He had made inquiries as to what law firm was most eagerly sought by aspiring young students. The biggest and most influential firm in New York was Evarts, Southmayd & Choate at 49 Wall Street. Green decided that in one way or another he would become affiliated with this firm. So he added his name to the long list and waited.

More than a year passed. At length he was offered the position of chief clerk. He promptly tendered his resignation to the library board, which wished well the young man "who had so capably filled the position of librarian for two years, and to whom the Association is indebted for so much of the good condition, excellent arrangement and efficiency of the library."

In the spring of 1868 Adolphus W. Green began work in the city's busiest law office. The firm included some of the nation's most prominent legal talent. One of the senior members was William Evarts, who was lawyer for President Andrew Johnson in his famous impeachment trial.

But Evarts was in Washington most of the time as United States Attorney General and later as Secretary of State. Adolphus Green did not see very much of him. Nor did he get to know another distinguished member of the firm, the brilliant Joseph H. Choate who was to become American Ambassador to the Court of St. James.

It was a third and somewhat less prominent member whom Green was to know best and whose influence on the young lawyer was to be most permanent. He was Charles F. Southmayd, another well-known lawyer of the era.

Gruff, short-tempered, Southmayd had no interest outside the law. He was completely devoted to his work, thorough in whatever he attempted. He had little or no social life and few friends. He dressed in old-fashioned clothes and walked rather than rode wherever he could. Whenever he signed his name, it was always, "Charles F. Southmayd in person."

Southmayd had a genius for law and was a lasting influence on the young lawyers who studied under him. He was one of the two men in Green's career who contributed not only to his legal outlook, but to the development of his personality.

This was an era when a prospective lawyer did not take formal bar examinations. Tests were mostly oral, and of a diverse and often unconventional nature. Sometimes the applicant was examined in open court, sometimes in chambers, sometimes in hotel rooms. Questions that justices would ask young law applicants were often comprehensive and searching; but on some occasions only one question would be asked, and sometimes just a good look at the applicant might be sufficient.

Having worked for four years in the leading law firm in the United States, Green had no difficulty in passing the bar examination. The more serious question before him in 1873 was where to set up practice. It was a depression year. Jobs were scarce. Thousands of people were hungry. There could scarcely have been a less favorable time for a young man to enter law practice. Nor were things better back home in Massachusetts. In Boston there were some thirty thousand people out of work and in many industries operations had been completely suspended.

Venerable Horace Greeley, the bewhiskered newspaper editor who was sometimes referred to as the "conscience of the nation," had been giving sage advice for many years to all who would listen: "If any young man is about to commence in the world, with little in his circumstances to pre-possess him in favor of one section above another, we say to him publicly and privately, go to the west; there your capacities are sure to be appreciated and your industry and energy rewarded."

Green, like many other young men, set his eyes to the west. Although the Chicago fire of 1871 had demolished most of the city, reports told of great opportunities. There was a need for almost everything and everybody who could contribute to the rebuilding. "It is easier to raise dollars in Chicago," one magazine stated, "than cents in New York."

Adolphus found Chicago, a city of almost 300,000 people, trying to rebuild itself; rough, tough, uncultured, without literary tradition. Philip D. Armour, the shrewd red-whiskered head of a growing meat-packing business, expressed the philosophy of other fabulously successful Chicago citizens of the day: "Of course I have no other interest in life but my business . . . I do not love the money; what I do love is the getting of it, the making of it . . . I do not read, I do not take any part in politics . . . but in my counting-house, I am in my element." It was reported that more than two hundred men in Chicago had amassed fortunes that were over the million-dollar mark.

Green, long used to poverty, was bent on making his fortune. But, because of his early upbringing, he was also interested in other matters: literature, painting, the theater. The crudeness of Chicago at first repelled him. Art and books were often looked upon with suspicion. The theater was condemned by preachers and the more respectable of the citizenry. The community was more inclined to be interested in Buffalo Bill than in an opera performance. Only the independent-minded millionaire merchant Potter Palmer and his beautiful, socially prominent wife were confident and powerful enough to dare to invite Madame Sarah Bernhardt to a reception in their home when she was on tour in the 1880s. For anyone less influential such an act would have created a scandal.

As might be expected, the booming frontier town was a happy hunting ground for lawyers. Green shortly found a law partner in Michael W. Robinson, a Missouri born farmer and Yale graduate. Both men were keen students of Latin, Greek and the classics. Both were active Democrats in politics. Both were great lovers of books. Between them they built up a promising practice.

Green developed a love for the practice of law, especially for the time he spent in the courthouse. His reputation as a brilliant trial lawyer spread. One of his friends was a big mustached post-office contractor named Charles Walsh. He had a daughter, Esther, a twenty-eight-year-old brunette. Although Green, eight years her senior, was looked upon by many as a confirmed bachelor, he surprised them all by announcing his engagement.

On the evening of July 3, 1879, an elegant wedding took place at St. James Catholic Church on Prairie Avenue, the marriage of Esther Walsh and Adolphus W. Green. Among those present were two of Adolphus' spinster sisters, Minnie and Nellie, who came all the way from Boston. Jane Green, his mother, was too ill to make the trip and died not long after. Typically, at Green's request, the ceremony conducted by Father P. W. Riordan was brief. The bride and bridegroom remained in their new home on fashionable Indiana Avenue for their honeymoon because Adolphus had legal work that needed to be done.

The next few years were busy ones. In twelve months the first of eight children was born. Times were difficult; money was scarce.

In addition to his regular practice, Green accepted the position of attorney for the Chicago Board of Trade, which brought him not only prestige but additional income.

He had little time for social activities. The only organization in which he was active was the famous Sunset Club of Chicago, a unique all-male businessmen's institution that met at dinner every other Thursday for short talks about current events. Here Green met people destined for prominence in the years ahead: Lyman J. Gage, who was to become president of the First National Bank and later Secretary of the Treasury in the McKinley administration; Victor Lawson, controversial Chicago editor; Carter Harrison, mayor of Chicago; Clarence Darrow, one of the nation's outstanding criminal lawyers; John P. Altgeld, who became governor of Illinois.

The most important influence on Adolphus W. Green was his friendship with William C. Goudy, founder of Chicago's Bar Association and one of the outstanding lawyers in the nation. In 1886, when he first became associated with the slightly built, heavily bearded Goudy, he was forty-three years old, some twenty years Goudy's junior. But the two lawyers had much in common. Goudy's great patience made a lasting impression on Green, as well as his perseverance and his singular thoroughness in everything he undertook. But like Southmayd before him, Goudy, though exceptionally able and successful, had his shortcomings. He had a frigid demeanor. He rarely smiled. He made many business acquaintances but few close personal friends. When he entered his office, he rarely spoke to anyone. But Green understood him. The two worked together well.

No lawyer excelled Goudy in the power of cold analysis, close logic, clear and cogent methods of arraying facts, and his skill of expressing in a few words the most involved legal problem. There was no practitioner in Illinois who had more cases before the State Supreme Court. Many were tried before the United States Supreme Court as well, either by himself or by his younger partner Adolphus W. Green.

Goudy was also a recognized leader of the Democratic Party in Illinois. To him was to go credit for nominating Grover Cleveland, the Democratic candidate in the Presidential election year of 1892. Green, a delegate-at-large to the National Convention, which took place in Chicago in June of 1892, made one of the seconding speeches for Cleveland, and cast Illinois' forty-eight votes for Cleveland's nomination.

In 1892 Goudy was to die suddenly. "Most people thought him cold-hearted," Green declared sadly. "His manner was not cordial, and there was none of the hail-fellow-well-met about him. But there was no man who could say less and do more to serve a friend."

Well before Goudy's death Adolphus Green had become a leading Chicago attorney, known even beyond the confines of the midwest. In addition to his law practice, he was also engaged in an area which increasingly was to occupy his time and attention.

This special interest started when a committee of prominent bakery owners from communities throughout the region came to his office and sought his assistance.

Green rolled back in his armchair as he listened attentively. It was an extraordinary occasion for these traditionally independent-minded men were not accustomed to confiding in one who was not of their industry. But it was known among businessmen of the day that the services of a capable lawyer were often necessary to solve certain complex problems. Green's growing reputation had prompted the group to seek him out.

A new wind was blowing in the last decade of the nineteenth century. Giant business corporations were being organized and achieving phenomenal success, sometimes almost overnight. The bakers, accustomed to traditional methods and ways of doing business, realized that they must change with the times. But how?

This was the question the bakers put to Adolphus Green who, as he listened in silence, wondered about his qualifications to serve them.

Downtown Chicago as A. W. Green knew it   ▸

Crackers

with Kerosene Flavor

SOME OF the most prominent bakers in the country were in the delegation that visited Adolphus W. Green at his LaSalle Street office: David F. Bremner, proprietor of the famous Bremner Bakery in Chicago; F. L. Sommer, owner of the nationally known Sommer-Richardson Baking Company in St. Joseph, Missouri, whose Premium Saltine won a prize at a country fair as far back as 1876; Louis D. Dozier, one of the nation's pioneer cracker bakers from St. Louis, Missouri; S. S. Marvin, who had worked in his father's Pittsburgh bakery since his discharge from the Union Army, and later introduced the Oyster Cracker; Benjamin F. Crawford, one of a long line of Ohio bakers, who was already a cracker manufacturer when young Green first began studying law in New York.

Nearly every town of any size in the United States had one or more cracker bakeries. Buying raw materials, baking and selling were done in comparatively small quantities. Since crackers and cookies were perishable and there were no facilities for keeping them fresh, it was necessary that deliveries be made quickly. The method of delivery was usually by horse and wagon, which restricted the territory covered by one bakery to the immediate area. Even then it was almost impossible, with existing organization and arrangements, to preserve the freshness of the crackers from bakery to dealer.

The quality of the product, too, was subject to great variations.

◀ *When cookies and crackers were sold from boxes and barrels*

Crackers might vary in size, texture or taste. Production plagued the bakers.

The most successful among them had learned to construct some machines to promote baking efficiency. They had, for example, converted their ovens to continuous firing. But most of the stages of the baking process were not mechanized. The assembly line was still unknown. Packaging, distribution, promotion methods—all lingered behind the needs of the rapidly changing times.

And it was indeed an era of change. The country was moving from a predominantly rural to an urban economy. The most fundamental habits of an entire people were in transition: eating, working, raising children, managing a home. The factory was becoming an important influence on the community and so were countless mechanical contrivances, from the telephone to the gramophone. Refrigeration was about to launch a revolution of its own in home and store.

Railroads transported food materials from farms to cities with unprecedented speed. Cities were mushrooming, attracting millions of people from the countryside as well as waves of immigrants from abroad.

Increasing export demand for wheat hastened the opening of the prairies. The steel plow helped break the plains. The fence problem was solved by the invention of barbed wire.

Women in cities found it more convenient and even economical to buy at the store the things they once had made at home. Many of the characteristics of the era were summed up by one word: "bigness." "Bigness in operations, bigness in the number of workers employed, bigness in profits," was the way one writer put it.

The problems the bakers described to Green reflected the impact of these changing times on their business. For generations each bakery had depended upon local good will. But, as new means of transportation made national distribution possible, the bakers found themselves harnessed to outdated methods and machines. How to keep apace with the times? It was evident that no one bakery could do it alone. The machine age had overtaken them, but they did not know what to do about it. Perhaps Green, sophisticated in corporate methods, could help?

Green did more than that. In the following weeks he spent hours studying the baking industry. It was a new world to him. He read everything he could find, spoke to everyone who seemed to know. He learned that biscuit baking was one of the oldest industries in the world, going back as far as the Stone Age. He read how it developed from Rome, through the age of feudalism, the European guilds, through Elizabethan England, and came to America along with the first colonists.

In the early days in America commercial baking was done on a minor scale, limited by the fact that most baking was done by the housewife in the home. The early biscuit business in the United States was not even recognized as an industry in the United States Patent Office. Registered inventions having to do with baking were classified under the arts.

Those were the days when bread was the mainstay of the dinner table; no meal was served without it. People were not afraid of starchy foods.

Women who did not bake their own bread ran the risk of being considered lazy. When a bride settled down at home following her honeymoon, she would find the various implements and ingredients for baking awaiting her, inevitable presents from relatives and friends. Nor was home cooking confined to bread; it also included gingersnaps, biscuits, macaroons, tea cakes, shortbread.

Although most of the baking was done in the home, in most communities there were small commercial bakeries. They were usually divided into two categories: bread; and crackers, biscuits and cookies. Frequently a single commercial bakery not only baked bread, crackers, cookies and biscuits, but also produced confectionery.

The baker worked from sunrise to sunset, mixing and shaping the dough, firing the huge brick oven and baking by its searing heat. He usually sold his wares in a shop in front of his bake room. The earliest bakers in America baked only on order. But as the colonial period ended, many bakers began to produce for the market. And, as the nation expanded, this relatively small operation expanded, too.

Many commercial bakers supplied products to sailing vessels. Those who sailed the ships needed a type of bread or biscuit that would not get stale or rancid or disintegrate during long voyages. The answer to this was hardtack or ship's bread. Other names were also used: army bread, captain's biscuit, cabin bread, pilot biscuit. These were handmade hard-baked biscuits, often produced under crude conditions, from light flour and a little moisture. The dough was pounded very tight to produce an almost white biscuit, so hard it often required a hammer to break it.

It was natural that bakeries supplying hardtack for sailing ships would be located in or around the port of Boston, where Green was born. The first cracker bakery in the United States of which there are trustworthy records was that of Theodore Pearson, established in 1792 at Newburyport, Massachusetts, at the mouth of the Merrimack River. Pearson's specialty was pilot bread or ship biscuit. In the Pearson bakery the dough was kneaded by hand with each biscuit rolled out and shaped separately. Then, with the aid of a long-handled shovel called a "peel," the biscuits were placed one by one on the floor of the old-fashioned, primitive oven, preheated by fire in the baking chamber.

A few years later, in 1801, another Massachusetts community, the town of Milton located six miles south of Boston, became the site of the second pioneer cracker bakery in the nation's history. It was owned by Josiah Bent, a former Yankee ship's captain who went into the baking business with the help of his family after retiring from a career at sea.

The captain's wife and children did the baking while the captain himself traveled about on horseback selling the products of his ovens which he carried in saddlebags. In addition to producing ship biscuit and hardtack, Captain Bent also introduced a new type of biscuit, the first plain, unsweetened biscuit other than pilot bread, ship bread or hardtack. The new products were called "crackers," probably because of the cracking noise they made when eaten.

Bent's original crackers were unleavened dough made only with water and flour. Since he rolled his dough many more times than his predecessors, he produced a fine grain which is characteristic of the cracker that, in some areas, still bears his name.

Encouraged by the success of Captain Bent, other bakers around the Boston area soon followed in his footsteps. A third major cracker bakery located in what is now Arlington, Massachusetts, was started in 1805 by Artemas Kennedy who manufactured crackers there and later in the nearby town of Milton. Kennedy did all of his work by hand. One by one, the crackers were tossed onto the hot floor of a Dutch oven. Boys in the Kennedy household would learn the art of cracker making almost as soon as they could walk.

The first crackers made by Kennedy were probably similar to the Pearson pilot bread and Bent's water crackers. But Kennedy introduced something new: the famous Kennedy Commons. These crackers were developed in the 1850's in Cambridgeport, Massachusetts, by a grandson, also named Artemas. It was here that "sponge" dough, raised by leavening, made its first appearance in commercial baking in this country. The term "sponge" is used to designate any cracker which relies upon the process of fermentation produced by yeast with flour and water.

In 1845, for the first time, the Kennedy bakery astonished towns-people by actually employing steam to run its machinery, replacing hand or horsepower. Production was so great that a fleet of wagons was needed to carry Kennedy crackers to towns within a radius of forty miles from Cambridgeport. Large shipments even went as far as California to feed miners prospecting for gold.

In the 1840's there were only five kinds of biscuits known in this country: the original pilot bread, the cold-water cracker, the soft or butter cracker, the square soda cracker, and the round sugar biscuit. The last three differed from the others in that they contained shortening—butter or lard—and were the result of a fermented dough. This fermentation, or raising, greatly lightened the texture of the cracker. In consequence, the crackers proved immensely popular.

Sweet crackers or cookies were slower to be made commercially available. Sweet biscuits that were imported from England helped develop the sweet tooth of America. As the demand grew, new machines were conceived by American bakers. By 1869 a brand-new type of oven—called the "reel" oven—began to replace the old-fashioned stationary "peel" oven that had been used by commercial bakers for generations. But the weight and requirements for floor space of the peel oven were great. Also, precise control of baking temperatures was impossible. If the peel oven was left idle too long, there was a danger of flash heats which resulted in excessive temperatures. The new reel oven replaced the stationary peel oven with a new moving type of machinery that was soon to revolutionize the baking industry and help it keep up with the expanding needs of the nation.

For its period the reel oven was certainly a marvel of ingenuity. It was usually built on the ground floor and basement* of the bakery building and worked on the principle of the Ferris wheel. On the ground floor portions of dough were deposited on the shelves that were suspended from the periphery of the revolving wheel. Each

---

* "Basement baking led to much criticism of the industry because it fostered unsanitary baking conditions," William G. Panschar points out in his *Baking in America.* "But basement baking was considered necessary because of the excessive weight of the huge ovens and the use of a gravity feeding system."

batch passed through the basement oven, whose temperatures could be accurately maintained. It was possible to control the cooking process by the speed with which the reel oven rotated. This reel oven made continuous cracker baking possible with the resulting increase in economy and more exact control of quality.

The Civil War upset much of America's economy. Its emergency demands brought changes in the industrial life of the nation, including baking. Soldiers needed food that would resist spoilage, dampness and rough handling. An unprecedented demand for hardtack therefore taxed the capacity of the cracker industry and helped speed wider use of the reel oven. According to Bruce Catton, in *Mr. Lincoln's Army*, "The hardtack was the great staple. It was a solid cracker, some three inches square, nearly half an inch thick; solid, hard, nourishing, and—by surviving testimony—good enough to eat when it was fresh, which wasn't always the case. Nine or ten of these slabs constituted a day's ration."

Many Union soldiers wrote home about hardtack that sometimes had to be broken with a hammer or the butt of a rifle before it could be chewed. Sometimes soldiers referred to it as "sheet-iron crackers" or "teeth dullers." This "portable" bread, however, did much to stimulate the growth of commercial biscuit and cracker production. The demand for such products, which, unlike cookies, had never been baked at home to any great extent, increased. A boom in cracker selling was on. Many bakeries, with reel ovens used exclusively, were built during the postwar period.

But with success came problems. America was expanding at an unprecedented rate. The frontier was disappearing; immigration was on the increase; the industrial revolution had arrived. And the baking industry, twenty-five years after the advent of the reel oven, found it difficult to keep up. Transportation, refrigeration, communication —all had created completely new demands. Local bakeries were not capable of supplying the needs of the times.

This was the background that Adolphus Green studied so carefully. Unlike the men who owned and managed the bakeries, Green had the advantage of viewing the situation as an outsider. For example, he traced the progress of a biscuit from bakery to general store. These stores were invariably crowded centers of business with miscellaneous goods for sale on counters, under counters, on shelves, hanging from ceilings, in cellars. Poorly ventilated, pungent with dozens of odors, the general store usually carried a wide range of articles from dry goods to candy, cigars, cutlery, groceries, tobacco, patent medicines, sugar, molasses, turpentine, pickled mackerel, calico, lamp oil, buggy whips, hardware, brooms and almost anything else that was needed in households of the day.

It was a combination drug, dry goods, liquor, hardware and grocery store. Most of the goods sold arrived in bulk and had to be cut, poured or measured before they could be made available to the customer. The merchant would scoop out rice or coffee from a tin; he would cut off a slice of tobacco; or he would count out a dozen biscuits. It was not until after the Civil War that paper bags were widely used. Before that the grocer improvised his own container for each purchase from a folded sheet of paper.

The store was generally heated in the wintertime by a cast-iron potbellied stove. In the summertime it was a popular gathering place for swarms of flies and other insects. It was often more than a place merely to make purchases. It was also a social center. In addition to housing the local post office, it was a gathering spot for gossips, for people who wanted a place to play checkers, to warm themselves by the stove, or just to nap undisturbed. There were "regular setters" and others who just dropped by occasionally.

If anything symbolized the general store and the traditional method of carrying on business, it was the cracker barrel. Individual packaging was unknown; crackers came in barrels or boxes that were placed on the store's floor, available to customers. The first customers would get the freshest crackers. As the barrel emptied, the crackers would become more broken, soggy and dirty. Frequently the housewife would open her container at home to find that the crackers she had just purchased were not only stale and dirty, but tainted with the odor and flavor of the adjacent kerosene tank.

The storekeeper might keep a cheesecloth covering over the cracker barrel, but the contents were always available to the unsanitary fingers of visitors. The clerk would invariably handle the crackers as he doled them out to the customer.

Screens did not come into use until the end of the Civil War, so the cracker barrel was a favorite spot for insects. Other living creatures would also make open barrels their homes. A customer might protest to the merchant that mice were living in the cracker barrel. "That's impossible," one wag of the times is reported to have said. "Mice could not possibly live in my cracker barrel. Because the cat sleeps there every night."

When the boxes or barrels in which the crackers had originally been shipped were empty, they were returned to the baker and used over and over again until they were worn out or became too filthy for use.

Because the grocer had to buy crackers and biscuits by the barrel or large box, he could hardly dispose of more than two or three kinds at one time. Nor did he have the ready cash to make a greater investment.

Green paid personal visits to grocery stores to observe how baked goods were sold. It did not require much study, however, for him to come to the conclusion that the cracker barrel was a symbol of an industry that had failed to keep up with the times.

Green saw at once that the biscuit business was ripe for unification. There was already a movement reported in the New York-New England area for the combination of bakeries in that region. So, in 1890 with the guidance of Green, a sizable number of baking firms, mostly in the midwest, joined to become the American Biscuit & Manufacturing Company, with offices in Chicago. The new company's first president was the reputable Chicago baker, David F. Bremner, who had led the delegation that met with Green months before. Included were such well-known bakeries as the Aldridge Bakery in Chicago, with four ovens; the Bremner Bakery in Chicago, eight ovens; Carpenter and Underwood in Milwaukee, five ovens; the Dozier Baking Company in St. Louis, seven ovens; the Langeles Bakery in New Orleans, four ovens; the Loose Brothers in Kansas City, four ovens; the Sommer-Richardson Bakery in St. Joseph, Missouri, three ovens. Altogether, the American Biscuit Company had some eighty-eight reel ovens, ten flat ovens, and approximately forty bakeries in Iowa, Illinois, New York, Maryland, Tennessee, Wisconsin, Michigan, Colorado, Missouri, Nebraska, Montana, Louisiana and Texas.

Other bakers now also sought Green's aid. A short time after the American Biscuit & Manufacturing Company was organized, Green provided the leadership for the establishment of the United States Baking Company with Sylvester S. Marvin, prominent Philadelphia baker, as president. The principal bakeries of the United States Baking Company were located in Ohio, Indiana and western Pennsylvania.

The demand for able counselors who could help corporations to merge was spreading. "In every industry, in every line and brand of trade, great consolidations and amalgamations were planned . . .

It was the great opportunity of the promoter," stated *The Commercial & Financial Chronicle*. In 1891 a group of Detroit companies needed assistance in amalgamation, and the services of Green were requested. He traveled to Detroit and assisted in the consolidation of a number of companies that formed the American Radiator Company, the biggest radiator maker in the country, with large financial resources at its disposal. For his services he charged a fee of $100.

Green had no intention of becoming a professional promoter of business combinations or "trusts" as they were called. His real love was—and continued to be throughout his life—the practice of law. But he became so absorbed in his investigation that he increasingly ignored his regular law practice. He was fortunate by 1892 in establishing a new partnership with Lockwood Honore and Frank Peters —to whom he could turn over his routine business with the knowledge that it would be competently handled.

Honore, the older partner, was a Harvard graduate and a brother of the famous Mrs. Potter Palmer, the celebrated Chicago socialite, art patron and feminist pioneer.

The other member of the firm, diminutive Frank Peters, was of Jewish origin, a balding, frail young man from New York City. Peters had come to Chicago as a boy and worked as a messenger for the firm of Goudy and Green. Adolphus Green was so impressed with Peters' earnestness and dedication that he helped finance his law studies at the Union College of Law in Chicago, where he attended evening classes. Peters was exactly the type of person to win Green's respect. In his own way he was a perfectionist, just as Green was in his. These were the two men who, together with Green, were to make up the firm of Green, Honore & Peters with fashionable offices in the "skyscraper" of the day, the Home Insurance Company Building, in the heart of Chicago's financial district.

But directing and guiding the two baking companies that Green had helped found—especially the American Biscuit & Manufacturing Company—increasingly absorbed his time and energy.

"Largely against my will, I was drawn into this company," Green pointed out. "But as time went on, I became more and more interested in it."

There would be times in the future when Green would regret leaving law for the responsibility of corporate business. But at that very moment another lawyer, whom Green was to know intimately, was enthusiastically adapting himself to high finance.

His name was William H. Moore.

THREE

Go East, Young Lawyer

WILLIAM HENRY MOORE came to Chicago in 1873 from Olympia, Washington, bringing with him a license to practice law and plenty of confidence and energy.

Moore was a large man in all dimensions. Someone described him as "important and at the same time ready to laugh about it." Born in Utica, New York, in 1848, William Moore came from a well-to-do family. His father, Nathaniel Ford Moore, was a highly successful merchant and banker. His mother, Rachel Moore, was a woman of independent character whose mind—as a contemporary put it—"was almost masculine in its exactness and clearness of judgment." She also came from a family of bankers, originating in Connecticut.

Young Moore was educated in a seminary near home and, at the age of eighteen, was admitted to Amherst College. He had finished only three years when, because of an asthmatic condition, he was forced to leave school and seek a climate more favorable to his health. He went West to the frontier town of Eau Claire, Wisconsin, where a year later he began the study of law in the office of the prominent midwestern attorney, William P. Bartlett.

Moore was quick to learn. It took him just two years working as a clerk in Bartlett's office to prepare for and pass the bar examination. Then he was off to seek his fortune in the far west. Moore loved horses, was an excellent horseman, and liked to ride through

◀ *Top, William H. Moore and bottom, James H. Moore*

the wilderness. Arriving in the territory of Washington, he sought to build a law practice in Olympia. But the going was not easy. He kept hearing that Chicago was an exciting city, second in population only to New York. Like Green, he was attracted by reports of opportunities for young professional men in this city which was being rebuilt following the disastrous fire of 1871. So in 1873 he packed his bag and said goodbye to his friends in Washington.

Arriving in Chicago months later, he became a clerk in a small downtown law firm at the very time that Adolphus Green was starting his law practice in an office a few blocks away.

Moore was a young man of great physical energy. Pacing up and down on the ground floor, waiting for the birdcage-like elevator, Moore seemed ready to burst with the momentum of youth. As often as not, he would take to the stairs, three at a time, to beat the elevator to his office floor.

Such youthful drive could not fail to attract the attention of a highly respected and prominent attorney, Edward Alonzo Small, who had offices in the same building. Himself of frail physique and delicate constitution, Small admired energy and strength in others. Needing a clerk, he offered the job to this curly-haired 200-pound human tornado. Moore accepted and quickly made the transfer. Within a year and a half he became a full partner in the firm. A short time after that he married his partner's daughter, Ada.

Ada was a tall dark-haired, animated girl, ten years younger than Moore. At the first meeting he was attracted to her. A whirlwind romance ended in marriage in November 1878. The wedding took place at the fashionable Small residence at 924 Indiana Avenue, not far from the house at 1086 Indiana Avenue where Adolphus W. Green was courting Esther Walsh. It was another—but by no means the last—of a series of coincidences that were to involve these two oddly different men.

The evening ceremony, performed by the Right Reverend Charles Edward Cheney of the Reformed Episcopal Church, was followed by a magnificent supper. Mr. and Mrs. Moore left that evening for a honeymoon in New York. The Moores were to have three children: Edward, Paul, and Hobart, who died at the age of twenty-five.

The firm of Small & Moore was counsel for a number of large corporations in Chicago, including the American Express Company, Adams Express, Merchants Dispatch, and the West Division Railway

Company. Over the years Moore established a reputation as the chief trial lawyer for the firm, although entirely in the civil courts.

The firm was gaining in prominence when, in the winter of 1882, Edward Small died. Shortly thereafter, William Moore formed a new partnership with his brother, James Hobart Moore. James was four years younger than William, even taller but not as heavy. The pair were inseparable in business as well as social life. What James lacked in cool judgment he made up in audacity. This was to prove a serious—even tragic—problem to both of them in the years ahead. Young James studied law for several years in the Small & Moore offices and was admitted to the practice of law in Illinois in 1881. Two years later he married Ada's sister, Lora Small.

As the years passed, the firm of W. H. & J. H. Moore became one of the most successful in the Chicago area, with a practice consisting principally of large business houses, trustees of extensive estates, and corporations such as the Elgin Watch Company, American Express, Adams Express, Inter-Ocean Publishing Company and the Diamond Match Company.

The professional services of William Moore were in increasing demand for the framing of charters, bills of incorporation, and other legal documents. It was inevitable that Moore and Adolphus W. Green would become acquainted in a town the size of nineteenth-century Chicago. But it would have been difficult to find two individuals less akin. Moore was outgoing, gregarious, active in the social community. He loved physical sports, horses, golf, dancing. His active participation in horse shows had already earned him the sobriquet of "Judge." It was to remain with him through life. Cultural activities interested him but slightly in his early years. He was a joiner. He belonged to the famous Chicago Club, the most exclusive of its kind in the city. His friends included the leading business and social leaders: George Pullman, president of the famous Pullman Palace Car Company; Philip D. Armour, head of the Armour Packing Company; Marshall Field, famous merchant; Robert T. Lincoln, eldest son of the President, who was to become head of the club and successor to Pullman. Moore loved a good story, seldom drank, never smoked. He radiated physical strength, good humor and self-confidence. He was a daring man—an optimist. In his professional work he was interested mainly in basic issues. He was impatient with details and willing to leave them to others. He was an organizer—of men and enterprises.

Adolphus Green, on the other hand, was almost everything that

Moore was not. His contacts in the community were almost exclusively based on his work in law and his cultural interests. Sports did not concern him. Exercise, he believed, was largely a waste of time. He had no feeling for horses; his family considered him the worst driver of a carriage or coupe that they knew. He loved the theater, books and music; smoked heavy black cigars; saw no reason to avoid alcohol; and joined clubs or organizations reluctantly and only when he found a compelling reason to do so. While he had business contacts with prominent financial leaders of the city, he did not number them as his close friends. He was more inclined to seek the acquaintance of members of the Sunset Club and was interested in discussing issues of the day, such as child labor or woman suffrage. Green was slow to act, cautious, given to careful consideration. He was a pessimist and a worrier by nature, nervous, humorless, dour. While he acted with great incisiveness once his mind was made up, it took him a long time to reach decisions. He tended to make enemies faster than friends because he was impatient and disappointed with the weaknesses and shortcomings of others. He was a perfectionist. He worried about every phase of his work. It was not enough to give instructions to subordinates; he had to supervise even the most minute details.

This was an era of new ideas and new opportunities. With the coming of new ways of doing almost everything, there developed a growing impatience with old, antiquated business methods. Bigness was the watchword; the elimination of the weaker competitor was an accepted necessity. There was a relentless drive for bigger volume, bigger mills, bigger profits, bigger plans for production, distribution and promotion. Men trained in finance and banking now began to exert a major influence on the development of business throughout the country.

Carnegie Steel was setting the pace in this trend toward bigness. Andrew Carnegie established such levels of efficiency that his company soon had a bigger volume, more plants, and higher profits than any organization in the land. John D. Rockefeller had tamed the wildcat oil industry and produced "stability" with the establishment of Standard Oil. "The trust was the logical result of Rockefeller's whole philosophy of business," wrote Stewart H. Holbrook, a student of the era. "He was one of the few men who understood that the old way of business had passed, the day when purely local concerns, working from limited supplies and for a limited market could survive. Rapid communication and transportation had changed that."

A whole new age of leaders, "fired by a passionate will to succeed," as Arthur Schlesinger described them, "came across the nation's horizon." Usually insensitive to the problems of those outside their ken, these men had, in the words of Holbrook, "a splendid audacity and vital energy that erupted in astonishing ways."

"Strong, ruthless men, bold and cunning and cunning in their boldness, were required for the work of crushing out the old cutthroat, haphazard, individualistic competitive system," wrote Arthur Gustav Myer. "Very expert destructionists were they. But they were also constructionists. They tore down to build up. A decayed, archaic industrial system, they replaced with one of a far more systematic order, the fore-runner of finer systems to come. Progress often works through clear instruments."

J. P. Morgan of New York was one of the earliest promoters who gave leadership to the new era. Mark Sullivan, the historian, states, "Morgan was in a class by himself . . . He was a bridge between two conceptions of banking, the older one which consisted solely of extending credit on approved security, and the newer one, which reached out for direct control of industries, used them as the basis for issuing stocks, and stimulated the sale of the stocks to the public."

While the nation was moving ahead at breakneck pace with its development of huge business enterprises, Adolphus Green and William Moore also moved steadily ahead—following independent paths —toward success in the practice of law in the Chicago area. Moore was also soon recognized as one of the most able financial organizers in the country. "It is doubtful," one publication said, "if Moore had a superior in the successful combination of purely business functions and legal practice."

As the industrial pattern of the nation shifted, the Moore brothers increasingly forsook their legal practice for corporate promotion and management. They were among the first to recognize the possibilities of industrial mergers in America and, next to J. P. Morgan, probably the most important in developing them.

In a matter of a few short years Moore's home-town newspaper was to report that his transactions "have astonished the best of the world's financiers."

Who could have anticipated, however, that the road to financial success at the turn of the century for both Moore and Green would be paved with biscuits?

FOUR

Battle of
the Biscuit Bakers

A SHORT DISTANCE from LaSalle Street—the Wall Street of Chicago —was Monroe Street. If you had walked along this street in the 1880's, you would have seen a sign "W. H. & J. H. Moore, Law Offices," in large gilt letters, repeated on eight windows of the third story of the American Express Building.

"In the history of the great movement for industrial centralization," one journalist of the day commented, "this 'law office' is a very notable landmark. No other office in the west is so notable in that respect, and, perhaps, none in the country aside from that of J. P. Morgan & Company."

The suite of spacious rooms occupied by the Moore brothers included a partners' room with several bookcases filled with calfbound legal volumes and, nearby, a stock exchange ticker providing instant information on the latest doings on LaSalle and Wall Streets. "The hinges of the law bookcases," it was said, "would have creaked from long disuse if anyone had thoughtlessly attempted to turn them."

Indeed, the firm of Moore & Moore had by the late 1880's evolved from a law office to a center of high finance. William H. Moore's interests had shifted from the practice of law to the more spectacular and remunerative business of counseling corporations in their efforts to combine.

As far back as the 1850's mergers were frequent, one of the

◀ *Hand-packing cookies and crackers at the turn of the century* largest being the formation of the New York Central Railroad in 1853. Following the Civil War this process accelerated. As the nation grew, in the words of Mark Sullivan, "Any new idea that promised to increase sales, reduce costs and multiply profits was eagerly seized. The promoter, the banker, the lawyer, were drawn into . . . service."

Of the many ambitious and resolute "captains of industry" who came forward during the 1880's, none was to display greater ability in industrial organization than William H. Moore. Industrialists increasingly sought his counsel. In 1881 leaders of the match industry called on the Moore brothers to assist them in solving some of their problems.

The friction match as we know it in America is believed to have been invented by a Connecticut man early in the nineteenth century. At the time of the Civil War, about a billion matches a day were being manufactured. With the growth of railroads this market grew so rapidly that the demand outdistanced available manufacturing processes.

In 1881 the country's largest match manufacturers had grouped together to form a single company, the Diamond Match Company. The most imaginative and practical inventions were employed to try to improve the quality of matches and the volume of their production. New machinery mechanized match manufacture by cutting splints from prepared wooden blocks and dipping and drying them in one continuous operation.

The Moore brothers, particularly William Moore, helped the Diamond Match Company transform itself from a Connecticut corporation with a $3,000,000 capital stock to an Illinois corporation with a $6,000,000 capital stock.

Among other industrialists who sought the services of Moore was a group of eastern bakers. Like Adolphus W. Green, whose office at the time was about a block away, Judge Moore became involved with an industry about which he knew nothing. He listened as the bakers told him their troubles, very like those that Green listened to so patiently that same year. The main difference was that the bakers who met with Moore were almost exclusively from New York and New England states. They included representatives of Brinckerhoff & Company, makers of the popular butter crackers and soda crackers; the Anger Brothers, manufacturers of zwieback; E. J. Larrabee & Company, who had made the first hard sweet biscuit in the United

States; Hetfield & Ducker, makers of lemon snaps as far back as 1862; Vandeveer & Holmes Biscuit company, founded in 1876, originators of the returnable glass-front cracker display can. Both Hetfield & Ducker and Vandeveer & Holmes claimed to be first in the manufacture of animal crackers. Others included Daniel Canty, known for its handmade butter crackers; Holmes & Coutts, who made a wide variety of sweet biscuits including early sugar wafers; and J. D. Gilmor & Company, maker of sweet crackers.

From the start Moore—brilliant at estimating the potential in a business situation—saw that the cracker business was different from other types of industrial enterprises with which he had been connected. He observed how difficult it would be to bring together bakers who had long traditions of independence. At the same time he realized the backwardness of the industry and the inevitability of change. He had also heard rumors of the coalescing of western bakers into larger organizations.

Moore was not the man to be discouraged by difficulties, not if there were economic potentialities in the situation. But achieving such organization was an expensive proposition. Fortunately Moore had excellent credit in important financial circles, particularly in Chicago. This permitted him to make attractive offers to independent bakers to place their assets at his disposal. Financing help came from Chicago businessmen like Philip D. Armour, George Pullman, and Chicago financier Norman B. Ream.

In the winter of 1889 he drew up final plans for the amalgamation of eight of the largest bakeries in the east. A corporation was officially organized under the laws of Illinois early in 1890 with its general office at 78 Monroe Street. It was named the New York Biscuit Company.

The original capitalization of the company was $5,000,000, representing 50,000 shares at $100 par. Later, the capitalization was increased to $10,000,000. Before the year was over, the New York Biscuit Company had brought within its organization a total of twenty-three bakeries in ten states, including almost a hundred and forty ovens located in such famous bakeries as Bent & Company, Milton, Massachusetts; John Pearson & Son, Newburyport, Massachusetts; Wilson Biscuit Company in Philadelphia; Parks & Savage, Hartford, Connecticut; J. D. Mason & Company in Baltimore, Maryland; the Burlington Bread Company in Burlington, Vermont; the New Haven Baking Company in New Haven, Connecticut; Treadwell & Harris in New York; and many others, including the eight bakeries whose officers had originally sought Moore's guidance.

Armed with sufficient capital to buy the assets of almost every bakery in the east that would sell, the New York Biscuit Company within a year had branches in many of the leading cities in New York and New England, and was producing some of the most popular brands of crackers and biscuits. An event of special importance was the entrance of the Kennedy Biscuit Works, largest bakery in America, into the organization of the New York Biscuit Company in May 1890. The Kennedy company had plants in Cambridgeport and in Chicago. So great had been the popularity of the Kennedy products that in 1878 it had established sales branches in New York and Philadelphia. The Chicago bakery, built in 1881, was under the management of Henry J. Evans, a big, burly former bakery wagon driver. When the plant was destroyed by fire in 1884, it was replaced by a new six-story building featuring, for the first time, ovens on the top floor rather than in the basement. Locating the ovens on the top floor permitted the lowering of the baked goods from floor to floor by the natural process of gravity, processing them as they went, thus avoiding the waste traditional in the bakery business.

The Kennedy works in Cambridgeport also had its own electric light plant and an automatic sprinkler system when it joined the New York Biscuit Company. At that time it employed 650 workers and owned 134 horses used for delivering its famous products. Immediately after the merger the veteran baker Frank A. Kennedy, president of the firm, resigned from active participation in management. Not until many years later was he to return to the baking industry.

William H. Moore became the first president of the New York Biscuit Company, Henry J. Evans vice president, and James H. Moore second vice president. One of Moore's first decisions was to erect a modern bakery in New York City on Tenth Avenue between 15th and 16th Streets. The enormous new bakery was, for years, the largest cracker-baking center in the world, occupying the whole easterly end of the city block.

The New York Biscuit Company prospered from the start. The fact that it was composed of some of the most celebrated and reputable baking firms in the country insured its success. The Moore firm contributed not only financing but also aggressive business leadership. Soon reports pointed out that the company was held "in the highest esteem and credit" by financial circles throughout the country. Earnings were high and the New York Biscuit Company was a popular investment on the stock exchanges of New York and Chicago. The American Biscuit & Manufacturing Company, on the other hand, was not listed, since its stock was entirely owned by the manufacturers themselves.

Thus by the end of 1890 the New York Biscuit Company in the east under the leadership of William H. Moore and the American Biscuit & Manufacturing Company in the west led by Adolphus W. Green confronted each other in a unique economic battle. The ammunition was not bullets or bayonets but graham crackers, ladyfingers, lemon drops, oatmeal cookies, oyster crackers, pretzels and gingersnaps.

From his offices on LaSalle Street, Green directed the activities of the American Biscuit & Manufacturing Company. The other western baking combination, the United States Baking Company, remained neutral. Green, now grudgingly giving almost full time to these activities, looked on the opposition as an almost personal act of animosity. He would not be dictated to by a group of eastern bakers led by a Chicago operator.

A few blocks away, on Monroe Street, William Moore was also becoming increasingly occupied with baking affairs. Genial, cool, deliberate in his professional decisions, Moore planned his moves carefully. Frequently he would differ with his more impetuous brother, James. William's method was to let his opponent make his mistakes, then move in with full force for victory. But Moore found Green a difficult opponent.

"The Monroe Street lawyers," reported the Chicago *Daily News*, "were eminently successful in the East, but they encountered stubborn opposition in the West. The large manufacturers in Chicago and west of this city refused to enter the combine." In short, Green refused to surrender his independence. He would rather fight. As a result, the *News* pointed out, "The Moores made war on the western people by cutting prices to a point where the independent bakers saw no profit in the trade."

Green took his first important step a year after the American Biscuit Company was founded. He tried to take business away from the New York Biscuit Company right in the heart of its own territory. The American Biscuit Company established a bakery at the corner of West and Bethune Streets in New York City, in what was once an old brewery. Green sent F. L. Sommer, president of the

American Biscuit Company and a respected baker in his own right, to take charge of the New York operation, with Shelby V. Timberlake as sales manager. Sommer's famous trademark, a parrot, had produced the popular slogan "Polly wants a cracker." Representatives of the American Biscuit Company in New York came to be known as the "Polly boys."

Many bakeries in this era named their products after local communities and regions. The Cambridgeport plant of the Kennedy Baking Company gave its products such names as Boston, Harvard, Cambridge Salts, Beacon Hill, Brighton, Shrewsbury, Melrose, the Boston Family, the Mayflower Milk, the Waverly, the Newton, Riverdale, Bedford.

When Green's forces invaded the eastern territory, one of their first acts was to drop all names resembling the rival Kennedy products. Instead, the American Biscuit Company products bore such urban names as Manhattan, Fifth Avenue, Albany Mixed, Jersey Toast, Manhattan Wafer (which was based upon the Kennedy Brighton) Iced Manhattan, Manhattan Jelly.

One of the reasons why Green entered the territory of the New York Biscuit Company was the fact that the Kennedy Biscuit Works was located in Chicago, the heart of the American Biscuit Company's activities. Green felt it was important to have representatives of his company in a position to challenge the prices and the products of his competitors on their home ground.

Green was not a sporting adversary. He had not entered the fray to reach a compromise; he had entered it to render his enemy helpless. It was his intention to blast the New York Biscuit Company from the face of the map and establish the ascendancy of the bakers west of the Mississippi.

Each side blamed the other. "We believe that the American Company was the aggressor," wrote an officer of the New York Biscuit Company, "and that the New York Biscuit Company has done nothing that it was not driven to doing. I am authoritatively informed that when the present difficulties commenced, every effort was made by the New York people to arrive at an amicable adjustment of all differences, but the New York people were invariably referred to Mr. A. W. Green, counsel for the company. The New York people could not get at the practical men in the American Company, but in effect, were limited to conferences with Mr. Green."

One of the most influential men involved was Frank O. Lowden, a young lawyer who, years later, was to become governor of Illinois. Lowden was the son-in-law of George Pullman, the railroad magnate, a large financial backer of the New York Biscuit Company. Pullman was uneasy about the biscuit warfare and hoped young Lowden, placed in a position of responsibility in the New York Biscuit Company leadership, could bring some order into the chaotic situation. It was a wise move. Lowden not only became a warm friend of William Moore but also ultimately won the confidence of Green as well.

Bringing the rival factions together was not easy. Green was suspicious, stubborn, uncompromising. Lowden reported that members of the New York Biscuit Company Board "were most positive in the position that the New York Company could not yield to what Mr. Green demanded even though the alternative might be a long and expensive war."

Lowden could see what the war was doing to both sides. "However expensive our present differences are to us," he wrote, "we must always remember that the American Company is suffering as much or more, and there seems to be evidence of demoralization all along their lines . . ."

Moore, genial and good tempered as he was, knew how to fight. Late in 1895 he ordered a 25 per cent reduction in prices. Crackers were thus sold below cost. He had first taken the precaution, *Everybody's Magazine* reported, to put his concern "on a stable war footing by persuading Pullman and Armour to agree to carry the floating debt and to advance what further funds might be needed. Thus assured . . . he proposed to keep up the fight until peace might be arranged on a satisfactory basis."

The new cut in prices was a blow which shook the American Biscuit Company to its foundations. There was talk of surrender. But a shattering event occurred which was to reverse the positions of the protagonists. The event would make front pages throughout the world, send stock markets crumbling, and establish new alignments in the financial leadership of the New York Biscuit Company.

The catalyst was the Diamond Match Company. The Moore brothers had had a direct hand in the amalgamation of Diamond Match. By 1896 it was one of the most widely traded stocks on the Chicago and New York exchanges. Early that year Diamond Match stock was not selling much over par. Negotiations were begun, however, that looked promising for the introduction of patents and processes of Diamond Match in countries overseas. Reports revealed that the company could make matches so much cheaper and better than any European manufacturer that immense profits could result. Rumors spread along Wall Street in New York and LaSalle Street in Chicago that Diamond Match was scheduled for a major boom.

The country was just emerging from a period of hard times. The time was right for speculation. The Moores, after the fashion of operators of the day, helped skyrocket the market value of both Diamond Match and New York Biscuit stocks through heavy purchases on margin. With their splendid credit position there was no problem in having bankers and businessmen accept these securities as collateral for large cash advances. The business of the Chicago Exchange during the summer months consisted almost exclusively of speculation in these two stocks.

Soon this speculation got out of control. Diamond Match became a craze among investors. Its stock went up almost without a break from 120 to 248. Trailing after Diamond Match came the stock of New York Biscuit, influenced by the fact that William H. Moore was the organizer of both companies. The Biscuit Company stock rose from 70 to 108 in a short time.

The urbane Moore brothers were thoroughly at home in this situation. They treated their colleagues with patience and did everything possible to realize a maximum economic advantage from the stock exchange development.

But catastrophe hovered overhead. Foreign negotiations of the Diamond Match Company moved too slowly, and doubts about the company's future began to be raised. And there were other factors involved, extending far beyond Chicago's financial district.

The year 1896 was a Presidential election year. Involved as they were in financial activities, leaders such as William H. Moore and Adolphus W. Green had little insight and even less time to pay attention to the social conditions of the country. They did not know— and probably would not have cared—that millions of workingmen, women and children were still suffering from the tragic depression of 1893. Tens of thousands were without jobs. There were no government agencies to help the needy or care for the helpless. Even those fortunate enough to be working were often compelled to accept wage cuts and insecure working conditions.

"Hundreds of banks closed their doors," wrote historian Henry S. Commager, "thousands of factories and mines shut down, one-fourth of the railroads went into the hands of receivers, and over fifteen thousand commercial failures testified to the breakdown of the economic system. That winter, and the next, millions of working men walked the streets in a vain search for jobs or shivered in long soup lines, for haphazard charity was the only answer that society had yet formulated to acts of God like panics and unemployment."

The employee in the biscuit manufacturing industry was typical of the new industrial worker of the era. He was without security; he worked long hours for meager wages under hazardous conditions. "In those days, we began work at four o'clock in the morning and finished at four o'clock in the afternoon with the minimum amount of time for breakfast and dinner," one worker recalled. And when the demand for products slowed down, working people found themselves unemployed, without hope of finding other jobs or anything to eat.

As one historian points out, "Though certain executives of some of the great consolidations took vigorous steps to maintain decent conditions for their employees, most executives as a class made their decisions largely on the basis of cost sheets, reports from minor executives, graphic analyses of business trends, and the prospective effect of their decisions upon dividends. There was typically a lack of realization of the effects in terms of human life of decisions to shut down plants, reduce operations, cut wages, substitute machinery for labor, throw orders to other plants."

Most working people attributed their problems to the "public be damned" attitude of industry. Hostility toward the new corporations increased. The nation was ripe for a tidal wave of reform. This movement was given its broadest expression in the nomination of William Jennings Bryan for the Presidency on the Democratic ticket in 1896.

"The humblest citizen in all the land, when clad in the armor of a righteous cause," said Bryan, "is stronger than all the hosts of error. I come to speak to you in defense of a cause as holy as the cause of liberty—the cause of humanity."

"What Bryan was really defending was the old and simple life of America," Walter Lippmann wrote. But business interpreted the candidacy of Bryan as a threat to its leadership of the nation. As a result, William McKinley, the Republican Presidential candidate, was given the united support of industry throughout the country.

It was against this background that the Diamond Match Company—so carefully established by William H. Moore—ran head-on into a crisis in the summer of 1896, just a few months before election day. Negotiations overseas for the introduction of patents and processes of Diamond Match failed to develop as speedily as had been anticipated, and speculation began to falter.

Some of those who had purchased Diamond Match stock began to unload. As one writer put it, "The Moore brothers were holding a bag which grew bigger and bigger and heavier and heavier every day."

"This frantic trading came to an abrupt and shocking end on August 4, when the heavily overextended Moores defaulted on their contracts." William Moore met with Philip Armour and others who had invested in the Match Company and the Biscuit Company and announced that he was unable to carry on. So devastating was the pricking of the Diamond Match balloon that the entire stock exchange in Chicago closed down in mid-August and did not reopen until three months later.

After the debacle a reporter who interviewed William Moore for a national publication noted that

His manner and conduct that day after the failure was probably as good a test of the man's temper as could be found, and none of the many callers at the Monroe Street offices could have told from the "Judge's" appearance or manner that a Waterloo lay just behind him.

Of course, it was not a joke, but Judge Moore took it with perfect coolness and absolute good humor . . . the smash had happened, and there was no time for reminiscences. The brothers set to work to get the wreckage untangled. And they addressed themselves to this coolly, rapidly, intelligently, with clear minds for the thing immediately at hand, just as they had done everything else. The day before yesterday, it had been the promotion of a company. Yesterday, it had been a big stock speculation. Today, it was clearing the wreck. Whatever it was, it was all in a day's work, a job to be done collectively and competently. There is no doubt that this composed, good humored attitude of the brothers had its effect in the reshaping of their fortunes. They took their failure so exclusively as a mere incident that other people accepted it in the same spirit. It was plain to everybody, even that first bitter day, that they had lost nothing but their money; that they had not lost their nerve; that their confidence in themselves, their firm, hearty confident grip on life was unimpaired.

A few weeks after the Diamond Match collapse William McKinley was elected President. Philip D. Armour wrote to a friend the day after the election, "We are all feeling better here this morning . . . We have the consolation of knowing that the country is safe for four years . . . It has been a fear as to what would happen all the time that has kept us unsettled. I guess in time we will come out of Diamond Match and [New York] Biscuit . . . without any bad scars on us."

Two days after the election the stock exchange in Chicago reopened. Said William H. Moore, "Just let us alone and we will work out after a while."

And that was precisely what he did. The Moore firm was never formally declared insolvent or put into bankruptcy. The settlements, in fact, were on the debtors' own terms. In less than five years the Diamond Match Company—finally able to install the new machinery and factory apparatus in England as it had promised—had regained its former position of prestige.

Judge Moore was to regain his own prestige many times over. It came as a direct result of the establishment of peace in the biscuit business.

The National Biscuit Company

PHILIP D. ARMOUR had his office in the same building as the law firm of Green, Honore & Peters. But unlike William H. Moore, Green had never taken the trouble to cultivate people of Armour's status.

Green knew that Armour, red-whiskered, baldheaded meat-packing industrialist, was a heavy financial backer of the New York Biscuit Company. And so was, Green realized, George M. Pullman, the railroad magnate who sat at the famous "millionaires' table" at the swanky Chicago Club.

Without the financial help of such men, Green knew, it would have been impossible for the New York Biscuit Company to have continued the rivalry which had been in progress for so many years. When he encountered Armour in the elevator, Green would usually stand stiff and erect and stare straight ahead of him.

Actually, there had been a possibility of unification within the baking industry prior to the Diamond Match fiasco. As a result of the shrewd negotiations of Frank Lowden, an agreement had almost been reached. It had been tentatively agreed that the New York Biscuit Company would more or less be contained within the eastern portion of the country, while the American Biscuit & Manufacturing Company would stay west.

But the Diamond Match debacle had revived Green's hopes of complete victory. When he heard the news, he excitedly paced his office, striding through the large open space where secretaries were

◀ *Chicago's first "skyscraper" and the first home of the National Biscuit Company*

transcribing, and then back to his desk again. He knew that the Moore failure was certain to weaken the bargaining position of the New York Biscuit Company.

Just as he anticipated, western bakers felt that uniting with the New York Biscuit Company at that particular time might actually prove more of a liability than an asset. But Green was convinced the time was right to strike a blow at the New York Biscuit Company that might end the rivalry forever. So he and the American Biscuit Company launched a new campaign of price cutting. "A week before the announcement of the reduction in prices was made," the Chicago *Daily News* reported, "The New York Company's shares fell about twenty points from the low figure consequent upon the Moore failure."

In the meantime the pressure of the Diamond Match crisis created a demand for new leadership of the New York Biscuit Company. In January 1897 the Moore brothers announced their resignations from the board of directors and a new board was named with Henry J. Evans, veteran baker from the Kennedy Biscuit Works in Chicago, as president; James W. Hazen, a baker who had risen from the ranks at the Kennedy plant in Cambridgeport, vice president; and directors Thomas S. Ollive, a New York baker; George H. Webster, a former partner of Philip Armour; J. D. Mason, a Baltimore baker; and Frank O. Lowden, a representative of the Pullman interests, general counsel.

The new board at first resolved to rally its forces and resume its price-cutting warfare with the western bakers. But since baked products could not be hoarded, retailers could take little advantage of the low prices.

A group was forming within the New York Biscuit Company that wanted an end to biscuit warfare. The man most directly responsible for the movement was Frank O. Lowden.

On numerous occasions Lowden brought Green and William Moore together for visits to New York, where both advice and funds were sought for the establishment of a unified baking industry. The Illinois Trust & Savings Bank of Chicago served as a trustee for the raising of subscriptions for a possible new company. The times seemed right. Scores of industries continued to consolidate: transportation, meat, watches, carpets, wallpaper, flour, glass, copper, rubber, coal, machinery, gas, lead, steel rails, stoves, slates.

"We were told so often," Green was to say later, "that the biscuit business was different from any other and we would not succeed in unification attempts." But Lowden, Moore and Green continued their efforts. The immediate requirement was for $12,000,000 to repay the various stockholders that might be involved in building a unified corporation. Another essential, in addition to money, was to convince scores of independent-minded bakers that their interests would be best served by unification. Problems as to how to bring the bakeries into the merger, how to finance expansion, and the underwriting of new stocks were involved in the concentrated efforts.

The fund-raising efforts proved successful. But leading bakers both east and west were still reluctant. And Green still remained a difficult man to do business with. As late as January 17, 1898, Armour told Lowden that he felt, as an investor in the New York Biscuit Company, that efforts toward consolidation must be pushed ahead more speedily. He suggested that the present number of bakeries was sufficient for the consolidation. "It will not do to let the matter drag along," he wrote, "as I think the company isn't gaining strength with the public by procrastination."

Lowden's diplomacy slowly inched the contemplated merger ahead. New investors were brought into the negotiations. They included Norman B. Ream, as well as Robert T. Lincoln, son of the late President who was shortly to assume the presidency of the Pullman Company.

On January 8, 1898, the *Chicago Economist* repeated its prediction that a plan for the consolidation of the biscuit companies was afoot. "As anticipated last week, the plan for the consolidation of the biscuit companies has been formally laid before the stockholders of the New York Company in a circular. The meetings of the stockholders of the American and the United States Companies will probably be called in two weeks to act on the matter."

The *Economist* had predicted accurately. On Thursday morning, February 3, 1898, three men met in the law offices of James B. Vredenburgh at 1 Exchange Place in Jersey City, New Jersey. It was beautiful and clear outside following the severe blizzard of the day before. The snow was so high that mail had been delayed and people were able to get about only by sleighs. However, the men scheduled to attend the meeting were present at noon when it was called to order by Vredenburgh. Present were Vredenburgh's law partner, Abram Q. Garretson, and Shelby V. Timberlake, sales manager of the American Biscuit & Manufacturing Company's Bethune Street plant in New York.

The meeting took place in New Jersey because that state was especially hospitable to companies seeking mergers. Some states were traditionally hostile to "foreign" corporations originating in other states. Under the provision of the New Jersey legislature it was specifically stated that, "The corporation is to have the power also to conduct business in other states and in foreign countries."

The three men went through the formalities of establishing a corporation. It required only a few moments. A few papers were signed. Then Vredenburgh dispatched an employee to the nearby telegraph station with a message to Adolphus W. Green in Chicago informing him that the legal act of establishing the company had been completed.

Far away in Chicago another blizzard had also caused major problems. "Miles of snow," as the newspapers described it, made walking comparable to "Alpine climbing in Chicago streets." The temperature was below zero.

Shortly before three o'clock Green received the telegram from Vredenburgh by special messenger at his LaSalle Street office. He had been expecting it. Calmly he put on his derby hat and heavy coat with the fur collar, thrust the telegram into his pocket, and took the elevator to the street. He carefully picked his way through huge drifts of snow to the office of the Illinois Trust & Savings Bank on the corner of Jackson and LaSalle Street, the bank founded years before by Philip D. Armour. A group of distinguished-looking men were awaiting him in the conference room there. Between them they manufactured a large percentage of the crackers, biscuits, cookies, candy, cake, lozenges and bread consumed in the nation. Never before in the nation's history had so many authorities on baking ever gathered together.

Green handed the telegram to Frank Lowden and pulled up a chair to the glass-topped table. Lowden read the text of the telegram Green had received from New Jersey. Representing the New York Biscuit Company, in addition to Lowden, were Henry J. Evans, the former New Hampshire farmer and truck driver; Thomas Ollive, bewhiskered British-born baker who had been in the baking business since he was fifteen years old; James W. Hazen, secretary-treasurer of the Kennedy Biscuit Works in Cambridgeport.

Representing the western bakers, in addition to Green, were Benjamin F. Crawford of Mansfield, the Ohio baker with his pince-nez and fancy cravat; Sylvester S. Marvin in his high stiff collar, head of the famous Marvin Baking Company of Pittsburgh and president of the United States Baking Company; Louis D. Dozier, president of the Dozier Baking Company and an officer of the United States Baking Company; Cornelius E. Rumsey, a baker from Pittsburgh, representing the American Biscuit & Manufacturing Company; distinguished-looking David F. Bremner of Chicago, president of the American Biscuit & Manufacturing Company; Harry F. Vories, from St. Joseph, Missouri, manager of the Lillibridge-Bremner Baking Company of Minneapolis and secretary of the American Biscuit & Manufacturing Company; and James S. Loose of the Kansas City Baking Company, an officer of the American Biscuit & Manufacturing Company.

In addition there were William T. Baker, president of the Chicago Board of Trade, and Norman B. Ream, Chicago financier, adviser and associate of such dignitaries as Marshall Field, George Pullman, Potter Palmer and William H. Moore. Abram Q. Garretson, who was to join the group at later meetings, was, of course, in New Jersey. Frank Lowden served as the meeting's temporary chairman.

The gathering was not simply to establish another corporate organization; it was to build peace out of chaos.

Adolphus Green announced the official name of the company as the National Biscuit Company. A unanimous vote of approval was taken. Then Bremner nominated Green for the presidency of the new company. Green declined.

In a short speech Green pointed out that he was not in a position to assume the leadership, that he felt a more suitable candidate would be Benjamin F. Crawford of the United States Baking Company, an organization that had been neutral in the recent struggle. Crawford was unanimously elected. Vories, from the American Biscuit & Manufacturing Company, was elected first vice president; Lowden, from the New York Biscuit Company, second vice president; Rumsey, from the United States Baking Company, secretary and treasurer. George E. West, from the New York Biscuit Company, was assistant secretary and treasurer.

Green was unanimously elected as legal counsel and chairman of the board of directors. All those present, with the addition of Garretson, were formally named directors of the newly established company. For services rendered in the formation of the new company, its principal promoters—including Moore, Green and Lowden —received large blocks of common stock. It is estimated that William

Moore alone received $4,000,000 in stock for his services, most of which he used to repay debts incurred in the Diamond Match incident. It would not be until years later that Moore would assume leadership of the company he helped create.

The certificate of organization of the company stated, "The objects for which said corporation is formed are, to manufacture, buy, sell and export, biscuits, crackers, cakes, Italian paste, confectionery and other food products . . ."

Green proposed that the cable address of the company be the one word "BISCUIT." It was voted that the home office of the National Biscuit Company be located at 205 LaSalle Street, the Home Insurance Company Building, where the firm of Green, Honore & Peters had offices. In fact, Green had already made the arrangements for a suite of rooms on the same floor as his own law firm.

Green thought it especially appropriate that the Home Insurance Company Building, the eight-story edifice on LaSalle and Adams Streets, be NBC headquarters. Located in the financial district of Chicago, the building was planned and constructed by William Le-Baron Jenney, a pioneering architect of the era. It was the first in the United States to use steel beams in its construction, its exterior wall being merely a shell supported by its steel skeleton. Thus, the first home of NBC was the first skyscraper in the country.

The modernity of the building pleased the leaders of the new corporation. A feeling permeated the meeting that history was being made. The next day, the Chicago *Daily Tribune* reported in a front-page article that "the biggest deal in Chicago's financial history," had taken place. "The new biscuit company was incorporated today . . . with a capital stock of $25,000,000 preferred and $30,000,000 in common . . . This morning, the new company is in possession of and operating all of the plants of the old companies."

The establishment of the National Biscuit Company was front-page news not only in Chicago, but around the country. "All the biscuit and cracker companies between Salt Lake City on the west, Portland, Maine, on the east, and St. Louis and New Orleans in the south, will tomorrow morning be under one management," reported *The New York Times*. There were 114 bakeries involved in the merger representing a total of slightly over 400 ovens.

The firm had the capacity of consuming 2,000,000 barrels of flour a year, and an output of 360,000,000 pounds of crackers annually.

The merger brought together the New York Biscuit Company, with its twenty-three bakeries and outlets in ten states, most of which were in New York and New England; the United States Baking Company with its thirty-eight bakeries in nine states, concentrated largely in Ohio, Indiana, Pennsylvania and Michigan; the American Biscuit & Manufacturing Company with its forty bakeries in fifteen states, concentrating in Iowa, Illinois and Missouri; and a group of smaller bakeries including the Decatur Biscuit Company, which had several plants in Illinois; the Hamilton Company, which was an offshoot of the American Biscuit Company in New Jersey; and the National Baking Company with several other plants in Illinois. Other independent plants were soon to be added to the group.

There were nineteen bakeries located in New York State in the original group that formed the National Biscuit Company, fourteen in Ohio, ten in Pennsylvania, nine in Illinois, eight in Massachusetts, seven in Iowa, seven in Indiana, and seven in Michigan. The newly formed corporation paid some $9,000,000 to the owners of the bakeries of the New York Biscuit Company, another $9,000,000 to the owners of the American Biscuit & Manufacturing Company, and $5,000,000 to the owners of the United States Baking Company. NBC, as the company was known, began its business with $6,500,000 in cash and supplies on hand. It was estimated that, in tonnage, the production of the companies making up the new corporation was about one-half the total production of the country. The larger companies, the New York Biscuit Company, the American Biscuit & Manufacturing Company, and the United States Baking Company were acquired by the exchange of securities. The other companies in the group were acquired by cash purchases.

There were about 1,300 shareholders when NBC was founded. Among the more prominent were the Moore brothers, Marshall Field, Chauncey Depew, lawyer and railroad magnate, Pullman, Armour, Lowden, Crawford, Ream, Vories, Rumsey, Kennedy, Green. It was estimated that investments from individuals who were not stockholders in the old companies amounted to between $8,000,000 and $9,000,000. William H. Moore, staying in the background during this final stage of the organization, together with his friends, distributed some $25,000,000 in preferred stock of the new company to pay for actual assets. Some $30,000,000 was issued in common stock largely representing good will.

"When the company drew its first breath," Adolphus Green

said later, "we were watching anxiously to see whether it would live or not."

The National Biscuit Company sometimes has been referred to as "the first of the new so-called trusts." According to *Everybody's Magazine*, practically all the corporate combinations that followed the founding of NBC "have been organized on the same lines."

Fortune magazine, however, claims that the National Biscuit Company was "never an honest-to-goodness trust to begin with. National Biscuit Company exercises no control over its raw materials —it can't corner wheat and eggs and butter. It has no patents to protect its products, no secret baking processes that are withheld from its rivals. Anyone can make a biscuit, anyone can try to sell it. The cracker trade, in point of fact, is a free-for-all fight in which no holds are barred."

Calling for unified efforts for the success of the new company, Green stated, "We should all fight together, not fight each other. We should all feel that there is just one thing to work for, and that is the success of the National Biscuit Company, and if we all pull together, there would seem to be no limit to the possibilities of our success."

And indeed, as the National Biscuit Company was launched on its career, there seemed to be no limit to its possibilities once the bakers scattered throughout the nation were unified as a team. But unification, as Adolphus W. Green was to discover, was far from easy.

Pioneer bakers: top left, David F. Bremner; top right, Thomas S. Ollive; ▸
bottom left, Benjamin F. Crawford; bottom right, Frank A. Kennedy

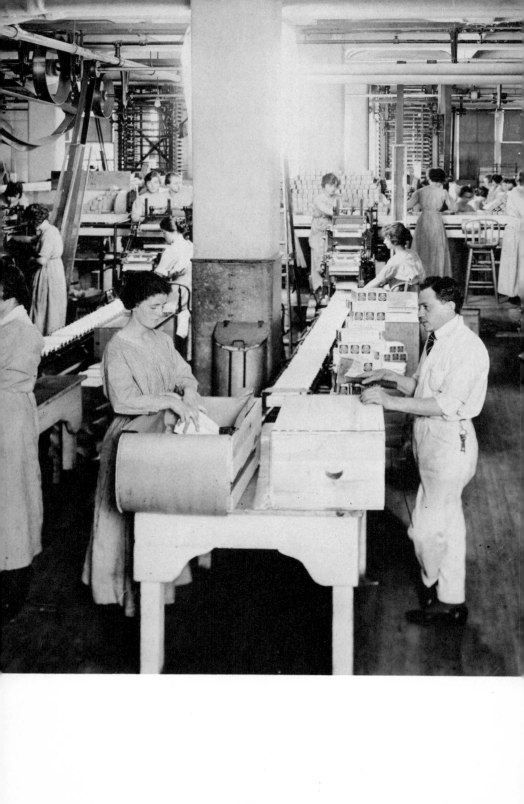

Left, wrapping "hard bread" and above, mixing dough in bakeries of yesterday

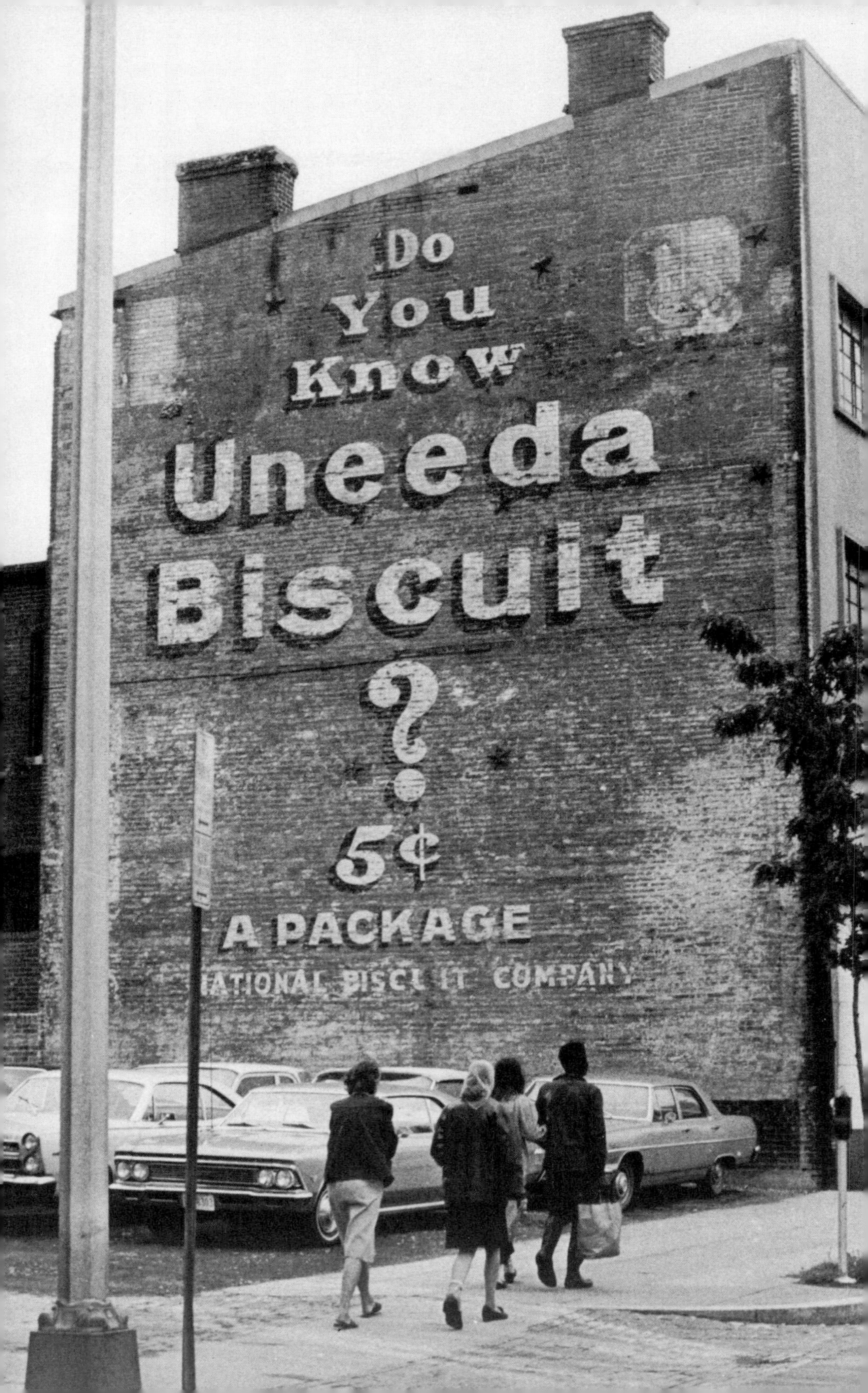
Do
You
Know
Uneeda
Biscuit
?
5¢
A PACKAGE
NATIONAL BISCUIT COMPANY

SIX

Birth of a Biscuit

THE CREATION of the National Biscuit Company, Adolphus W. Green realized, marked the beginning of the end of the cracker barrel as an American institution.

Green was conscious of the anonymity of the crackers and cookies people ate. The name of the maker of the cracker, if it had a name at all, was unknown to most consumers. If a baker's name appeared on the barrel, it was most likely on the head, which was usually destroyed when the barrel was opened. Thus, crackers in barrels often had no identity.

This knowledge influenced the thinking of Green as he pondered the future of the giant new company. Although Benjamin F. Crawford was the company's formal president, Green was its actual chief executive. When Judge Moore sold most of his NBC holdings to help meet his various financial obligations, responsibility for the company's leadership was placed squarely on Green's shoulders.

Moore, free of the biscuit business for the time being and also free of debt, now turned to other activities. By the winter of 1898 Moore's reputation as an authority on corporate combination had spread. He was besieged by requests to help organize corporations, as he grandiloquently put it, "from the marshes of Maine to the Pacific coast." Before the year was over he had organized the American Tin Plate Company. A few months later he brought together the National Steel Company. In April 1899 he organized the Amer-

◀ *Removal of building reveals famous advertisement*

ican Steel Hoop Company. In May he proposed to take over the giant Carnegie Steel Company, and he almost did.

In another year, he would show his organizational wizardry further by helping to found the largest industrial corporation in the history of the country. By 1900 Moore had closed his law office.

Green, now fully involved in NBC management, turned his law practice over almost completely to his associates. He knew that the affairs of the biscuit company would require all of his time and attention. He realized from the beginning that to survive, the company would require more than mere bigness. In some respects the very size of the company—its unwieldiness and lack of unity—was its most serious problem.

Green set about improving this by closing down a number of bakeries which he thought were economically unsound. He dropped thirty-one bakeries in the very first year of the company's existence. The following year he closed down six more, and seven more in the year after that. In addition he scrapped many products that were being produced by various NBC bakeries. Instead, he concentrated on certain products that could be nationally identified with the new company.

Green was groping for a formula that could transform a group of heterogeneous bakeries, scattered about a huge nation, into an entity. He realized that many of the bakeries that made up NBC had developed, over the years, excellent local relationships. But the new company needed something more than *local* business assets. It must become national in fact as well as in name if it was to succeed.

To bring this about, the company must find ways to make its name and products known to the *entire* country, and quickly. Of the scores of large corporations that came into being around the turn of the century in the great surge toward business unification, many failed dismally. Unimaginative leadership could fragment the National Biscuit Company rather than consolidate it.

Each member baker, from one end of the country to the other, had his own ideas of how the mother company should operate. Each baker had his own loyalties to his own baking methods, products and community. In addition there was inevitable antagonism among vetteran bakers and the lawyers and financiers who made up the NBC leadership. Although the assets of the member companies had been purchased, this did not necessarily mean that good will and teamwork were assured.

"A company like ours must have a fixed policy," Green insisted. But how to evolve such a policy? And how to make such a policy acceptable to everyone involved?

Green was certain of only one thing. Every cracker that the National Biscuit Company produced had to be a "top of the barrel" cracker.

The situation was complicated by the fact that more than the member bakers needed convincing. The American housewife had to be educated to the idea of buying baked products. "More and more women have learned to buy from the grocers instead of doing their own baking," an early company statement pointed out, "but too many still cling to the task of spending hours beating batters and watching them in the oven, when they might buy cakes and cookies that rival their own. Every woman's baking day can now be banished in the limbo of tallow dips and home spinning.

"Today, there are so many interesting things for every woman to do, that few can say they do not need more time for their families and the world outside their homes as well."

Aware of such considerations, Green set about organizing his company around a single idea. A single product must become thoroughly identified with the company. It must be new, and it must be popular. But what was that product to be? Green pondered the problem in his office and at night at home as he paced the floor of his bedroom.

Of course, there were many fine products to choose from. The Kennedy Biscuit Works had its famous Common cracker as well as zwieback, pretzels, jumbles, gingersnaps and scores more. NBC's Philadelphia bakery made oyster crackers, Sultanas and Social Teas. A bakery in Milwaukee made Bismarcks, animal crackers, ladyfingers, Boston butter crackers and Newports. In Mansfield, Ohio, the bakery of Crawford & Zeller produced thirteen different varieties of oyster crackers alone in addition to Cornhills, lemon biscuits, oatmeal crackers and others. The New York bakery on Bethune Street was turning out Bee Hives, Baseballs, Alberts and Bridal Veils, Manhattan Wafers, Vienna Creams and Paris Bars. There were countless other delicious items available for promotion.

But only one product appears to have had the special characteristics that Green was looking for. This was the soda cracker. It was by far the most popular of all varieties of crackers and cakes in the land. The soda cracker had a long and honorable career. As far back as 1840 four kinds of crackers were known in the country. There was the original pilot bread, the hard cold-water cracker, the soft or butter cracker, and the soda cracker. The softer butter cracker and the soda cracker differed from the others in that they contained shortening and were the product of a fermented dough.

Green believed the flaky soda cracker had universal appeal. He also realized that the customary handling of the soda crackers in barrels, boxes and returnable tin cans meant that the consumers were frequently getting dirty, soggy and stale crackers. His plan was to produce the best soda cracker ever made and to protect it, if possible, with some sort of a package that would preserve its crispness and cleanliness.

From the very beginning Green decided to give this cracker a unique appearance. He therefore experimented by clipping off the corners, producing an octagonal shape that was like no other cracker on the market at that time.

Of course, it was difficult if not impossible to obtain any unified NBC support for Green's idea. "You'll never make a biscuit dough in that way," critics warned, "and you ought to know better than to try."

Such opposition from experienced bakers might have discouraged a different type of man. But determined to succeed almost to the point of fanaticism, Green was well able to act alone if necessary. He sat for long hours at his desk in his office, staring out of the window and puffing a black cigar.

One day he announced to his associates that the soda cracker would be the first new nationally produced product of the National Biscuit Company.

The decision having been made, the next question was what to name the new product. Here was a problem of crucial significance. Corporations were just learning the importance of brand names. Names that were easy to read, pronounce and remember. Green, scribbling on bits of paper for weeks, tried to decide what the name should be. He asked for suggestions. Hundreds were received. The most important was contributed by a stranger destined to play a strategic role in the development of the company.

When Green was an active member of the Sunset Club, where civic-minded Chicago business leaders met weekly to discuss current events, he had met Victor F. Lawson, the crusading publisher of the Chicago *Daily News*. Among Lawson's many claims to public prominence was his refusal to condemn men on strike against George M. Pullman's railroad.

Green had been impressed with Lawson's integrity and particularly his desire to reform the advertising business of his day. Like Green, Lawson had a sharp tongue. He railed against the practice of early advertising agencies collecting as much as the traffic would bear from advertisers, then paying the newspapers as little as could be negotiated. Lawson sought to establish definite rates and ethical business principles in advertising as well as in other fields.

On August 15, 1898, Green received a letter from Lawson which mentioned the name of Henry N. McKinney of N. W. Ayer & Son, an advertising agency with headquarters in Philadelphia. "Mr. Mc-Kinney's firm is the largest of its line in Philadelphia," wrote Lawson, "and, I believe the most skilled in handling advertising in all its aspects. And this I *know—they're honest.*

"I have known them for 20 years and on both sides of the business. They have placed advertising in my newspaper, and I have placed advertising through them in other newspapers—and always with entire satisfaction. I believe that Ayer & Son can handle the advertising of the National Biscuit Company with better results than can any other advertising agency in the country."

Green was interested. When he received a letter from McKinney shortly thereafter, he invited him to Chicago for a talk.

"I found myself in his reception room awaiting an audience, and wondering what a lawyer knew about advertising," McKinney recalled later. "Shortly after, I was ushered in and found myself busy answering the questions asked by him, as he endeavored to find out what I knew about it, and he kept me so well occupied at that end of the discussion, that I forgot whether he knew much or little . . ."

A tall man with dark eyes and a prominent chin, McKinney was born in Natal, South Africa, where his parents were missionaries. He came to the United States as a young man and entered the advertising business. McKinney had his own special way of obtaining advertising accounts for the Ayer company. He studied the field in which the company worked, checking where the company might go as well as where it had been. It was only when he had worked out a full program right down to its advertising techniques and slogans, that he actually approached the company. At that point he seemed to know more about the company than some of the people who ran it.

McKinney informed Green that his agency solicited "No business from manufacturers or dealers in alcoholic beverages, no patent medicine advertising, no questionable financial or speculative propositions.

"The proper foundation on which to build a great business," he advised Green, "is to make a good article and then advertise it widely and make the consumer demand it, and thus be independent of the dealer."

This was exactly the way Green saw it. The Ayer agency was selected to handle NBC's advertising.

Green and McKinney agreed that the first step was to name the new product. At this McKinney was far from a novice. During his career he had originated many brand names that had become known throughout the country including Karo, Keds, Necco, Meadow Gold.

"Altogether too little attention is paid to the name," McKinney stated. "Looking ahead, the manufacturer knows that if his article is a success, scores of imitators will try to steal the benefits of his success, by making their products, as near as the law will permit, like his in name and appearance. He must, therefore, insure his future sales by adopting a name and trade dress which will belong exclusively to him by trademark and trade right."

Green was certain of part of the name. The word "cracker" had too long been associated with stale and soggy products. The word "biscuit," on the other hand, used to describe a thin, hard bread that would keep without spoilage for some time, had a more dignified status. It was used more by the British than Americans and to most people represented, Green thought, a higher grade of product.

But the specific name for the soda biscuit that Green planned to promote still eluded them. He asked the agency to think about it and suggest possible names. "The biscuit we propose to get out," he explained, "is not, in the strict sense, a new biscuit. It will be, in fact, the ordinary soda biscuit, but made of excellent material with great care and of a little different shape than the ordinary biscuit . . ."

Green followed his request that the agency produce a name by submitting his own list. As might be expected, they largely reflected his classical interests and academic training. They included Pherenice Biscuit. The word "Pherenice," Green explained, was a Greek word signifying "thirst," pronounced in English "very nice." Verenice was another suggestion. Bekos Biscuit was another. "The word 'Bekos,' " Green explained, "is an old Greek word signifying bread." Another suggestion was Trim, "because," wrote Green, "we propose to trim the corners of this biscuit. We could also connect it in its advertising feature with Corporal Trim, the well known character of *Tristram Shandy*."

Green submitted other suggestions. Dandelo was named after a celebrated Doge of Venice. Another suggestion was Veronese, which Green explained was a name "taken from Paul Veronese, the celebrated Italian painter." Also listed were Fireside biscuit or Fireside cracker—"Baked at the fireside, eaten at the fireside"; Nabisco biscuit —"this, of course, is a coined word from National Biscuit Company"; and, the last name, Bisco biscuit—"a word coined from Biscuit Company." (It was not until the year 1966 that the company was to make use of the name "Bisco," applying it to the famous Nabisco sugar wafer.)

A few days after Green's list was received, McKinney wrote to Green telling him—with great diplomatic skill—that he, too, had done a great deal of thinking.

The name must be simple and easily pronounced and as nearly as possible capable of only one pronunciation. It must also sound well and be easily spoken. Taking up names you suggested, saying frankly how they impressed me:

"Pherenice"—too difficult for the masses.

"Verenice"—ditto. Try a dozen of the medium class and see how few will make it sound anything like "very nice"—it's also too long.

"Bekos"—better, but doesn't strike me as *the* right name.

"Trim"—meaningless until the cracker is seen and not striking enough to fasten itself on the memory.

"Dandelo" and "Veronese" have no connection other than a fanciful one and do not strike me favorably. I am afraid it is a sad fact that the great mass of cracker users are entirely ignorant of *"Tristram Shandy"* and the "Doges of Venice" and "Paul Veronese" and therefore, illustrations in connection with these names would have to be accompanied with a lesson in history to bring out their full value. "Fireside" is a good name, but its rise in so very many things takes away the effect that would go with a newer and striking name that never has been, and never could be, used by anyone but yourselves.

"Nabisco" is, I think, along the right lines, but a little long and to my ear, not smooth and pleasant. "Bisco cracker" comes still nearer and to my mind, is much the best of any name yet mentioned, and yet I am not quite satisfied with it.

Do you say—it's easy to criticize, but why don't you suggest something better? I have made no suggestions as yet because I have not had an inspiration. Nevertheless, I have done a good deal of trying. My thought is that the name should be simple, plain, novel.

Working along this line, I have made many lists; out of them all, the only ones that have any possible value are the following, and none of these suit me.

"Taka Cracker"—"Hava Cracker"—"Usa Cracker"—"Uneeda Cracker" —"Takanoo Cracker"—"Racka Cracker"—"Wanta Cracker"—"Nati"— "Pauco"—"Tanco"—"Onal"—"Biscona."* I know the name should be settled promptly, but I feel so sure that the question of name is so important that delay is preferable to error. If not then too late, I hope to bring some helpful suggestions when I come next week.

Green studied McKinney's suggestions. He could tolerate criticism only from people whose opinions he respected. There was one name among the group that appealed to him. That name was "Uneeda." Adolphus Green underlined it in red ink.

Thus, on September 6, 1898, the name was selected that was to be described as "the best-known trademark in the world." It had thirteen letters, and there were those who would claim that the name was worth "at least a million dollars a letter." One newspaper editor described the word as "the greatest triumph of human ingenuity among mere word marks. It is easy to understand. It speaks the common language of high and low, or rich and poor." Green himself later described the word as "the most valuable in the English language." On December 27, 1898, the word "Uneeda" was officially registered with the United States Patent Office.

Adoption of the name was a signal to move ahead on other fronts. "We must have," said Green, "if we are going to advertise a soda biscuit, the best soda biscuit that has ever been made, and that is not enough; it must be put up in a new kind of package, a package that will keep it as good as we send it out."

Thereupon, McKinney was dispatched to Europe to study the moisture-proof packaging techniques of bakeries abroad. "While you are in London," Green told him, "I wish you would find the time to examine such packaged goods as you may run across. You may find something there in the shape of a moisture proof package not of metal. Also investigate, if you have an opportunity, just what their pasteboard packages are and how they put up their labels, whether by hand or by machinery."

* Suggestions made by McKinney contained no "descending" characters or letters whose lower section descended below the reading line. Evidentally, McKinney believed that this made the word more readable and pleasing to the eye.

McKinney was to write Green telling him how little new information he was finding and adding hopefully, "I hope that at your end of the line you are making valuable discoveries and that when I come back, I will find many of these problems solved."

Green was indeed carrying on his own experiments with a package that would keep the Uneeda Biscuit fresh, clean and unbroken. "Barrels are the most objectional form of package," he said. "Wooden boxes the next most objectionable. Pasteboard cartons as we prepare them, keep the moisture away from the cracker reasonably well, but of course, as soon as the carton is opened, the moisture gets to the biscuit. Moisture knows a good thing when it sees it, and is always seeking to get at our goods."

Discovering a method of wrapping the Uneeda Biscuit was even more difficult than finding a name for it. Green's idea was to put out Uneeda Biscuits in small-package units for national distribution. It was a simple enough matter to get away from the cracker barrel and the big box by using the small paper carton. That is, it would have been simple for almost any other product. But crackers were highly perishable; even a tightly wrapped carton of ordinary pulpboard would not suffice to keep out moisture.

While McKinney was away, Green and his colleagues conducted experiment after experiment to try to concoct a package that would keep out the moisture for a sufficient length of time to permit the cracker to travel from the oven to the consumer's table.

George E. W. de Clercq, who had risen from an office boy at the Kennedy bakery in Chicago to become an expert on packaging operations, was an aide to Green in 1899. De Clercq later recalled one of the first moisture-vapor tests used in packaging of Uneeda Biscuits.

"We took two pickle crocks," stated de Clercq, "and placed two porous bricks in each and put water in the bottom, but only enough so that the test packages could be placed on top of them without touching the water. In one jar we put sample packages in which we used a wax-impregnated paper; in the other, samples in which we used a wax-coated paper. We sealed the jars by putting paper tightly under the crockery lids. We left the samples 72 hours. On examination, we found the crackers in the packages with the wax-impregnated paper to be so soggy that they were unfit to eat. The others, enclosed in the package with the wax-coated paper, appeared to be unaffected by moisture and were in excellent, fresh condition."

But, despite such experiments, success was elusive. In a further effort to solve the problem, Green consulted as many experts in the packaging field as he could. Among these was Robert Gair, pioneer packaging industrialist who was invited in the summer of 1899 to Chicago from Brooklyn, New York, at the expense of the National Biscuit Company to discuss the problem.

A Scotsman by birth, Gair had started his paper manufacturing in 1864 in New York, where years later he conceived of the multipurpose cutting and creasing die. This paved the way for the massproduced folding carton which was a predecessor to the fiber shipping box. He listened to the problem as Green described it, and agreed that the days of the cracker barrel were numbered. He told Green how he had introduced the paper bag to the grocery business and thus helped bring about a sweeping change in the method of dispensing foodstuffs in stores all over the country. Gair discussed the possibility of NBC using folding cartons made in his Brooklyn factory. However, the problem of how to package the biscuit so that it resisted moisture was still to be solved.

Other experts were consulted. W. B. Howe, president of the Howe & Davidson Company of Chicago and Marseilles, Illinois, met with Green. His firm made a side-opening tuck-in folding carton for many products which needed a special wax-treated paper for special protection. He stated his belief that a tuck-in carton was the thing "for use in all your factories." But no tuck-in carton alone could give moisture protection. To exclude air and water vapor, and to prevent absorption of shortening which hastens rancidity, the carton required some sort of inner liner of waxed paper. But how could the waxed paper be used economically to enclose the product?

While experts like Howe and Gair provided some assistance, the solution to the problem was to come from a completely different and unexpected quarter.

Price list for NBC products, 1908 ▸

PRETZEL VARIETIES

	Bxs.	Lge. Cans
Machine Made Pretzels	7½	7½
Machine Made Pretzelettes	7½	7½
Hand Made Pretzels	9	9
Hand Made Pretzelettes	9	9
Fancy Pretzels (Hand Made)		12
Salt Fish Pretzels	10	10
Alphabet Pretzels	10	10
Oyster Pretzels	10	10

BULK GOODS

	Bxs.	Cans
Currant Fruit Biscuit, Plain or Iced		
Dandy Buttons	10	10
Dinner Biscuit	10	10
Fancy Macaroon Rings		20
Fig Dips, Assorted and Chocolate	18	18
Five O'Clock Tea Biscuit, Assorted, Chocolate and Plain	14	14
Fluted Cocoanut Bar		16
Fudge	10	10
Full Moon		16
Ginger Drops		16
Ginger Snaps, N. B. C.	8	8
Ginger Wafers, Famous	12	12
Golden Crisp	7	7
Graham Crackers		16
Graham Wafers	8	8
Grandmother's Cookies	8	8
Hand Made Jumbles, Plain	12	12
Hand Made Jumbles, Chocolate	8	8
Household Molasses Cookies, Plain and Iced		16
Household Sugar Cookies, Plain and Iced		16
Ice Cream Cake, Assorted	8	8
White	8	8
Jars		
Jumbles, Macaroon	16	16
Klips	12	12
	8	8
	16	16
	22	

BULK GOODS

	Bxs.	C
Albert Biscuit		1
Alphabets	10	1
Animals	10	1
Arrowroot Biscuit		1
Asters		1
Atlantics	10	1
Bolivar	10	1
Bostons, Kennedy's	9	
Brightons, Plain or Iced	12	1
Brownies	11	1
Butters, Eagle, N. B. C.	6½	
Butter Scotch		1
Butter Thin Biscuit		1
Butter Flakes		1
Candidate Cake	10	1
Cartwheels	8	
Cavalier Cake	14	14
Cheese Biscuit		1
Chocolate Bar		1
Chocolate Imperials	16	1
Cinnamon Bears	9	
Cocoanut Creams	10	1
Cocoanut Cream Sandwich	12	1
Cocoanut Jelly Bar	12	1
Cocoanut Macaroons	16	1
Cocoanut Rosettes		1
Coffee Cake, Plain or Iced	10	1
Combination, or Tea Mixed	14	14
Commons	6½	
Cracknels	16	1
Cracker Meal	6	
Cream Blossoms	22	22
Crown Assorted	9	9

Two early bakeries: above, Chicago; opposite, New York

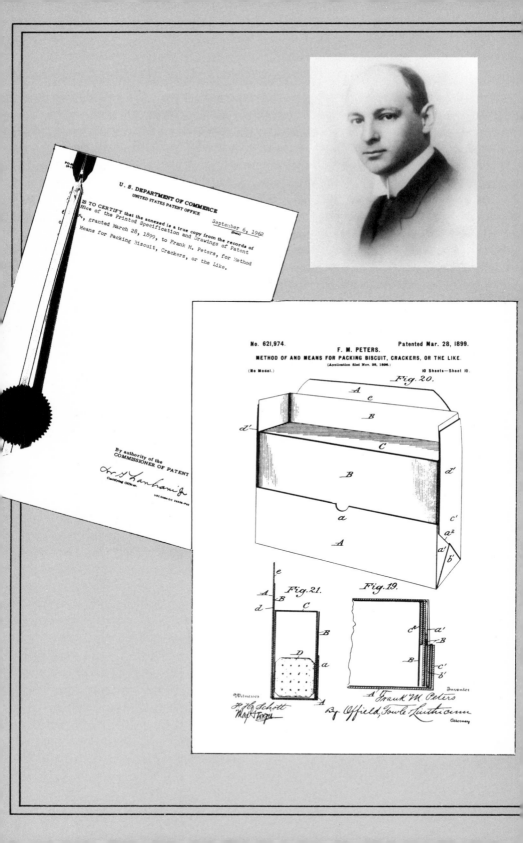

No. 621,974.   Patented Mar. 28, 1899.
F. M. PETERS.
METHOD OF AND MEANS FOR PACKING BISCUIT, CRACKERS, OR THE LIKE.
(Application filed Nov. 25, 1896.)
(No Model.)   10 Sheets—Sheet 10.

Fig. 20.

Fig. 21.   Fig. 19.

Witnesses
Inventor
Frank M. Peters
By Offield, Towle, Linthicum
Attorney

Mr. Peters

to the Rescue

"A WONDERFUL FELLOW," Adolphus Green once said of his youthful law partner, Frank Peters. "I expect he will soon become a scientific baker, something we have not got in the National Biscuit Company."

Although he was charged with carrying out much of the business of the law firm of Green, Honore & Peters, Peters was inevitably and increasingly drawn into NBC's endless activities. Since he had a scientific bent of mind, the problem of devising some sort of a machine which could package goods efficiently fascinated him.

Peters had no formal workshop. However, to the consternation of his wife, he used the kitchen table, to which he had fitted a simple foot treadle. After months of experimentation, he finally worked out a method of putting a piece of waxed paper on a carton blank and folding and interfolding the two into a box with airtight and moisture-proof qualities. Peters found that when a square block of wood, operated by the foot treadle, was lowered onto a flat carton blank with the waxed sheet placed on top, it provided the form about which the operator could interfold the waxed paper and lock the carton and flaps so that the container was set up and ready for filling and closing. By this means the contents were thoroughly protected against contamination of any sort.

His aim, Peters pointed out, was "to provide a package which, at an expense practically no greater than that of the ordinary lined

◀ *Frank M. Peters and his revolutionary In-er-seal carton*

carton package, will effectually protect the goods and preserve their freshness."

Although Peters' idea seemed absurdly simple and obvious, just wrapping up crackers and biscuits in cardboard rather than paper, it was decided that he should at least make an effort to obtain a patent. So in the winter of 1899, just a year after the company's first birthday, he traveled with his wife to Washington, D.C., to investigate patent possibilities.

Peters was confident that he had conceived of an important idea. "While I have described my improved package and method of making same as applied more particularly to the packing of biscuit, crackers, or the like," he stated in his patent application, "it is obvious that the same package and method may be employed for other articles— as, for instance, lard and similar compounds . . ."

Even Adolphus Green did not think that there was much possibility of a patent being granted. So he was delighted when Peters wrote to him from Washington:

"The patent on the Uneeda package was fully allowed. I put up the package before the eyes of the examiner (had my wooden block along), then after the box was completed cut off the carton, as we have done so many times, and showed him how the crackers were enveloped in the waxed paper. He wanted no further argument and said he would give me the strongest patent he possibly could. He was much impressed with the novelty of the package and it was unnecessary to use the affidavits of Mr. Bremner and Mr. Evans, which I had taken along to be on the safe side . . . Altogether, it was a very successful trip!"

Even Peters did not appreciate how successful his trip had been. His invention, demonstrated in the packaging of Uneeda Biscuit, helped launch what amounted to a revolution in the food packaging industry of the country. His packaging ideas were to contribute to ushering in an era of packaged food, self-service, and, ultimately, the supermarket. Just as Peters anticipated, countless other products soon began to move out of bulk boxes and barrels into clean, neat, convenient packages—bread, milk, butter, cheese, lard, flour, rice, molasses, pickles, coffee and tea. This, in turn, was to revolutionize means of distribution and sales.

Peters' invention was soon licensed overseas and helped pioneer a package revolution in Europe as well.

The firms of Robert Gair in Brooklyn and Howe & Davidson

in Chicago were given the assignment of producing the carton to Peters' specifications. The paperboard was purchased from a number of paper mills. In time the demand for cartons was so great that National Biscuit purchased the Howe & Davidson plants outright.

In March 1900 it was decided to name the Peters carton "In-er-seal," a variation of innerseal, which was to represent the idea of freshness and cleanliness as contrasted with all the shortcomings which had characterized the cracker barrel for so many years. As Green expressed it, we have "destroyed confidence in the doubtful depths of bin and barrel, and created a commercial value for wholesomeness and freshness . . ."

Now came the need for a visual symbol of the Uneeda Biscuit in particular and the company generally. Prior to the Civil War, and immediately afterward, few manufacturers labeled their goods. In 1871 there were only 121 registered trademarks in the entire United States Patent Office. But as the industrial tempo of the nation quickened, manufacturers sought to protect their goods by special brand names, slogans and visual emblems. By 1875 there were over a thousand trademarks registered. This was to increase tenfold in the next quarter of a century. Many slogans and trademarks became known in every household in the land. Some of these included "Absolutely pure"— Royal Baking Company; "You press the button: we do the rest"—Kodak; "It floats"—Ivory Soap; "The Prudential has the strength of Gibraltar"—Prudential Life Insurance; "The beer that made Milwaukee famous"—Schlitz; "All the news that's fit to print" —*The New York Times;* "If you see it in the *Sun,* it's so"— the New York *Sun;* "Pink pills for pale people"—Dr. Williams' pills.

In 1893 the Chicago World's Fair was visited by more than twelve million people who had a glimpse of many exciting new gadgets and inventions. It was the era of the first long-distance telephone, the moving picture, the telegraph, automobile and X ray. It was a period when the foundation was laid with the help of advertising, for other companies such as Sears Roebuck, Quaker Oats, Shredded Wheat, Postum Cereal, H. J. Heinz, Gold Dust.

But it was particularly an era of trademarks. There was that picture of a woman carrying a tray for Baker's Cocoa. The Quaker Oats man was known all over the country. The curly-headed boy of Hires Root Beer was a friend to millions. So was the Scott's Emulsion cod-liver oil fisherman with the huge fish over his shoulder.

The National Biscuit Company—more than many other firms—

needed product identification. Now Green addressed himself to this problem. As usual, his thinking took a scholarly direction. He spent hours browsing through books in the library of his Indiana Avenue home. Always fascinated by bindings, he had for years collected old books.

Late one night, long after his family had gone to bed, Green was thumbing through an ancient volume containing medieval Italian printers' symbols. One of them was a cross with two bars and an oval, representing—so it said—the triumph of the moral and spiritual over the evil and the material. He read with growing interest how, during the fifteenth century, this symbol was used as a printer's mark by the Society of Printers in Venice. Green felt certain that he had found the proper trademark or "coat of arms" for his company. The next day he proposed to McKinney that the symbol be officially adopted. McKinney agreed.

Countless other details confronted the company; and Green insisted on being personally involved in all of them. There was the question of designing the package itself. Again Green went to his library for inspiration and found a sixteenth century Grolier volume with a hand-tooled binding. Its border design was adopted by the company as part of a proposed package design which Green sent to N. W. Ayer in Philadelphia in November 1898.

He then went on to help choose the style of type to be used. Frederic W. Goudy, a young artist, was engaged to design the words "National Biscuit Company." He was later to recall: "The Commission came through their advertising executive, James Fraser, who did not tell me that twenty-five or more other designers had also been given the same commission at the same time. A few days after I had delivered my drawing to Fraser, I received a telephone message from him requesting my presence at his office. On arriving there I was shown some forty other drawings of the same words I had drawn, and was then told that mine had won the competition. If I had known it was a competitive affair I might not have accepted the order at all, although *all* the drawings were to be paid for. One nice thing occurred when I presented my reasonable bill: Fraser surprised me by tearing it up in my presence, and asked me to make out another for double the amount."*

Green also decided upon the color, purple with white lettering

---

* Twenty years later Goudy, now a world famous type designer, was engaged to design a special company type which was named "Nabisco."

except the name, Uneeda Biscuit, which was to be printed in purple in white sub-panels in the center of two opposite main panels. Green personally proposed the design for the package end seals which were to be reproductions of the biscuit, true as to shape and coloring and of a size as large as the dimensions of the ends of the carton could allow.

At this crucial point there was no way to convince Green to delegate authority. He personally made sketches of how the labels on the packages should appear, passed judgment on the ink, reminded the agency of how the packages were to fit into shipping cases, decided whether the typography should be in capitals or lower case.

"The care used in designing the words and the detailed shape of each letter is unbelievable," an employee of Green's recalls. "The variation in the size of some letters and the irregular spacing was all Mr. Green's."

Much anguish went into the writing of the brief sales message that appeared on the first Uneeda package. McKinney drafted one version. Green was critical and changed it. It finally emerged: "Uneeda Biscuit. Served with every meal; take a box with you on your travels; splendid for sandwiches; perfect for picnics; unequalled for general use; do not contain sugar. This is a perfect food for everybody, and the price places them within the reach of all. National Biscuit Company."

On the reverse side of the package appeared another message: "Uneeda Biscuit—to protect, preserve and deliver to the consumer our new and splendid Uneeda Biscuit, as fresh and crisp as when just from the oven, we have devised this moisture proof package. Carefully remove this wrapper and after the biscuits are eaten, you have a school children's lunch box. Serve these biscuits in this original package. Keep the box closed. This preserves the crispness."

Green was haunted by a fear that—under the pressure of these and many other details—he might not place sufficient emphasis on the highest standards of product quality. He knew that the company could not continue to grow in prestige and public acceptance if the product itself did not have both quality and uniformity. No amount of promotional verbiage could substitute for the basic excellence of the products themselves.

So the first factories which Green assigned to the production of Uneeda Biscuit were the old American Biscuit Company bakery on Bethune Street in New York; the D. F. Bremner plant in Chicago, which had eight reel ovens; the Kennedy Biscuit Works in Chicago, with fourteen reel ovens; the Dozier bakery in St. Louis, with seven reel ovens; the Loose Brothers bakery in Kansas City with four reel ovens; the Lillibridge-Bremner bakery in Minneapolis with five reel ovens; and the Sommer-Richardson bakery in St. Joseph, Missouri, with three reel ovens.

It was not easy convincing the various bakeries of the necessity of speed, efficiency and uniformity.

"You have already made a contract with Howe & Davidson, as I understand it, for 2,000,000 cartons of the size and quality agreed upon," Green wrote to a subordinate in November 1898. "You must see that those cartons are ready to be delivered to the different factories who will be authorized to make this biscuit . . . I wish each of these factories to have a number. If there is a number already in the general business of the company used for these factories, then I should use such a number. If not, commence with the numbering for this particular work, Bremner, #1; Kennedy, #2; etc. That number wants to be on each carton delivered to the factory, as that will be the only way in which we can distinguish where the goods were made when they are out to the trade. You will have to make an estimate of how you are to divide, as far as these numbers are concerned, the order of 2,000,000."

Even such a detail as whether the printed cartons were dry was a matter that Green could not pass over without comment. "You should arrange in the contract with Howe & Davidson," he wrote to James H. Douglas, recently named sales manager, "that those cartons should be thoroughly dry when sent out by them, and to be packed in such a way that they will keep dry in transit from them to the factory. It is absolutely necessary that the cartons should be of exactly the same size, and strong provision in the contract with Howe & Davidson should be inserted to that effect."

Like an army officer, Green dispatched orders to his staff: "There are certain matters in regard to the Uneeda Biscuit of which I wish to have you take charge," he wrote to D. F. Bremner, "and for the prompt execution of which I shall hold you responsible. The form of the biscuit has been decided upon. The formula by which it is to be made is to be ⅔ patent flour and ⅓ a first quality of straight flour, and is to contain 22½ pounds of lard. The crackers to be made and packed so that the box decided upon, which is 8½ inches long, shall contain 21 crackers, which together shall weigh seven ounces."

No detail was too small for Green in his almost fanatical effort to achieve success with his Uneeda Biscuit. "The cracker is to be well baked," he told Bremner, who had spent a lifetime in the bakery business, "so that each cracker shall show a good color.

"Each factory must be in condition to turn out these biscuit ready to deliver to the trade on Tuesday, December 27," he ordered.

Although Green tried to let his subordinates reach their own decisions, he very frequently found it impossible to resist worrying. "I shall not pretend to dictate to you the details of how this [the baking of the goods] is to be accomplished, but I will make the following suggestions: There is at present no cutter ready to make these goods in a commercial way, but one is being prepared, as I understand it, at Richmond for that purpose. That should be gotten ready as soon as possible and taken to the Bremner bakery, and an experiment made upon large enough lines to demonstrate that the cutter is all right . . . We propose to have a girl instructed here by Mr. Peters in the proper way of setting up the boxes and packing the goods; perhaps two or three girls and you [Bremner] should take one of these girls with you to each factory to instruct the girls at that factory. Directions for making this biscuit should be put in writing, giving the manner of setting up the boxes and packing the goods."

Green even discussed such details as the handling of dough. "My observation leads me to conclude that the proper handling of dough is of extreme importance, and that upon this kind of goods there is a great difference between the different factories, and in fact, between goods of the same factory at different times."

Green would ask the various bakers to reply in writing, "accepting the important trust that I have put in your hands." To H. F. Vories, manager of the NBC package department in those hectic November days in 1898, Green wrote, "I wish you to consider the best plan of distributing these goods from the factories that make them to our other factories. I do not wish our other factories to stock up with these biscuits. I wish to take every measure possible to get these biscuit as quickly as I can from the mouth of the oven to the mouth of the consumer."

And still there were vital decisions to be made, such as the question of price. Green believed in low priced package goods. He felt, in order to attract large numbers of consumers, that it was necessary to keep prices low. He also wanted the package itself to be restricted to a size containing no greater quantity than could practically be consumed while in a palatable condition. He was adamant in resisting efforts to increase the size of the package and the price. He felt that success or failure depended largely on whether the consuming public detected an obvious difference in quality and taste between Uneeda and other biscuits.

Nearly all his associates hinted to Green that the price must be higher. They insisted that the five-cent price would make the success of the venture impossible. Naturally, those who had invested large sums of money in the company wanted a higher price to guarantee a quick return on their investment.

But Green resisted. And Frank O. Lowden supported him. Lowden also saw the possibility of tremendous volume at a small profit per unit. But, beyond that, Green had a vision of mass distribution and sales far beyond anything that had been attempted previously in the baking industry.

He told the stockholders in January 1899, "We shall continue to improve the manner of making our goods, and of packing them so as to get them in better condition to the consumer. Reduction in prices will also, in its turn, increase consumption and in itself enable us to decrease our percentage of profit on sales without diminishing the aggregate volume of our profits."

As usual Green and Lowden saw eye to eye on the necessity, for the time being, of low profits. Green did not consider profits in percentages, but in dollars and cents. He was satisfied that such a package as he had in mind for Uneeda could be produced at a profit—a small one to be sure—per package. And he was willing to look for large profits in dollars and cents through a large volume of business. This concept, at the time, was considered highly questionable. For many it was even shocking. But Green was not to be diverted.

Although haughty in the face of opposition, Green could display amazing humility. In a letter to Lowden, in which he asked advice on financial matters, he said that he had no doubt, "that when you return and look the matter over for yourself, you will be of my opinion. If you are not, then I shall be pretty sure that my opinion is wrong. When I cannot bring you around to my opinion in this business, I am pretty well convinced that my opinion is not the right one."

The business of launching the new product was now approaching its climax. Green was feeling the results of the mounting pressure.

He had taken on the full responsibility; the strain had been more than he had anticipated. As he wrote to Lowden, "I am very tired."

Yet the most important aspect of launching the Uneeda Biscuit and starting the new company on its career remained before him.

EIGHT

A Little Child
Shall Lead Them

AT THE TIME advertising was not in good repute. It was confined largely to patent medicines, tobaccos, seeds and farm implements. With few exceptions, advertising appeals to the consumer were limited to small enterprises or those with very specialized products to sell.

But it was time for a change. The country had been, as Peter Lyon puts it in *Success Story* "bursting its britches along every seam; from 1880 to 1900 the population rose fifty percent (from about fifty million to about seventy-five million); and the national wealth shot up twice as fast. During the decade 1874–1883, the annual flow of goods to the consumer was worth, in the average, about 12 billion dollars; by 1894–1903, the value had more than doubled, to better than 25 billion dollars a year."

In the expanding nation there was a demand for almost everything. But the more sagacious realized the necessity of informing the population of the new methods, new products, new services. Advertising was the most efficient means of doing this.

Green astonished his board of directors early in 1899 when he requested a substantial sum for national advertising. Within the first decade, Green put in McKinney's hands $7,000,000 for national advertising. The announcement in the press of the first year's appropria-

◄ *His uncle asked him to pose*

89

tion caused a sensation from coast to coast. It was hailed as the largest advertising commitment ever made.

The NBC promotional campaign was based on the principle of moving the company closer to the consumer by selling direct to retailers without benefit of wholesalers or jobbers. The only way this could be done was by the most intensive and imaginative type of national advertising.

The handling of NBC's account by N. W. Ayer & Son broke new ground in American advertising. N. W. Ayer provided precisely the type of advertising counseling that NBC needed. The agency demonstrated mature judgment, imagination, and the ability to get along with NBC people who had strong opinions. Green was, of course, not an easy man with whom to work. "We cannot do a company's work *for* him," an Ayer executive wrote. "We must do it *with* him. His knowledge, assistance, and cooperation is of vital necessity. We have no cut-and-dried, bound-to-succeed scheme to propose or endorse."

The advertising agency tried to use every available talent. It "set a precedent by placing at the disposal of an advertiser the expanded facilities of a modern advertising agency," McKinney pointed out. "And here, as never before, the advertising agency amply proved its ability to expand and execute advertising as an integral part of a selling campaign. The Ayer agency and the National Biscuit Company worked in such close cooperation that one cannot say which made the greater contribution."

Early one January morning in 1899 residents of Chicago were baffled by a mysterious new word in bold type printed in their newspapers. It was the single word "Uneeda." They found the same message on billboards and street cars.

"Uneeda Biscuit."

In a few days this unidentified message was changed to a query: "Do you know Uneeda Biscuit?"

This was followed by still another question: "Do YOU know Uneeda Biscuit?"

Then: "Do you KNOW Uneeda Biscuit?"

After that: "Of course Uneeda Biscuit!!!"

A little later: "Uneeda Biscuit—certainly!!!"

This advertising was expanded until it covered the entire country including not only newspapers, billboards and painted signs but magazines, theater programs, posters, window and cutout displays, store banners and booklets.

The "teaser-type" campaign officially presented Uneeda Biscuit to America almost a year from the day the company was born. "The startling advertisements took the public eye and captured the public taste," McKinney recalled. "Demand was created at once. It seemed as if success had been won in a breath."

"It was a gigantic task which NBC advertising assumed," a company official commented, "namely the breaking down of habit and ignorance, the habit of buying from barrels, bins and boxes, and ignorance of what that meant."

Then one effective advertisement followed after another. Some ideas were conceived by McKinney; some by Green; some by James H. Douglas, NBC sales manager.

N. W. Ayer & Son established the first full-fledged copy department in 1900. Among those on McKinney's staff was a bright young copywriter named Joseph J. Geisinger, one of the advertising industry's first full-time copywriters. He addressed himself to the difficult job of inventing a symbol that could reflect—in an attractive way—the unique products and services that NBC offered the consuming public. Geisinger first thought of a fisherman, clad in a slicker, eating dry biscuits out of a dry package, an interesting concept which made the point that NBC products were always fresh and crisp. But the fisherman idea did not appeal to Green; the agency was asked to give more thought to the problem.

Now Geisinger happened to have a five-year-old nephew named Gordon Stille, a plump-cheeked, bright-eyed boy with a winsome look. His uncle asked him whether he would be willing to pose for an advertising photographer, dressed in boots, oil hat and slicker, with a box of Uneeda Biscuits under his arm. The child agreed. So did his parents. Pictures were taken. The rest is history.

When Adolphus Green saw the proofs, he was enthusiastic. The pictures appeared to have the human quality needed to appeal to the consuming public. Henceforth, the portrait of the boy in the slicker clutching the Uneeda Biscuit box became one of the most widely used advertising motifs in the history of the advertising business. Because of the popularity of the boy in a slicker, a number of people insisted that they were the ones who posed for the original picture. One person even insisted that he had been the original slicker boy and that he had been kidnaped, knocked on the head and forcibly photographed!

The picture was reproduced on streetcar cards, posters, advertising banners, moving picture slides, cartoon strips, booklets, reprints, and a wide variety of other media. Countless children throughout the country dressed up to imitate the slicker boy at masquerade parties and parades. There was scarcely a small boy who was not a Uneeda boy at one time or another.

The Uneeda Biscuit boy helped usher in a new era. The day of anonymous foods was, as one magazine pointed out, "definitely at an end. The era of brands and trademarks had begun." And NBC had helped to do it in scores of ways.

Poems were submitted to the company glorifying the cracker:

> I am Uneeda, I defy
> The roaming dust, the busy fly.
> For in my package, sealed and tight,
> My makers keep me pure and white.

Uneeda Biscuits became so popular that they frequently were used as props in motion pictures and the theater. To exploit this the company invited its employees to report the name of any theatrical presentation that used an NBC product.

The editor of *Comfort* magazine recounted how he had purchased a package of Uneeda Biscuits, put it under the back seat of his Peerless automobile, and forgotten it. The package was bumped and jogged wherever the automobile traveled. One day, about two years later when the car was overhauled, the package was discovered. It was taken from under the seat and opened. The inside moisture-proof preservative paper was, it was testified, in perfect condition. "Inside was a neat row of 23 whole and unbroken Uneeda Biscuits. The state of the crackers was one of remarkable preservation—almost unbelievable."

By 1900 sales for the Uneeda Biscuit were topping 10,000,000 packages a month. This happened at a time when all other packaged crackers would scarcely, it was estimated, total 500,000 a year. Uneeda Biscuit became an accepted part of American life. Cartoonists and photographers made frequent use of the package as they would of scenes of the Grand Canyon or Niagara Falls. J. N. Darling, the cartoonist known as "Ding," told a representative of NBC that, "I had no thought of distributing free advertising when I made the cartoon [that included a Uneeda Biscuit package]; but Uneeda Biscuit packages are so much a part of the scene on any picnic ground that I could hardly make a picture without it."

A writer for *Printers' Ink* defined the Uneeda Biscuit as, "an agent of Americanization." He recommended that the immigrant coming to the shores of America be Americanized with the help of Uneeda Biscuit.

Uneeda Biscuit eating contests were held in store windows. Toys were fashioned to look like miniature packages of Uneeda Biscuits and the Uneeda horse-drawn wagons. A town in West Virginia was officially named Uneeda. A minister in Albany, New York, used Uneeda Biscuit as a subject for a Sunday sermon: "Whether you ride in the train, sreetcar or automobile, you see again and again the suggestion, 'Uneeda Biscuit.' Wherever you go, you can't miss it; it is omnipresent. The National Biscuit Company has said Uneeda Biscuit so often and with such consummate skill that it has succeeded in convincing the people of the United States that Uneeda Biscuits are vitally necessary to them. No better illustration can be found of the possibility of creating a demand where none exists and intensifying the desires normally present in all of us."

The Uneeda campaign was the largest conducted in the country up to that time. It was the first to feature a staple food, ready for consumption, and sold in individual packages.

Of course, many grocers saw less possibility for profit in packaged crackers than those sold in bulk. A cartoon was printed showing an old gentleman sitting in a country store next to a cracker barrel saying, "The idea! Spendin' their money for advertisin'! I tell ye, boys, th' only formula fer a rattlin' good grocery bisness is checker games, with plenty o' free crackers."

But Green brushed aside such conservatism. "Uneeda is and will be the foundation of our business all the time," he said. "The more of them you sell, the more of your other goods you will sell." For him the campaign amounted to almost a personal crusade.

In May 1898 the first NBC dividend had been declared. "This new consolidated company has declared its first dividend on its $23,537,000 of preferred stock," the Chicago *Chronicle* reported. "The dividend is a quarterly one of 1¾%, payable May 31, and is reported to have been more than earned. Business is improving, but it has been decided not to begin disbursements on the common stock until a considerable cash surplus has been accumulated."

Green's intention was to hold off paying dividends on common stock until such time as more or less intangible assets represented by this stock had been written off the accounts. It was this philosophy that was largely responsible for the ultimate transferring of such stock into assets representing truly tangible values.

At the turn of the century the company had realized a year's sales representing $35,651,898. Profits for the twelve months to January 31, 1900, represented $3,302,155, with a per cent of profit on sales of 9.26. By the end of 1900 the sales figure had increased to over $36,000,000, with profits up to $3,318,355, and the per cent of profit on sales 9.11. A year later the sales had increased to $38,625,134 with profits at $3,670,455, and the per cent of profits to sales was 9.50.

At the completion of NBC's sixth year of existence, Green informed the stockholders that the company has "paid regular quarterly dividends on its preferred stock at the rate of 7% per annum since its beginning. The first dividend of 1% [meaning 1% of par value, a customary manner of reporting dividends in this era] on the common stock was declared August 15, 1899 . . . and since that time dividends have been paid on the common stock regularly every quarter at the rate of 4% per annum.

"We bent our energies to improving the quality of biscuit. We have succeeded in making great advances. We set about securing the best possible package to keep them in. The result was the air-tight, moisture-proof In-er-seal package. We put our advance quality of biscuit in our advance style of package and advertised these trade-marked goods. The public began to buy superior biscuit protected and sold in a superior way under our In-er-seal trademark. The sale of In-er-seal goods has been phenomenal. People who never before used biscuit are now constant buyers. Our trademark brands have become common bywords."

Just as Green had foreseen, the success of Uneeda Biscuit "created a new demand for biscuits of all kinds." The company extended its advertising to several other products selected as having good potentials.

As the name National Biscuit Company became associated with freshness, wholesomeness and reliability, NBC products became so popular that distribution facilities lagged behind demand.

In the old days Josiah Bent and his family used to bake crackers three days a week and carry the product around in baskets to their customers the remaining three days. Bent's system of distribution approached perfection for the territory he covered. He knew every cracker was fresh when he handed it to his customers; and he was in constant personal contact with them.

This simple plan could not, however, meet the requirements of millions of people. The cracker business evolved into a wholesale business in barrels and boxes, a business of jobbers and warehouses and wagon "peddlers" instead of market baskets. But the cumbersome system of distribution in quantity meant that more time must elapse between the baking and the eating. As a result, freshness suffered.

It was necessary to devise a method—now for a huge nation—that had been used successfully on a local basis by Bent, Pearson and Kennedy decades earlier. The first thing to do was to get back to the *small unit* of Pearson's day. This NBC was in the process of accomplishing. Now it was necessary to devise ways and means of making this small unit speedily available to the consumer.

From the beginning the company established wholesale selling branches or distribution agencies. These were supplied by shipments from the bakeries—now reduced from 114 to about 80. And each agency, in its turn, supplied the grocer customers of the company. In this way a direct and prompt service to the consuming public was organized.

For the first decade all store door deliveries were made by horse and wagon. In those days the maximum range for delivery was within a radius of ten miles. A two-horse team was often hitched up Monday morning and returned Wednesday night.

The horse was an important and often bothersome factor in distribution. Not only was it necessary to buy horses, wagons and accessory equipment, the animals had to be stabled and fed and space made available for the vehicles. Men had to be hired to drive the wagons, keep equipment in repair, and care for the horses.

There were special Uneeda Cadets, young men who went around the country visiting stores, one after the other in systematic fashion. They would buy up old Uneeda Biscuits that were not fresh and get rid of them. This was done on a surprise basis, because storekeepers tended to hold on to merchandise rather than turn it in.

It was necessary for the company to constantly insist that its salesmen, accustomed to selling crackers in bulk, push its packaged goods. "We rely upon you," Green said in a letter to his salesmen in 1901, "to see that . . . goods are prominently and conspicuously displayed in every store, that the package may at once connect itself with the advertisements in the consumer's mind. This accomplished," concluded Green, "the rest is assured."

James H. Douglas, a sales manager who had valuable experience as a baker in Iowa and Nebraska, repeatedly reminded his salesmen that their "future with the company must depend upon the success you have in placing of our packaged goods." He tried to instill a crusading spirit in the sales force.

But no amount of salesmanship could succeed if there were not sufficient products to sell.

One day Green picked up the telephone. The excited voice on the other end was that of C. L. Holt, the usually calm manager of the Uneeda bakery in New York City. The first words Holt spoke were "The trade here is furious."

Green was startled. But the next sentence was even more disturbing. The trade was upset, it was revealed, because the demand for Uneeda Biscuits was not being met. Green learned that Uneeda bakeries were operating about 20,000 dozen *behind accumulating orders!*

When the big Uneeda Biscuit plant had been completed in New York City in May 1899, National Biscuit Company employees had proudly paraded through the streets, boasting of the opening of the biggest bakery ever. A platoon of mounted policemen cleared the way for the procession, headed by the 23rd Regiment band and followed by no less than 112 gaily decked horse-drawn bakery wagons, each bearing the words "Uneeda Biscuit."

There were floats, too, one representing the famous Ferris wheel with huge Uneeda Biscuit boxes for cars. Another carried an immense parrot, nine feet high, holding in one of its talons a proportionately large Uneeda Biscuit.

It had seemed unlikely that this bakery's full facilities could ever be completely utilized. But now Holt was telling Green that the plant could not even keep up with demands!

And neither could most of the other bakeries which were making Uneeda Biscuits. Production was lagging everywhere. It was encouraging to know of the demand for Uneeda. But to have created the demand and not be able to fill it! This was indeed a blow.

Green now announced that he needed a vacation. From price war, to peace, to launching the new company, to conceiving Uneeda Biscuit, Green had been constantly under pressure. His irritability had increased, but his perceptiveness was never more acute, his grim determination never more effective. In a letter to Frank O. Lowden, one of the few men in whom Green could confide, he wrote bitterly:

I have been obliged to order advertisements stopped in the newspapers until we can get in shape to supply the demand.

I certainly am glad that I am going away. If I stayed here I believe I would eat my heart out. We have ovens down East that cannot be run for want of proper machinery . . . Some people still believe that this Uneeda business is only temporary. Of course, I am very much disappointed that I have been unable to carry out my advertising plan as I have laid it out. We will be unable to tell this year just what the limit is for the demand that we can create . . .

Is not that a strange condition of affairs? When the company started, it was believed that the [New York] plant would never run full. A number of days when I was down there last, they were running full and running overtime in the evening. If the quarter just closed does not show a large profit, then the fault is in our manufacturing department, and I have become convinced more and more every day that there is where the great weakness of our company exists . . .

The subject about which I am going to speak at the directors' meeting and I wish to advise you of now . . . is the enormous waste that is going on in the manufacture of our goods. If Uneeda has done nothing else, it has disclosed the almost criminal method in which our business is carried on. I will venture to say today that we are wasting enough in this company to pay 3% dividend on our common stock, and this is a most conservative estimate.

Take Uneeda Biscuit as an example. Some plants are producing from a barrel of flour 500 packages of Uneeda Biscuit. Some plants have fallen below 400 packages. The average should be about 480 packages, but it falls much below this mark . . .

This arises from two causes. First, carelessness in handling the doughs whereby the crackers are too heavy; second—the amount of crippled and broken crackers; the latter ranging from one pound and a half a barrel in the best plant to nine or ten pounds to the barrel in the worst plants. Two pounds to the barrel is as much as any plant should have . . .

You know me well enough that I cannot rest satisfied while this state of affairs continues. Up against this problem, with the struggles I have made in the last few months, and the little I seem to have accomplished, I begin to feel that the job I have undertaken is too big for me. Some few of our people . . . are thoroughly alive to the importance of this question. But others, and I regret to say, some in high stations, are apathetic. To their minds the situation exists, and has existed. Therefore, it is useless to try to remedy it. They look upon me as an idealist . . .

I am glad that the time for my vacation approaches . . . And yet I hate to go and leave this company in its present state. I have as fully as I could laid down the policy that I wish observed while I am away, but it is very difficult to get the policy observed. It is broken into every few days now by orders given in violation of the policy. What will become of this policy while I am away? The Lord only knows.

I hate to burden you with all these troubles when you are away on your vacation, but I feel that I must unburden myself a little to somebody, and I know that I can count upon you to sympathize with me. I can tell you one thing, if I had known the condition of our manufacturing department, I never would have become Chairman of the Board of Directors, or what I am sometimes called, the "Boss of the Biscuit Business."

Production problems found their inevitable solutions. Ultimately his reports to the board of directors reflected an increasing optimism.

"We have had a very large increase in the sale of our package goods . . . This package business has reached its present volume because we have what the great consuming public want, of which we have apprised them by our extensive advertising.

"This increase in the sale of our package goods has not been confined to any one city or state, but is well distributed over the entire country . . ."

Despite the spectacular career of Uneeda, the phenomenal success of the National Biscuit Company was not the result of any one product. It was the result of the qualities of many products—long regional favorites—but never before packaged and promoted on a national scale.

An early store display and an original advertising agency sketch ▸

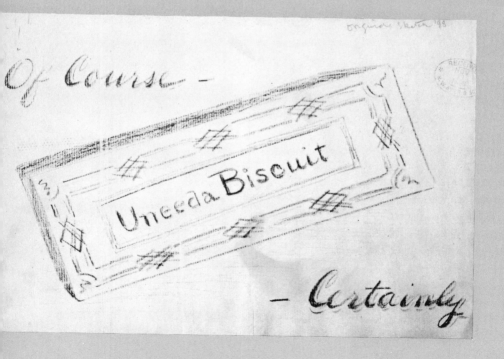

Of Course -

Uneeda Biscuit

- Certainly

From Animal Crackers to ZuZus

—————

ALTHOUGH Adolphus W. Green had six children whom he loved dearly, he was no prouder of them than of his special creation in the world of baking, the Uneeda Biscuit.

But the proud father also had other relatives demanding attention. The National Biscuit Company had inherited some of the world's finest names in cookies, crackers and biscuits. Despite his fanatical emphasis on the launching of Uneeda Biscuit, he realized that it was unwise to build a business on one item alone. NBC would succeed only to the degree that it was able to produce, package and promote a complete line of products.

One such product was first conceived by an ingenious inventor in Philadelphia, James Henry Mitchell, who specialized in the creation of mechanical devices for the baking industry. Mitchell's inventions, some dating as far back as 1872, included a dough-sheeting machine, a sugar-wafer machine, a machine for the treatment of cakes, a machine for coating cakes, and grain-weighing apparatus. So useful were the results of his efforts that in 1874 he received a citation from the highly respected Franklin Institute in Philadelphia.

For some time Mitchell had been working on a challenging new idea. He sought to create a machine that could simultaneously make a cookie and fill it with a preserve or "jam." The device, as he designed it, produced a "pie," that is, jam surrounded by dough. It ac-

◄ *The first use of "Nabisco"*

tually resembled a funnel inside another funnel, or a tube within a tube. The inner funnel or tube carried a stream of jam. The outer tube formed a hollow tubelike stream of dough. This dough was formed into a sort of casing which completely enveloped the jam. Both jam and dough could be simultaneously extruded in an endless ribbon of cake or pie, which was then cut into slices.

In 1892 Mitchell applied for a patent for his new machine, which was granted. Although he had no name for his "pie," he thought the idea might be of value in commercial baking. So in 1892 he persuaded officials of the Kennedy Biscuit Works, which had recently become affiliated with the New York Biscuit Company, to try out his new machine, which he shipped to Cambridgeport.

Mitchell personally installed the machine and supervised its functioning, experimenting with its workings as well as with the formula for the jam. One of the earliest machines included instructions to make certain that dried figs are "soaked over night; in the morning, they are drained and ground. They are then cooked in a steam jacket kettle with an equal amount of granulated sugar; pound for pound."

When the day came for the first major trial of the machine, officials of the New York Biscuit Company as well as the Kennedy bakery gathered round. A number of experimental batches were run. The machine seemed to work splendidly. The professional bakers tasted the final result, found it good and went away impressed.

This was the era of the price war between eastern and western bakers. Here was a new biscuit that might help the east win the war!

But promotion could not start until a name was selected. Already, cookies and crackers had been named Brighton, Boston Family, Cambridge Salts, Beacon Hill, Shrewsbury, Melrose. The exciting new product of the Mitchell machine needed some such name. Later an assistant to James Hazen, manager of the Cambridgeport bakery, recalled, "The name was taken from the name of the town of Newton —a suburb of Boston." When this name was selected for this new product, it reflected a practice—by Mr. Hazen, who was manager of this plant—of using the names of towns and cities in the vicinity of Boston.

The original Newton-baking machine was eventually packed up and sent to the Manhattan bakery of the New York Biscuit Company, where it was used for some time. Meanwhile, production of the Newton continued at Cambridgeport.

Word about the Newton spread so that a demand to manufacture them arose in other locations. The Philadelphia branch of the New York Biscuit Company was particularly enthusiastic when it sampled the Newton and announced, "A recent development of a wonderful and intricate machine . . . Think of baking a pie completely by machinery, the biscuit themselves being the product of such an amazing invention."

F. A. Russell, manager of the Philadelphia branch obviously unaware of the process by which the new product had been named, said, "They are worthily christened, having the name of so eminent a philosopher as Sir Isaac Newton, one whose name is always thought of in connection with science."

Although Russell was incorrect in his facts, he was correct in his optimism. The new Newton sold like hotcakes. Gradually, the fig content, most frequently used for the "jam," began to be associated with the name. Before long, instead of being listed as Newtons, the new product was rechristened "Fig Newtons," and became one of the mainstays of the National Biscuit Company.

Adolphus Green was aware of the sales potentiality of the Fig Newton, which NBC promotion lyrically described as a "unique combination of cake and figs—puffy little bolsters of flavorsome, golden brown cake with a generous filling of fig jam, one of the many varieties that have made the name of the National Biscuit Company a byword for biscuits." Soon Fig Newton cakes were encased in the famous In-er-seal package and sold, not only in bulk in the traditional manner, but also in small packages whose popularity was to grow and grow.

Another popular product at the time of the birth of NBC was the ginger cookie. Gingersnaps were baked commercially as far back as 1862. A decade later a variety of ginger products were on the market including ginger cakes, ginger fingers, ginger jumbles, gingernuts, gingersnaps.

Green recognized the possibilities of a well-packaged mouthwatering ginger product. Therefore, following on the heels of the Uneeda Biscuit and its companion cracker, the Uneeda Milk Biscuit, came the Jinjer Wayfer. In the year 1899 alone some 65,000,000 packages of Jinjer Wayfers were sold.

A brand new product and honorable descendant of the gingersnap was the ZuZu. Although opinions differ, there was one theory that the "ZuZu" was taken by Green from the name of a character in a play he had enjoyed, *Forbidden Fruit*, by Dion Boucicault. The ZuZu was a spicy combination of ginger and sugar-cane molasses. Aided by its In-er-seal package, its brilliant yellow cover, and a highly imaginative promotional campaign, it became one of the most popular cookies ever baked.

As a result all sorts of enterprises requested permission to use the name of ZuZu: a dance orchestra on Long Island; a manufacturer of cigars from Pennsylvania; a candy maker in New York; a ginger-ale company in Waco, Texas; a chewing-gum packer in Quincy, Illinois; a flour manufacturer in Atchison, Kansas. As the fame of the ZuZu spread, a baby zebra in New York Central Park Zoo was christened after it.

The company used all of its promotional ingenuity to popularize ZuZu. One idea provided free ZuZu Clown costumes to youngsters throughout the country. "No matter where the children live, each year finds dozens of them in all parts of the country becoming versatile actors in the character made famous by advertising, the ZuZu Clown."

Another goodie destined for glorification was the sugar wafer— a best seller everywhere. At the time of the founding of NBC, most bakeries made sugar wafers in one form or another. But there were no nationally known, uniformly baked sugar wafer brands.

Green grasped the opportunity to order the manufacture of a top quality sugar wafer, to be branded with the NBC trademark and introduced with an extensive campaign of advertising. Again the problem of a name arose. However, ever since Green had submitted his list of name suggestions for a soda cracker, he had kept one of them in the back of his head. This name, "Nabisco," had been politely but firmly turned down by McKinney as "a little long, and to my ear, not smooth and pleasant." Now, Green thought, was the moment to revive the name. This time McKinney voiced no objection. It was decided that the new NBC sugar wafer would be called "Nabisco."

Sales and advertising plans were carefully developed and Nabisco Sugar Wafers appeared for the first time in June 1901. They were first packed in tin boxes, later in the In-er-seal paper container. The Nabisco, in lemon, orange, chocolate, vanilla and mint flavors, met with instantaneous success. One company spokesman, throwing caution to the winds, stated, "In my opinion, Nabiscos are one of the major gastronomic achievements of the human race, as important as the development of ice cream."

Advertising copywriters were lyrical. The flavors of Nabisco Sugar Wafers, they wrote, "tempt beyond resistance those who love life's sweetest joys." They even resorted to poetry:

"Now you must tell me true," she cried,
      When he declared his soul was raptured,
"For I must feel your love is tried,
      Before I yield my heart as captured."
"See! here above thy head I hold,
      'Nabisco' sweet, and all my treasure,
And you must tell me, lover bold,
      Which choice will give you keenest pleasure."
"Fair one," he cried, "here at thy feet,
      'Tis hard to choose 'twixt one and tother,
So just to prove my taste is sweet,
      I'll eat the one, and keep the other."

Another NBC product, the graham cracker, was also popular throughout the country. It had been a favorite since it was created and introduced in the early part of the nineteenth century by Dr. Sylvester Graham, an eccentric but sagacious expert on health foods. He promoted it widely as part of a campaign to encourage the use of unbolted, unsifted wheat flour.

The graham cracker had been sold by bakeries for decades. The New York Biscuit Company and its rivals to the west all sold it. However, it remained for the National Biscuit Company to stabilize its production, package it, and give it national promotion.

There were many other famous cookies and crackers baked by NBC ovens. About the time that Green and Moore were, as young lawyers, descending upon Chicago, a special type of soda cracker was being produced by the F. L. Sommer Company in its huge bakery in St. Joseph, Missouri. It was called "Premium Saltine." At first it was made only in the west. But its popularity spread and soon it was in demand all over the country. The Premium soda cracker was the greatest thing that had happened to the Sommer company since its government contract for half a million pounds of hard bread for distribution to Indian tribes. The Premium soda cracker or saltine was to become—although not without opposition from Green—one of the most valuable assets that NBC inherited.

Then there was the famous tea biscuit, forerunner of the Social Tea Biscuit, which came into existence in the spring of 1889. Both the name and the product were originated by Holmes & Coutts, New York bakers who later became part of the New York Biscuit Company. Social Tea Biscuits were being packed and sold in large glass-front cans and wooden boxes before the turn of the century.

As early as 1899 the National Biscuit Company, recognizing the popularity of the Social Tea Biscuit, had packaged it in its In-er-seal carton, trademarked and promoted it. One of the first sweet biscuits to be placed on the market in packages, its immediate success pointed the way for many more to follow.

The smallest item on the NBC list was the oyster cracker in wide demand prior to the turn of the century. In 1879 the Wilson Biscuit Company, manufacturers of American Biscuits in Philadelphia, listed Oyster Crackers 1, Oyster Crackers 2, Oyster Cracker Standards as well as Pearl Oyster Crackers. While most bakeries did not have that large a selection of oyster crackers, almost all had one type or another of oyster cracker. The Kennedy Biscuit Works in 1890 had no less than eight different types of oyster crackers available.

NBC considered the oyster cracker an important product and conceived a new name for it, "Oysterette," registered in March 1901. The Oysterette or oyster cracker "to be eaten with oyster, and containing no oysters" was to become fabulously successful even where oysters were unknown.

Animal crackers were created and achieved fame many years before the advent of NBC. In the beginning they were just called "Animals." They were imported from England when "fancy" baked goods first began to be in demand here. In the latter part of the nineteenth century they were manufactured domestically by Hetfield & Ducker in Brooklyn as well as Vandeveer & Holmes Biscuit Company in New York. Both firms eventually became part of the New York Biscuit Company and "Animals" were one of their staples.

When "Animals" were adopted by NBC, their name was changed to "Barnum's Animals Crackers," named after P. T. Barnum, showman and circus owner who was so famous during this era. Barnum's Animals Crackers provided the nation with a new type of animal cracker, produced in a small square box resembling a circus cage with a tape at the top for easy carrying. Barnum's Animals appeared during the Christmas season just three years after the Uneeda Biscuit. What was originally a seasonal novelty proved so popular that it became a steady seller. Soon Animal (the s was dropped) Crackers became part of the American scene and of almost every

American household. Animal Crackers became such an integral part of the life of the country that Christopher Morley wrote:

> Animal Crackers and cocoa to drink,
> That is the finest of suppers, I think;
> When I am grown up and can have what I please,
> I think I shall always insist upon these.*

An article entitled "Cruelty to Animal Crackers," appearing in the New York *Evening Journal*, said, "Zoos in some of our cities are so incomplete that the only way a lot of kids can learn anything about wild beasts is from Animal Crackers. One father was so careful about his baby that he wouldn't even let his child have an Animal Cracker for a pet. Once he did buy him a lion made out of cookie dough, but he was so cautious that he put a muzzle on it. . . ."

A strip in the cartoon *Reg'lar Fellers* by Gene Byrnes (George Mathew Adams Service) ran like this:

(*Character appears in a grocery store.*)

"Gimme five cents' worth of Animal Crackers."

(*Character walks along the street eating.*)

"I think I'll eat an elephant an' then a tiger."

(*Character still eats.*) "Now I'll try a giraffe an' a buffalo an' then a lion."

(*Character leans against a fence eating.*) "I'll bet there's a regular circus going on inside of me."

In a similar vein, an NBC advertisement ran:

> A cracker lion cannot roar,
> And wouldn't if he could;
> But kiddies like him all the more
> Because he tastes so good.

The famous Arrowroot Cracker was made from wheat flour, combined with arrowroot flour, which was obtained from rhizomes (underground stems) of a tropical American plant. This was supposedly the most easily digested of all starches and in demand for youngsters. At the other end of the alphabet was zwieback, from the old German word meaning twice baked, also a NBC best seller, which had been on the bakery lists for many years.

---

* *The Philosopher Poet*, by Christopher Morley, copyright 1917, Doubleday Doran & Company.

Zwieback is believed to have been invented by Harry Trueller, a German baker who made a cutter out of his wife's old sewing machine to increase production. (In August 1964 Trueller GmbH became a part of National Biscuit Company.) Ludwig Anger, a New York baker, started to bake zwieback back in the mid-nineteenth century. He wrapped it in paper bundles and continued to sell it that way for some thirty years. In 1879 young Anger began to pack zwieback in cartons under the name of "Anger's Celebrated Zwieback." The Anger Brothers bakery became part of the New York Biscuit Company and later was incorporated into NBC.

And so the parade of popular products went on . . . and on. It was fortunate that Green was no sentimentalist. Cookies and crackers associated with childhood memories have a special hold on many people. But Green was firm in his decisions as to what products to keep and what to discontinue. In a few years he had eliminated much of the bread and confectionery from NBC's list of products. But he also reduced the number of biscuits, cookies and crackers from thousands to four or five hundred. NBC's lists were still crammed with names that almost everybody knew and loved. With Uneeda Biscuits leading the way, there were Social Teas, ZuZus, Premiums, Ginger Snaps, Nabisco Sugar Wafers, Jinjer Wayfers, Graham Crackers, Fig Newtons, Bonnie Doones, Snowflakes, Crown Pilot Crackers, Saratoga Flakes, Baronets, Juniors, Melodies, Cameo Cream Sandwiches, Mary Anns, Oatmeal Cookies, Lemon Snaps, Saltinas, Coconut Dainties, Vanilla Wafers, Chocolate Wafers, Festinos, Cheese Tidbits, Five O'Clock Tea Biscuits, and so on . . . and on.

By 1908 the National Biscuit Company was manufacturing some forty-four products packaged in its now famous In-er-seal carton, and numerous others sold in bulk. There was much duplication, since most products sold in the In-er-seal carton were also available—if the consumer wanted them—in bulk. In addition, there were nineteen products especially packaged in fancy tin containers.

Some crackers—traditionally popular in certain regions—were retained. But all items had to pay their own way; if one did not prove nationally popular, Green ordered it cut from the list. Either the biscuit would reflect NBC's high standards of quality or it would have to give way to other products. Next to quality came service.

Green's promotion was primarily aimed at attracting consumer attention and support. Today it seems odd that this was once considered unusual.

NBC aimed to produce top quality merchandise, package it under a copyright label, advertise so aggressively that the grocery trade would have no choice but to handle its goods in response to consumer demand. Green figured that if production was at a high enough level, if advertising and promotion were carried on intensively, sales personnel could be regarded as merely "service" functionaries. According to this philosophy, the wholesaler was invited to "get out of the way" and the retailer was relatively unimportant. It was not until many years later that the Green philosophy, so effective during his own era, was re-examined in light of changing conditions.

"When the company started," said Green, "it was an aggregation of plants. It is now an organized business . . . We do not aim to sell all the biscuit consumed in this country . . . The results have exceeded even our expectations . . . The great body of the consumers have become our allies in this great enterprise. So far as we have any monopoly in this business, it is one that the people have voluntarily conferred upon us."

But success bred imitations. And this created the most difficult problem that confronted the young company.

Uwanta, I-Lika, Iwanta

A TORNADO raging through the Texas area struck the National Biscuit Company agency there many years ago, destroying it almost completely. When the manager could dig himself out of the ruins, he wired his general office, "Nothing left but our reputation."

But it was the reputation of the company—so carefully built under the watchful eye of Adolphus W. Green—that was really its prime asset, in some ways even more important than the products it made.

On the subject of competition, Green said, "We do not pretend to sell our standard goods cheaper than other manufacturers of biscuits sell their goods. They always undersell us. Why do they not take away our business? First, because they cannot make goods equal in quality to ours. Second, because they cannot put them in the In-er-seal package. Third, because they cannot give the trade the efficient service we furnish ./. ."

In addition to the good name that the National Biscuit Company was earning, there was also a very favorable profit picture that attracted competitors. By the end of 1901 NBC's profit figure began to approach the $4,000,000 mark. For the first time profits topped $4,000,000 in 1907. "Our business is increasing and becoming each year more secure," stated Green, "because we offer for sale the best

◀ *An early competitor*

goods, put up in the most attractive manner, and give to the grocer the most effective and satisfactory service."

It was inevitable that there should be attempts to infringe on the various symbols of a company which had achieved such success in such a short time.

Imitations were not unknown during this period. The then famous "Jap-a-lac" in the hands of imitators became "Jac-a-lac"; the name "Cottolene" became "Cottoleo"; Pears' soap became "Peer's" soap. One writer described this trend as one in which, "Thousands of women are fooled; trapped into supporting a moral thief and a business coward—a man whom decent businessmen shun—getting a cheaper article at a cheaper price. A woman sometimes fails to realize that she has it in her power to raise the standard of American business honesty by her refusal to patronize such imitations."

Any corporation would have rallied to protect its good name and products from imitations. The National Biscuit Company was well equipped—with so many lawyers among its leaders—to seek legal redress against unscrupulous competitors.

The firm of Green, Honore & Peters, which had done so much to assist in the founding of the Biscuit Company, occupied adjacent offices to it on the top floor of the Home Insurance Company Building on LaSalle Street. The firm had become increasingly involved with NBC problems, almost to the exclusion of other business. Green himself was completely occupied with his work as general counsel and chairman of the board of the National Biscuit Company.

Peters, too, became more occupied with the new company, particularly with the invention of packaging devices. From the kitchen of his home, where he first worked, he moved to a little room on North Clark Street. This, too, became too small and he had to seek larger quarters on Illinois Street; then he moved to a fully equipped machine shop on Michigan Street.

Many of the mechanical contrivances which NBC introduced into its bakeries in the early years had their inception in Peters' workshop. His many patents—numbering some twenty-four in all—ranged from machines for packing crackers to a new type of oven, anticipating in many ways the "traveling" oven of the future. In the spring of 1901 Peters formally left the law firm and officially joined the National Biscuit Company.

Only Lockwood Honore, the third member of the firm, failed to concentrate on National Biscuit Company affairs. He was busy elsewhere, particularly in Democratic politics. After running unsuccessfully once for a circuit judgeship, he was elected in 1902 and resigned from the law firm.

Green now had to find a new partner. A young lawyer from Detroit, Earl D. Babst, had been of occasional assistance to the National Biscuit Company in the past. A handsome young man, sharp-featured, with thick hair and an agile mind, Babst came from a pioneer Ohio family of lawyers and bankers. A great lover of the arts and a patron of music and the theater, he was also a good lawyer. A graduate of the University of Michigan, Babst had been admitted to the Michigan bar in 1894. He then opened up law offices in Detroit and, because of his knowledge of new corporate structure, became a consultant to the National Biscuit Company. He appeared to be just the man to fill the vacancy. In the latter part of 1902 the firm became Green, Peters & Babst.

There was also the fifty-five-year-old Charles K. Offield of the firm of Offield, Towle & Linthicum, a widely respected Chicago law firm specializing in patent problems, located in the nearby Monadnock building on Jackson Street. Offield was strictly a legal counsel, declining—so it was said—to participate in scores of cases involving promotional matters. He had also been legal counsel for the Pullman Palace Car Company, the Armour Company and the Singer Manufacturing Company.

The Company needed these legal talents. The trend of competitors in the baking business to adopt trademarks, package designs and product names easily confused with those of the National Biscuit Company increasingly threatened the very existence of NBC. In some instances such resemblances were coincidental. But nothing made Adolphus Green more furious than the thought of his handiwork being imitated or violated by competitors.

"The true purpose of these imitations of our trademarks and trade names was not to flatter, but to steal," Green bitterly reported to his board of directors, "to steal from us some part of what we had created, and to deceive the consuming public." Green knew, above all, how painstaking had been the effort to build the image of the company on responsibility, service, freshness of products, care of packaging. The symbols so carefully conceived by Green and McKinney had to be protected if the company was to survive. The names of the products, the carton in which they were packed, the now famous Grolier border, the graphic package design, the typography in which the product name was printed, represented the company's new approach to the biscuit business. So did the term "In-er-seal" and the colophon—that oval with the double bars which Green had discovered.

Under the law anyone can make a soda cracker or a gingersnap. It is only when the article suggests some other, better-known brand —and tends to deceive—that the law intrudes.

On April 17, 1899, the first legal test of the right of Uneeda Biscuit to its name, design and package came before the courts. The issue was whether the National Biscuit Company was entitled to the exclusive use of the word "Uneeda" and competitors could be barred from trying to capitalize on its popularity. (The mark "Uneeda" is still a registered trademark of the National Biscuit Company for biscuit products.)

The NBC objection was that a competitor was producing a soda cracker in a box generally similar to the Uneeda Biscuit box, even including somewhat similar scroll work, and using the name "Uwanta," a close imitation and simulation of the trademark.

Evidently the issue involved was as clear to the court (United States Circuit Court in Chicago) as it was to the National Biscuit Company. The right of the National Biscuit Company to its trademark and name was upheld and a permanent injunction was issued enjoining the competitor from "using or causing or permitting to be used or affixed to or upon any biscuit, crackers or other bakery products or packages manufactured by them . . . the word Uneeda, or the word Uwanta, or any word or synonym thereof, or any word calculated to deceive or mislead, or any word colorably different therefrom, and from affixing to any package, biscuit, crackers or bakery products, any wrapper, label or other covering having thereon a border in parallelogram arrangement and accompanying letters in substantial imitation of the wrapper, label, and package or box arrangement of the said complainant. . . ."

The victory was a substantial one. But it was just the beginning. A long list of legal actions followed to protect the company from similar infringements. In June 1899 NBC won an injunction to prevent the use of the word "Iwanta" by a Pittsburgh bakery. In July of 1900 an injunction was granted to prevent a Chicago concern from using the Kennedy name on its biscuits.

In a case appealed in 1904 the court stated, "The use of a trademark is to distinguish one's goods. No man has the right to use or imitate the trademark of another, and thus represent his goods as the goods of another. However broad the field of competition, it does not include the use of a rival's trademark, either directly or covertly, for the purpose of deceiving the public and marketing his own goods as those of his rival." (Circuit Court of Appeals of the United States, 6th Circuit, January 21, 1904.)

In another case a perpetual injunction was granted against a company using "Ulika Bis-kit." In another, NBC lawyers traveled to Maryland to defend the company's insignia against the use of the name "Eta Hargrave Biscuit." The name and symbols of the company were safeguarded from one end of the nation to the other.

One case was before a New Jersey court for five years and stubbornly contested by the defending company. Testimony was taken in numerous regions of the country and there were no less than 2,500 printed pages of court records with hundreds of exhibits. The court finally granted an injunction stating, "The law relating to fraudulent or unfair competition between traders is so firmly established and has been so lucidly illustrated and defined by the courts of England and of this country, that extended citation of authorities would be profitless. The underlying principle that no man has a right to palm off his wares as those of another, thereby cheating the purchasing public and filching the business of a rival, is so essentially an element of national justice, and so solidly embedded in our jurisprudence, that all that is necessary to quicken a court of equity is to show that in the particular instance the offense has been committed. The case cited by counsel in their briefs exemplifies the illimitable conditions and circumstances under which this simple doctrine, requiring men to be honest towards each other, may be invoked."

Still the infringements continued. The ZuZu Cracker was the basis for a host of imitations, including "BuBu," "Za-Zon," "Lu-Lu," "Zulu," "Su Su," and "Hoo Hoo." Other products involved in infringements included Nabisco Sugar Wafers, Social Tea Biscuits, Oysterettes, Zwieback and many others. By 1906 there had been 249 cases in which competitors had been compelled to abandon products or their names or symbols or packages. By 1915 the number of cases won had risen to 833.

The most frequent violations had to do with the In-er-seal trademark. Some 145 cases involved competitors forced to abandon their activities because they were imitative. There were fifty-eight cases involving Uneeda Biscuit, forty-eight involving the Graham Cracker,

thirty-five involving the ribbon-tying design chosen by Adolphus
Green, thirty-seven which had to do with the Mary Ann, thirty-five
with Social Tea Biscuit, twenty-one Royal Cracker, nineteen Oysterettes, eighteen ZuZu, thirteen Lemon Snaps, thirteen Five O'Clock,
twelve Saratoga Flakes, ten Faust Cracker, eight Jonnie. Altogether,
about forty products of National Biscuit Company were involved in
such imitative practices.

"We have concluded nine suits instituted in the Federal courts
against those infringers of our trade rights, in all of which we have
been successful," Adolphus Green reported to his board of directors.
"The courts will not allow unfair competition of this character to
go unpunished whether the misrepresentations are made by word of
mouth or more subtly by simulating the collection of details of appearance by which the consuming public has come to recognize our
products.

"It is fair to say, however," Green continued, "that many manufacturers, when we have written them calling attention to their imitations, and stating that we would be obliged to enforce our rights
by instituting suits unless such imitations were discontinued, have
abandoned the use of the imitations without suit."

But all efforts to defend the National Biscuit Company in the
courts were not successful. In the spring of 1900 Adolphus Green
wrote a letter to Charles K. Offield calling his attention to a number
of companies that were producing packages for biscuits that might
be infringements on the Peters patent.

"We hand you herewith a package of 'Uneeda Biscuit' lined
with wax paper under the patent of F. M. Peters, #621,974, March
28, 1899," wrote Green. "We also hand you the following packages:
'Abetter Biscuit'; . . . 'The Annen Biscuit'; . . . 'Annen's Purity
Milk Biscuit'; . . . 'Old Grist Mill Kookies' . . .

"These four packages seem to us to be infringements of the
Peters patent. Will you please examine the same carefully and give
us your views in regard thereto. These goods are sold in various parts
of the country, and if they are infringements should be suppressed."

Offield agreed with Green. A suit was filed in the Circuit Court
of Appeals against one company for alleged violation of the Peters
patent. Offield, Babst, Peters and others presented lengthy testimony
for NBC before the court. Circuit Court Judges Willis Van Devanter
(who was to become a United States Supreme Court Justice), Amos
M. Thayer and Walter H. Sanborn heard the case.

"It is the primary object of my invention to . . . provide a package which, at an expense practically no greater than that of the ordinary lined carton package, will effectually protect the goods and preserve their freshness," Peters told the court. A score or more of visual exhibits demonstrated the function and purpose of the In-er-seal wrapper.

But the court disagreed with the NBC argument. Judge Thayer pointed out, "If what Peters accomplished rises to the dignity of an invention, it is because he was the first to suggest the idea of laying a sheet of waxed or paraffined paper on top of the blank carton and folding them together so as to form a unitary structure. This method of making a carton, it was said, was of great importance, because it had the effect of interfolding the ends of two protecting envelopes in such a way as to more 'effectually close these ends, and at the same time, prevent any movement of the lining relatively to the box,' and because more dampness and dirt were thereby excluded from the enclosed article. Did this suggestion involve the exercise of the faculty of invention? We think not."

In its ruling the court stated, "In the case in hand it is plain, we think upon a fair consideration of the state of the art at the time the patented suit was applied for, that Peters' patent is lacking in patentable novelty, and that he is not entitled to a monopoly of the manufacture, use and sale of the article in question . . ."

The loss of the suit was a blow to the company and particularly to Peters. But Green was quick to point out that when the patent was first obtained, he himself had been surprised. He was not particularly dismayed when the court disallowed its exclusive use.

Another serious problem was the attitude of many state governments toward the new corporation. Legally, the corporation which was founded or had its home office outside any particular state was looked upon as "foreign." The question arose: "Can a state disbar a company from practicing within it merely because it has located other branches outside the state, or perhaps was incorporated in another state?" If this were so, a national company such as NBC would find it impossible to function. Ohio was a particularly difficult area, even though the National Biscuit Company had several branches there and NBC president Benjamin Crawford himself had owned a bakery in Mansfield.

The Ohio situation seemed likely to set a national precedent. Earl Babst, who had been born in Ohio and had many contacts there, was assigned to pursue the matter. He encountered another young and ambitious lawyer, Frank Monnett, recently named attorney general of Ohio. Monnett was deeply concerned about the role of the big corporation or "trust," and he was responding to popular "trust-busting" sentiment when he refused to permit "foreign" corporations to operate within his jurisdiction. There were, indeed, justifiable apprehensions concerning dangers that lurked in irresponsible corporations. Nevertheless, national companies were already providing products and service which had not been possible on a smaller scale. Answering the accusation of monopoly, Green replied, "The consumer is not obliged to buy our goods; there are plenty of the biscuit of other manufacturers on the market which he can buy at any time, if he so desires; but he does, in fact, buy our goods in an increasing quantity because the quality suits him and the price is satisfactory."

In 1899 the Ohio case came to trial with Monnett claiming that the National Biscuit Company "being a foreign corporation . . . has not . . . procured from the Secretary of State a certificate that it has complied with . . . requirements of law to authorize it to do business in this state. . . ."

The company denied the trust charge, stating that it "has not prevented competition . . . by compelling its customers and the citizens of the state of Ohio to buy bakery goods . . . There are eight other factories in the state of Ohio engaged in the business of manufacture and sale of crackers, biscuit and the like, besides hundreds of smaller bakeries . . ."

So important was the case that Adolphus Green himself was present at the trial. After lengthy testimony, the case was finally dismissed.

After months of negotiation between Babst and Monnett, a formula was finally devised by which an entrance fee would be paid by the corporation based upon a comparison of that part of the company's property which existed in Ohio with its total holdings. This formula permitted National Biscuit Company to manufacture, distribute and sell its products within the state of Ohio. It soon became a recognized practice for corporations throughout the nation. "This development," Babst stated, "took the status of the corporations out of the colonial period."

There were still other problems that did date back to the colonial period which the National Biscuit Company faced. One of these had to do with the whole system of state food laws, which the company encountered as it sought to sell its products. Individual states appointed special food departments to supervise food by weight, value and other standards. Each state had a different type of law and it was almost impossible for a national corporation to comply with each. Retailers handling goods of a non-complying company, however, could be prosecuted.

The states' concern was justified. There was no way for a consumer to differentiate between good or bad products. There was no Federal law to insist that manufacturers use only certain types of materials in their food products, that they prepare them with an eye to the public welfare, or that they list the ingredients of the product on the label.

It was not that American merchants and manufacturers were especially vicious or dishonest [Mark Sullivan wrote]. They had as high an average of uprightness as any other class. Human nature had not suddenly changed. The trouble had its roots in the evolution that had taken place in business, the substitution of the corporation for the individual, and the injection of distance and middle men between producer and consumer.

The corporation threw about business a cloak of impersonality behind which practices would be carried on, which under the older system would have brought odium to their perpetrators, which enabled men who wanted to be dishonest to be so, and to put their honest competitors under a disadvantage. Conscientious manufacturers found it difficult, if not impossible, to compete with their less ethical business rivals, and were driven in self-defense to emulate their meretricious trade practices. Many manufacturers gave sympathetic support to the movement for a pure food law . . .

The National Biscuit Company was such a company. In state after state it was faced with widely differing regulations, passed to safeguard the public safety, which made operation for a national company practically impossible.

Laws to insure wholesome food sometimes made impractical and even impossible demands. For example, in some states each package had to be individually weighed by hand. Others demanded that certain statements appear on the exterior of the package. Other states required different types of statements. Even states with similar rulings often gave varying interpretations. It was almost impossible for a national company, even if interested in observing the law, to know the varied regulations, much less observe them.

In the face of these threats to its existence NBC had to find a way of working with state governments. The assignment of trying to establish such working relations again fell to Earl Babst, who had done so well in helping solve the "foreign" corporation impasse a few years before.

Babst visited the various states. He called upon hundreds of grocers, listened to their opinions and problems. He studied their customers. He saw the old cracker barrel still in use. He poked around and kept his eyes and ears open.

Then he visited public officials involved with enforcing state pure food laws. What he found was discouraging. In North Dakota, for example, he talked to the commissioner. Babst claimed that NBC had raised food standards far beyond what they had been before. He asked how it would be possible for the company to continue in operation with the widely varied state regulations which were in force.

After listening for a while, the official slammed his hands down angrily on the arms of his chair and said, "By God, no eastern lawyer is going to tell me what we can eat out here in North Dakota!"

Babst launched a campaign for the liberalization of food laws. He presented the NBC position before committees of state legislatures in Nebraska, North Dakota, Michigan, Kentucky and Iowa. For one interview he arrived with some eight hundred products, bought from local grocery stores, to support his arguments. He tried to demonstrate how modern machinery and mass production made it impractical and even impossible to conform to each local law. Babst invariably met with opposition.

The only answer to the chaotic conditions that existed was national legislation. There had been a growing movement for national pure food laws for many years, supported by farmers, dairymen and many manufacturers. One of the organizations with which the National Biscuit Company worked closely during this period was the National Association of Retail Grocers, founded in 1893 to operate in the interests of the community food store owners and the consuming public.

Babst, Peters and other representatives of the company appeared at numerous hearings in Washington. They pointed out that the National Biscuit Company's products were among the most widely distributed of all food companies, even exceeding that of the packing industry. They sought legislation that would standardize the various laws, permitting standard operations in areas throughout the country.

Among the advocates of such a law was Porter J. McCumber, United States Senator from North Dakota. A graduate of the University of Michigan, where, like Babst, he had studied law, McCumber told his fellow senators that "Every honest manufacturer in the United States is pleading for this bill because he says that if he manufactures his goods in accordance with the pure food laws of the several states and territories, it is impossible for him to compete justly and fairly with the bogus articles that are put in competition with those manufactured by him."

Opposition to the law was strong, especially from "states rights" advocates and manufacturers of imitation whiskey and proprietary drugs. Only in the United States and Britain, proclaimed the spokesman for the Proprietary Association, are the people so free that they can "talk as they please, worship God as they please, and prescribe for themselves. Where liberty reigns, there you will find proprietary medicines."

But on June 23, 1906, the Federal Pure Food and Drug Act passed the House of Representatives and President Theodore Roosevelt signed it a few days later. On January 1, 1907, it went into effect.

Lack of proper legal guidance during this period might have resulted in the downfall of the company even before it was able to prove itself. As Green had been trained by Charles F. Southmayd in New York, and later by William Goudy in Chicago, so he had trained Frank Peters, Lockwood Honore, Earl Babst, Frederick W. Waller and others.

Now a new lawyer was about to come forward in the Green, Peters & Babst firm. Tall, handsome, quiet spoken, a graduate of the University of Wisconsin, young Roy E. Tomlinson seemed particularly promising to Babst. He asked Green if he could have him transferred to his NBC staff. Green agreed, and starting in 1902, Tomlinson was to become increasingly involved with NBC affairs. Their association was to continue for more than half a century.

Meanwhile, the aging Adolphus Green's exploits were by no means at an end.

NATIONAL BISCUIT CO. NEW YORK CENTRAL LINES SPECIAL

ELEVEN

Boss of
the Biscuit Bakers

ON THE MORNING of July 2, 1913, a young man stood on the deck of the steamship *Mauretania* waving to those on shore as the Cunard Line vessel slowly moved out to sea. His name was John Henry Mears. He was a reporter, dispatched by the New York *Evening Sun* on a round-the-world junket in an effort to beat the record of thirty-nine days, nineteen hours and forty-three minutes set two years previously by André Jaeger-Schmidt on a trip from Paris.

Mr. Mears said in an interview before his departure, "In the matter of food I am fortunate. My uncle, A. W. Green, president of the National Biscuit Company, is, of course, a food expert. He is naturally taking considerable interest in this project and, being a great traveler, he has been able to give me invaluable tips concerning the safest and best foods to eat in different parts of the world.

"I am not carrying a medicine chest, not even a flask," confessed Mr. Mears. "I don't expect to need any doctoring." However, Mr. Mears was carrying a package of Uneeda Biscuit encased in a metal container which his uncle, Mr. Green, had persuaded him to take along. Green wanted to see how the biscuits would withstand the sea air and various climates. He also appreciated the valuable publicity possibility in the race around the world.

Mears left the *Mauretania* at Fishguard, Wales, took a train to London, crossed the English Channel and continued on to Paris, Berlin and St. Petersburg. From Russia Mears and his package of biscuit

◀ *William H. Moore, Adolphus W. Green, Mrs. Esther Green and Miss Mary Green aboard* Nazu

crossed Siberia to Manchuria along the Siberian Railway. Then over to Japan and back to New York by way of Vancouver and Seattle.

Along the way he was photographed clutching the Uneeda Biscuit package at Napoleon's Tomb and the Louvre in Paris, while crossing into Siberia, in a rickshaw in front of the United States consulate in Yokohama, Japan, and beside the statue of Peter the Great in St. Petersburg.

When he returned to New York some thirty-five days later, he had smashed the record by going around the world in thirty-five days, twenty-one hours, thirty-five minutes and four-fifths of a second! Newspapers rejoiced that the record of Phileas Fogg, made famous by Jules Verne in *Around the World in Eighty Days*, had been broken. In addition Mears had also drastically cut the time of seventy-two days, six hours and eleven minutes established by the famous Nelly Bly in 1889.

A few days after Mears's triumphal return Green tore open the Uneeda Biscuit package in the presence of a committee of impartial observers. The contents were, as Green proclaimed, in "first class condition. The biscuits were found as fresh and crisp as the day they were packed." A brochure entitled *Around the World in Thirty-Five Days with Uneeda Biscuit* spread the news.

NBC salesmen were urged to tell grocers "of the perfect condition of the perfect soda cracker, Uneeda Biscuit, after its world's record trip . . . When everybody knows that Uneeda Biscuit are perfect, everybody will eat more, creating more business for the grocer—thus making its profits greater."

Some years earlier Green had confided to Frank Lowden, "Some people still believe that this Uneeda business is only temporary." By 1915 he would be able to proclaim that Uneeda Biscuit had been "more widely used than any other food product has ever been," and, indeed, it was not unusual to see horse-drawn wagons lined up for three blocks outside a bakery waiting for their cargo of Uneeda Biscuit. Shortly after NBC was born, shareholders were receiving dividends at the rate of four dollars a year, largely as a result of such imaginative promotion of Uneeda Biscuit as well as other products. By 1915 the dividend rate had climbed to seven dollars annually.

But production continued to lag behind promotion. The bakeries absorbed by the National Biscuit Company at its birth were unable to keep up with the demand. Green had little difficulty in convincing his board of directors that new bakeries should be constructed.

In Chicago a site for a new bakery was selected on Washington Boulevard, adjacent to the old Kennedy works at Morgan and Carpenter Streets. When the bakery was completed, the NBC plant covered almost an entire block and included a Uneeda bakery, a Nabisco bakery, the Chicago sales agency and a power plant. The establishment employed about a thousand workers, mostly women.

In New York the completion of a huge new bakery was celebrated with a colorful parade of 112 NBC delivery wagons, many bands and much fanfare. The new building was adjacent to the original bakery built by the New York Biscuit Company on the east side of Tenth Avenue at 15th Street. Later, four more "fireproof" structures had been added, making NBC the largest manufacturing establishment in the City of New York. Two of these buildings were devoted entirely to the baking of Uneeda Biscuit. Another produced only Nabisco Sugar Wafers.

Most industrial buildings in those days followed an architectural style known merely as "mill buildings." Many architects were not interested in designing factories, which tended to be drab, unimaginative red brick boxes, from two to six stories high, with no aesthetic pretenses. Turrets atop the buildings often contained huge water tanks, which fed a primitive sprinkler for fire protection.

Green had no patience with such outworn patterns; NBC's new bakeries were to pioneer in certain construction innovations. He would hound his engineers for new ideas that would create a neater and more orderly appearance. When individual motor-driven control equipment was introduced around 1912, Green insisted it be introduced in new bakeries so that all ugly belts and pulleys could be eliminated.

Green also insisted on "advanced" facilities for employees—locker rooms, special compartments for clothes changing, well-equipped washrooms.

In New York City the new bakery was opened with a special luncheon. Four hundred NBC members of management and distinguished guests were served in one of the huge bakery rooms, transformed into a magnificent banquet hall for the occasion. The caterer was the famous Delmonico.

The aging A. W. Green, dignified and erect, presided at the head table. Behind him was a huge picture of the famous Uneeda Biscuit Boy in his yellow slicker and rain hat, a box of Uneeda Biscuit in his arms. Green replied to a tribute from those assembled with a lengthy address saying in part, "I cannot but be deeply touched by such a demonstration, but I am not vain enough to believe that it all comes to me as a personal tribute. I rather take it as a tribute to the high ideal that I had a share in setting for the National Biscuit Company.

"In this age, business must and will be done by corporations. The individual as an independent businessman in large enterprises is fast disappearing from the face of the land. In his place has come the corporation. In the conduct of that corporation, what shall our ideals be? Shall we conduct a corporation on a line different from that on which our private individual life is conducted? Shall the officer of a corporation have two lives—his life as an officer of that corporation, doing anything not forbidden by law, steering as close to the wind as the law will permit, or even defying the law? Or shall he apply the same standards in the conduct of that corporation that he applies in his own private life, in his relationship to his family and in his relationship to his God?

"These corporations, gentlemen, have a great mission to fulfill in this country. Whether for weal or woe, they are here, and here to stay. The future welfare of this country must depend in large measure on the manner in which these corporations shall be conducted, and, to my mind, it behooves every officer of a corporation entrusted with its management to so manage its affairs that it shall commend itself to the public sentiment of the country—of all the people of the country—to the end that the attitude of the people towards these corporations shall not be hostile, but friendly. . . ."

Another speaker at the luncheon was Henry N. McKinney, originator of the word "Uneeda," and a trusted adviser to Green ever since. "When we began to tell the world about Uneeda Biscuit," McKinney told the audience, "we found two enemies strongly entrenched—ignorance and habit; ignorance of the fact that the ordinary soda cracker sold in a bag, as it had been heretofore, began to deteriorate the moment it came from the oven and touched the air, and was further spoiled by contact with dirt, dust and odors . . . the housekeeper from time immemorial had been accustomed to send to the grocery store for five cents' worth of soda crackers in an ordinary paper bag.

"As we gather today the very air seems to be full of victory; we almost count the battle won; but it is not won, it is but begun. What we have done in the past is nothing to what we shall do in the future . . . When we gather the next time to open another building, alongside of which this shall seem very small, I hope then to be present to again answer to the toast to Uneeda Biscuit, the soda cracker that has made a nation hungry."

Since the New York bakeries and the City of New York increasingly became the center of NBC activity, Green decided to move the executive offices there. "Many businessmen were being attracted to New York City," says Marian V. Sears of Harvard University, discussing American business at the turn of the century, "because it was the financial center and New York financiers were becoming prominent in the management and on the boards of big business."

The executive offices moved to New York in 1906. In the ensuing years all departments were transferred from Chicago to New York.

Green and his colleagues were understandably proud of the New York complex of buildings. It was the biggest baking center not only in America but in the world. When the wind was right, seamen and stevedores coming off the North River docks could sniff appetizing smells of Vanilla Wafers and Marshmallow Fancies. On other days, the aroma of Animal Crackers and Fig Newton Cakes contrasted sharply with the smells emanating from taverns along Ninth Avenue. "An air of innocence," one writer put it, "clings to the National Biscuit Company, as it must to any business where grown men concern themselves with a ginger snap named ZuZu. . . ."

Alert as he was to the value of public relations, Green arranged for a special visitors' gallery in the New York bakery around the sifting floor of the tenth-story mezzanine. A passenger elevator conveyed visitors to this gallery where the entire baking operation could be seen.

In addition it was probably the only factory at that time constructed to permit a New York Central Railroad train to actually run through the plant to pick up and deliver freight.

Thousands of employees, also mostly women, were hired in New York as in Chicago. Many were recent immigrants. Most factories constructed during this era were located in the very heart of a city, close to the railroad and to where people lived. Employees either walked to work or used trolley cars.

Still the demand for fresh biscuit grew. In 1914 another bakery on Eleventh Avenue was constructed. Spanning the entire block from

Tenth to Eleventh Avenue and from 15th to 16th Street, the new bakery was eleven stories high and provided an additional 650,000 square feet of space.

Included in the huge square block of red brick buildings was the New York sales agency, which was the central office of the sales department for the entire company as well as for the New York territory. When yet more space was needed, a building at 85 Ninth Avenue was purchased for the executive offices.

In 1903, NBC's president Benjamin Crawford, never very active, retired. Two years later Green himself assumed the presidency of the company. The position of chairman of the board, previously held by Green, was not filled.

As he grew older, Green became increasingly irritable and impatient. Never easy to get along with, he now inspired fear and terror among his colleagues. Doubtless the fast changing nature of industrial America was a constant source of frustration to him. Although immensely successful, Green faced an accumulating series of critical problems, most of which he could not resolve, or even comprehend. As a result he attempted to apply an individualistic code of conduct —product of the eighteenth and nineteenth centuries—to the new and complex twentieth. Stern and rigid paternalism did not fit the needs of a new era of American industry.

One of Green's regulations, strictly enforced, forbade the privilege of a private office to anyone but himself and a few selected exceptions. Even department heads had their desks in open areas, making it easy for Green to see at a glance if everyone was at his desk hard at work. Green's own office was spacious, paneled in dark mahogany and equipped with a fireplace. Each day on the dot of twelve noon Green left his desk for the big company lunchroom. It was a signal for his vice presidents, hungry or not, to follow. All ate lunch together at a large round table, not used when Green was away on his frequent trips about the country.

Green relentlessly applied the only brand of leadership that he knew. His intolerance and burning passion for perfection created more problems than they solved. Lack of opportunity for his subordinates to make even the smallest decision led to demoralization. But the more diffident he found his colleagues, the greater became Green's determination to steer his company to new successes. Since nobody seemed to measure up to his standards, he tried to do the entire job of running the company himself.

Late in the year 1910 another grand bakery opening took place at Houston, Texas. Green arrived in his private railway car to tell the guests assembled at the luncheon that he had "never misrepresented anything, nor must you. Our customers don't know me; they know you. You are the National Biscuit Company. I hope that every business transaction of this company will forever be on the square, with an honesty and integrity which has characterized the upbuilding of this corporation, and which has made it the grand success it is today."

In September of the following year the most elaborate and impressive ceremony to date took place in Kansas City: the opening of a new plant, located in the community where the National Biscuit Company's most able competitor, the Loose-Wiles Biscuit Company, had its main plant. The Loose-Wiles Biscuit Company became the Sunshine Biscuit Company, acquired by the American Tobacco Company in 1966.

Invited guests from points all over the country converged on Kansas City. Some twenty-five private railroad cars, as well as the famous Twentieth Century Limited, congregated at the Kansas City depot, carrying officials and directors of various companies, including forty bank and railroad presidents. It was the first time that a train ever traveled from New York to Kansas City without a changeover.

City officials and several hundred managers, sales agents and salesmen, all Kansas City's guests for the day, formed a huge automobile parade, headed by a corps of mounted police and a forty-piece band. Included in the line of march were horse-drawn delivery wagons, just painted, as well as newfangled motor trucks.

The parade toured the business district for an hour before it reached the new bakery on Central Street and Milwaukee Avenue. Escorted by the mayor, Adolphus Green entered the building and ceremoniously touched a button throwing back a secret panel on one side of a conference room. This launched a tour of the bakery, one of the most modern in the country, and every feature of its construction had been supervised personally by Green.

City officials, company directors, presidents of other large corporations, all marched through the eight-story factory, poking into flour bins, watching mixers and peelers at work. Under Green's watchful guidance, they did not miss a detail. Baking was done on the top floor in these days, where mixing and proving rooms as well as the machines that stamped out the biscuit and the ovens were located. The biscuit then descended on automatic conveyors devised by NBC vice president, John G. Zeller, to a lower floor where they were packed in the famous In-er-seal carton. Each machine in the plant was driven by an individual motor. The heat for baking was supplied entirely by oil piped into fire boxes or furnaces beneath the oven on the fifth floor. Oil was also used for the steam boilers supplying heat and steam for the building and equipment.

The fifth floor provided an innovation for industrial edifices, modern toilet rooms and shower baths for employees and dressing rooms where employees could exchange their street clothes for white uniforms especially designed for bakery use. In the corners of the building were fire towers, each built to connect directly with the outside and containing fireproof stairways leading to the street. The stairways were so constructed that smoke would not reach them and thus one of the most frequent causes of panic was avoided. The basement contained a large refrigerated room for fruit, butter, eggs, milk and other provisions.

"As you go through the factory," Green pointed out to the visitors, "I ask you to look at the provisions we have made for sanitary surroundings of our help. I wish you to observe particularly the conditions under which our girls work in this factory. I think they will average up certainly as well as the average collection of ladies in Kansas City, and that is going some. Just look at them, but don't look too long. If you do not say that they are well cared for, I shall be very much mistaken, because I have had that at heart ever since this company was formed—the care of our help, the sanitary conditions under which they work . . . I want you to see if they are not a happy and contented lot of girls."

In a newspaper interview Green spoke of the new bakery's possibilities. (The Kansas City NBC bakery continued in use until August 31, 1951.) "Our new factory will be a beauty. It will have ovens capable of turning into biscuit two carloads of flour a day. I don't know how many biscuit that will be, but there will be a lot. Of course, we are proud of this new factory, but, after all, it is only a 'tangible asset' and 'tangible assets' don't cut much ice with the National Biscuit Company, in view of the fact that it is founded on a word."

"A word?"

"Yes, a word," said Green, "Uneeda Biscuit. If an earthquake or Halley's comet should destroy everything we have, the word Uneeda would still be worth a fortune to us."

It was not until mid-afternoon that the hungry visitors concluded the tour and sat down to lunch. But before the food was served, Green expounded further on the role of the corporation as he saw it. "The officer of every corporation should feel in his heart—in his very soul—that he is responsible, not merely to make dividends for the stockholders of his company, but to enhance the general prosperity and the moral sentiment of the United States," Green stated. "Such is the ideal I have set up for this company . . ."

"If I can say when I come to die, that through this corporation which I am managing, I have contributed one iota towards higher and better ideals, then I shall feel that I have accomplished something in this world of ours."

The opening of the new bakery and the remarks made by various company spokesmen received much attention in the newspapers. "If all men responsible for the management of large corporations acted upon the ideas expressed the other day by A. W. Green, president of the National Biscuit Company," the Chicago *Daily News* stated editorially, "the attitude of the general public towards large corporations would be different from what it is, or at least has been in the recent past . . . The sense of social responsibility must be developed in the corporation as the successor of the individual in the field of business . . . It is encouraging to find the head of a large business concern thus pointing out that the corporation has responsibilities to society as well as to its stockholders."

The Chicago *Record-Herald* stated, "Sound, progressive, refreshing views regarding the policies and methods of corporations were expressed at Kansas City on Saturday at a remarkable luncheon. Corporate righteousness should be preached and exemplified by the corporations themselves. To ask this is to ask nothing unreasonable or Utopian. Enlightened corporations know that, like individuals, they can prosper and grow without frenzied finance or abnormal, unethical methods."

And the Fort Worth *Record* stated in an editorial, which it entitled "A Corporation That's Different," that Green "is a representative of a new type of corporation managers . . ." Quoting Green's statement "I feel in the conduct of this corporation the same responsibility to my country and my God as I do in my conduct to my own family. Can you ask more?" the editorial answered, "No!

So long as Mr. Green lives up to these high ideals, he and his company will enjoy a deserved popularity . . . If other great captains of industry would follow Mr. Green's example, the trust problem would solve itself in short order."

When the Kansas City bakery opened, the National Biscuit Company had some fifty-four bakeries around the country, of which thirty-two were owned and twenty-two leased. By 1915, in response to steadily mounting demand, Green reported the construction of eleven new bakeries, all as he described them, "models of manufacturing efficiency and safety." The bakeries were so located that no town in the nation was more than an overnight trip from an NBC bakery.

While Green was the dynamic guiding spirit, the success of the National Biscuit Company was the result of efficient organization of its countless phases, the result of efforts by many individuals—salesmen, drivers, peelers, packers, executives, lawyers, regional directors, technicians. Local sales and distributing agencies were established in all the principal cities and towns in the country. Whenever possible the agency was housed in a building constructed according to a standard NBC plan. Here, at seven o'clock each morning, the driver would load up his wagon—or sometimes, in winter, a sleigh—and start a day which lasted until all the goods had been delivered.

Late in 1903 the necessity for collecting from old or slow accounts led to the organization of a treasury department. NBC encouraged grocers to place frequent orders, as many as twenty a month, in order to be sure the crackers reached the consumer in good condition. Good risks got thirty-day credit; poor risks paid cash to the driver of the delivery wagon. Discounts were allowed on the basis of thirty-day volume. With this system Green discouraged the grocers' practice of purchasing a large order once a month which resulted in stale crackers in faded, torn packages.

Other departments were established as new needs arose. In New York an engineering department created early in the company's existence included a mechanical engineering and experimental shop. Laundry divisions in the larger bakeries furnished clean, attractive uniforms to employees. The operating department, purchasing department, packing division and others all helped to increase efficiency and to coordinate the many divergent elements of the company.

As the National Biscuit Company grew, it became too large even for a man of Green's energy and fanatical determination to supervise completely. Reluctantly and with some misgivings, he delegated authority. John G. Zeller, a former partner of Benjamin F. Crawford, was appointed superintendent of construction, a position he had held in the United States Baking Company. The self-effacing but capable Zeller, who lived to be ninety, gave decades of service to the company.

Frank M. Peters, Green's law partner turned inventor, remained Green's associate for years and provided many of the mechanical ideas which revolutionized the packaging industry. In 1905 Peters was elected a director, and the year following he became a member of the executive committee.

Earl D. Babst, who had played such an important role in the early years of the company, became the company's general counsel when Green became president. In 1915 Babst was elected a company director and first vice president. Roy E. Tomlinson, the youthful attorney who had become assistant general counsel to Babst, displayed a quiet efficiency which both Babst and Green liked.

Frederick W. Waller, recruited originally by the firm of Green, Peters & Babst, became Green's personal secretary. In 1912 he was made a member of the board of directors and rose to the position of vice president.

Charles F. Bliss, who started his long career in the baking industry in 1885, served as a general clerk of the country department of the American Biscuit Company. A veteran of the "biscuit wars" before the founding of NBC, Bliss organized sales agencies in the nation wherever these were not physically connected with existing bakeries. All other sales agencies were supervised by the heads of the various bakeries.

But it was to Frank O. Lowden, the son-in-law of George Pullman and future governor of Illinois, that Green looked for counsel and friendship more than to any other man.

With these men Green shared—sometimes reluctantly—the responsibilities and activities of company operation. The first operating board probably was created in Chicago before the company moved to New York. In operation until about 1917, the board met frequently. "Any member could raise objections," one NBC officer recalled, "and, if reasonable, the matter was postponed for later consideration. If no objections were raised, at the time, all members had to keep silent forever after . . . Mr. Green was very strict on timing and the members had to pledge an accurate time schedule on each project they had charge of and live up to it . . ."

A newspaper reporter asked Green to what he attributed his success. "Hard work," Green replied, "this is the secret of any man's success."

"But surely one must have brains to succeed," the reporter said.

"Nearly all men have brains enough to succeed in one thing or another," said Green. "They only lack the strength, the will to keep at anything until they get the best of it. Some men make a temporary success through mere cleverness, but permanent success is only gained through hard, hard work. It is a continuous fight, and the greater the prize, the harder the struggle."

"Of course," the reporter asked, "you do not mean to say that man should not have any recreation. Do you?"

"Certainly not," said Green, "a man must have some. But the majority of men think they need more than they really do."

Green's policies, aided by a growing national population and a revolution in eating habits, began to pay off. The first dozen years of the company's existence were indeed bright years of progress. And among the brightest aspects were the company's products themselves.

Adolphus W. Green at grand opening of Kansas City bakery in 1911 ▸

Composite drawing of NBC bakeries and sales agencies operating across the nation in 1920's

MADGE BELLAMY *as*
LORNA DOONE
in Maurice Tourneur's Motion Picture
ENJOYING
ORNA DOONE BISCU

TWELVE

"If You Please,
My Name Is Lorna Doone!"

THE BIG CHALLENGE for the National Biscuit Company in the first decade of the twentieth century was to invent or revive an ever increasing variety of cookies and crackers to fill the demand and, at the same time, maintain standards of quality and service.

English bakeries were making fancy sweet cakes long before the Civil War, when American consumers were still munching soda crackers. However, as America became a significant market, English bakers began to send shiploads of sweet biscuits here. Soon they had established sales agencies in nearly every large city in the country, even as far west as California. Their goods were sold in virtually all of the principal grocery houses in the country.

It was obvious that there were profits in America's developing sweet tooth. Domestic bakers began to send to England for special machines in an effort to keep up with foreign competition and changing American tastes. In the decades that followed, America not only equaled England in the production of cookies of all flavors, sizes, shapes and appeals, but began to manufacture many types of baking machines of its own.

The expanding population of the United States was becoming accustomed to the notion of buying more of its food in newfangled tin cans and ready-made paper packages. Chain stores—offering lower

◄ *Posters in grocery-store windows promoted a movie and a biscuit*

139

prices and a wider choice than the traditional retail store—were multiplying.

"For all practical purposes," Hampe and Wittenberg state in *The Lifeline of America*, "the modern chain store in America dates from the founding of the A. & P. in 1859. The public liked the idea of buying a staple such as tea at lower-than-usual prices, and within six years there were twenty-five red-front stores under the name of the Great American Tea Company." By that time success led the company to add a line of groceries. In 1869 the name "The Great Atlantic and Pacific Tea Company" was adopted. By the turn of the century there were 200 stores in the A. & P. chain. By 1915 there were 1,670.

Meanwhile, other grocery chains came along. The Jones Brothers Tea Company of Brooklyn—later to become the Grand Union Company—was created in 1872. Bernard H. Kroger founded the Great Western Tea Company in 1882.

Other famous store chains included H. C. Bohack (1887), Brooklyn; Gristede Brothers (1891), New York; National Tea (1899), Chicago; Ralph's Grocery Company (1873), Los Angeles. First National Stores was organized in 1926, although some of its founders date back before 1900.

Then—by the 1920's—came self-service. It was a new concept which at first annoyed many consumers and was viewed with skepticism by many storekeepers. But the innovation offered an opportunity to display a wider variety of products directly before the eyes of the shopper, to be felt, pinched or hefted, as the consumer desired.

Almost from the start the chains were the National Biscuit Company's best customers. This was financially rewarding, but it also presented a problem. The chains demanded a constant supply of new and different products. As a result, executives of NBC sales and manufacturing departments met almost daily to discuss how to satisfy this growing demand for new cookies and crackers. It was not easy. Finding names for new products became a nuisance, too. It reached a point where salesmen were told to list the names of Pullman railroad cars so they could borrow when a name was suitable.

Shortbread had for long been a challenge to the big biscuit bakers. This small buttery cookie of Scottish origin seemed impossible to manufacture by mechanical mass-production methods. However, it was rumored that in Detroit an inventive molder had been experimenting with a machine that might do the job. This man was Frank

Werner, founder of the Werner Machine Company, Grand Rapids, Michigan, and he knew that shortbread had been made by Scottish housewives as long as memory could extend. He also realized that molding such cakes according to tradition demanded the use of wooden molding blocks. It was generally assumed that commercial production of shortbread was impractical.

However, Werner, a man of both imagination and persistence, began to experiment. The idea of a mechanical application of the hand process haunted him, and eventually he devised the first crude mechanism which made quantity production of shortbread possible.

News of the machine reached the National Biscuit Company in New York. "We heard so much about shortbread," said Earl D. Babst, "that it was a subject of discussion at almost every meeting of executives of our sales and manufacturing departments. The need for more products was urgent and shortbread was one of those we most frequently discussed."

Most of the executives were against shortbread. Not only was it difficult to produce, but they said, it just "wouldn't appeal." But Babst, who like Green possessed a certain arrogant independence, was not one to be discouraged. "Whenever I have all of you against me," he would say, "I think I have a success." He persuaded his colleagues to try the new machine.

Experiments proved successful. A satisfactory formula was devised for the dough. Now a suitable name—so important in merchandising cookies—was needed. Since shortbread was Scottish in origin, Babst concentrated on a Scottish theme.

This was the era when *Lorna Doone*, a nineteenth-century Scottish romance by R. D. Blackmore, set in Exmoor, was required reading in schools and popular in cultured households.

" 'My name is John Ridd,' " one bit of dialogue in the novel read. " 'What is your name?' "

" 'Lorna Doone,' she answered in a low voice, as if afraid of it, and hanging her head, so that I could only see her forehead and eyelashes. 'If you please, my name is Lorna Doone.' "

When Babst visited Exmoor, the chauffeur of his rented automobile pointed to the surrounding countryside saying, "Sir, this is Lorna Doone country."

Perhaps it was the sentimental flavor of the name. Or perhaps Babst dimly recalled the fact that Blackmore had a way of describing "hot mutton pasty" or picturing a "currant loaf." No matter, Babst felt that the name "Lorna Doone," besides having a Scottish connotation, might well appeal to American tastes.

One day in March 1912 Babst sat down at his desk and wrote a short letter to the operating department of the National Biscuit Company.

"Gentlemen: I suggest the word 'Lorna Doone' as a name for biscuit."

The suggestions of Earl Babst, like those of his immediate superior, A. W. Green, carried weight. Production of the new type of shortbread was pushed. The operating department notified Babst that "we are putting through a requisition today changing the name of 'Hostess Jumbles' to 'Lorna Doone Jumbles.' "

In a relatively short time Lorna Doone became one of the company's popular products. It was sold both in bulk and in the In-er-seal package. Soon its popularity far exceeded even that of the book. In 1923 a silent motion picture entitled *Lorna Doone* was produced by Thomas H. Ince, featuring the popular actress Madge Bellamy. NBC put its entire promotional machinery to work to publicize the movie. Brochures were dispatched describing "*Lorna Doone*–a good picture," and reminding readers that Lorna Doone was also "a good biscuit."

NBC's admiration for the film was reciprocated. "I think that 'Lorna Doone' biscuit a very delicious little cake," commented Madge Bellamy graciously, "and I want to thank you very much for the interest you have taken in the advertisement of my latest picture, *Lorna Doone*."

More than thirty years later a new film–a talkie–entitled *Lorna Doone* was produced, this time by Columbia Pictures, featuring Barbara Hale. Again there was full cooperation between the film makers and the promotion department of National Biscuit Company, whose full sales force of more than three thousand men assisted in the promotion.

During those early years Lorna Doone was not NBC's only new cookie success. On April 2, 1912, the company's operations department announced to its managers and sales agents that it was preparing "to offer to the trade . . . three entirely new varieties of the highest class biscuit packed in a new style . . . The three varieties of biscuit . . . will be known as the 'Trio.'

"The varieties comprising the 'Trio' are as follows, namely:

"Oreo Biscuit—two beautifully embossed chocolate-flavored wafers with a rich cream filling at 30¢ per pound.

"Mother Goose Biscuit—a rich, high class biscuit bearing impressions of the Mother Goose legends at 20¢ per pound.

"Veronese Biscuit—a delicious, hard sweet biscuit of beautiful design and high quality at 20¢ per pound . . .

"This 'Trio' is an exciting innovation, and we are quite sure it will immediately appeal to public favor."

NBC promoters grew eloquent over the sales possibility of the Mother Goose Biscuit, describing it as "of the highest quality." Designs stamped upon it, the company said, "representing all the jingles of the Mother Goose rhymes, will make it especially attractive, recalling as they do the happy memories of childhood." The Veronese Biscuit ("Veronese" was one of the names suggested in 1898 to Henry McKinney by A. W. Green for the soda cracker eventually named "Uneeda") was described as "the highest class of hard sweets of exceptionally rare quality and should have a leading place in our growing list of biscuit of this high character."

The two members of the trio most lavishly promoted in the initial announcement have since disappeared. But the third, Oreo, was evidently just the kind of cookie the American consuming public wanted. Somewhat similar to a previous product named "Bouquet," the Oreo consisted of two firm chocolate cookies with rich vanilla frosting in the middle. The first Oreos were slightly larger than today's product, but always round. Within a short time Oreo, which resembled an English biscuit, became a fantastically good seller among NBC sweet goods. Today the company claims it is the most popular cookie in the world.

The origin of the name is not really known, although one possibility is that it came from the Greek *oreo*, meaning hill or mountain. Supposedly, either in testing or when the product was first produced, it was shaped like a baseball mound or hill—hence, an "oreo." This has a certain validity in view of A. W. Green's tendency toward classical names. Oreo was officially registered in 1913 as "Oreo Biscuit." By 1921 it had become "Oreo Sandwich" and by 1948 "Oreo Creme Sandwich."

Variations have been tried—a vanilla Oreo, a single-cracker Oreo, and in the 1920's a lemon-filled Oreo was introduced. The size has undergone changes, too. Today's is about midway between the largest and the smallest. Through all shifts in public preferences, Oreo has remained one of the nation's most consistent favorites.

As frequently happens with popular products, there are people who fancy that they contributed to its creation. An Oreo admirer once wrote to the company, "During the early 1920's you had a contest offering a cash award for a suitable name for this particular cookie. I entered this contest and submitted the name Oreo. Time passed, I learned or heard nothing concerning the matter, so gave it no further thought until this past Sunday night . . . If you will kindly check your records concerning the said contest, I am sure that in them you will find I am the one who submitted the trade name, Oreo."

The company answered, "We think that you must be confused about the origin of the trademark Oreo. It was not originated as the result of a contest in the early 1920's or at any other time. It was originated by our advertising department, and first used on March 6, 1912."

On November 13, 1913, another famous cookie was born. Mallomar was described as "a delightful combination of marshmallow, jelly and layers of cake covered with chocolate icing." For several years before Mallomar, the company made a product called "Marshmallow Cream Sandwich." It was also covered with chocolate but only sold in bulk. When the formula for Mallomars was perfected, it was decided to make them a specialty and to pack them in the In-er-seal package. Later it, too, was made available in bulk. Although A. W. Green was sternly against bulk sales of products, the demand for bulk cookies and crackers persisted. Not until relatively recent times did the package almost completely supplant bulk sales.

As older products outlived their popularity and were dropped from the production list, new products such as Mallomar were introduced. During the early 1900's the company produced scores of products whose names are unfamiliar to most of us today: Saratoga Flakes, Festinos, Lillian Russells, San Juans, Hippodromes.

Green's genius for promoting and advertising set a precedent that had a permanent influence on food promotion. The company's first advertising manager, John D. Richardson, was an able and dignified baker who joined with David F. Bremner to build one of the most successful bakeries in the midwest prior to the origin of the National Biscuit Company. Because Green was so gifted in advertising techniques and intolerant of subordinates, Richardson's contribution consisted mostly of executing orders. Henry N. McKinney of the N. W.

Ayer agency, whom Jarvis A. Wood, a senior member of the firm of Ayer, called "the greatest developer of advertising," had become head of the New York branch of the Ayer agency by 1911. He was thus available to National Biscuit Company and to his close friend Green whenever needed.

When NBC's general offices moved from Chicago to New York in 1906, Richardson remained in Chicago as vice president in charge of the western department. Alfred C. Mace, a twenty-six-year-old former commercial artist, was transferred to New York and put in charge of advertising. Mace had previously applied to NBC for a position in its advertising department, but none was available. Determined to be associated with the company, which he knew to be a creative power in advertising, he had taken a position as a clerk in the package department at forty dollars a month. He worked over ideas and sketches for advertising promotion at night and submitted them to Richardson. One day A. W. Green saw some of them. He was impressed. After that, Mace's rise was assured.

It is difficult today to realize the importance at that time of car ads and billboards. Elevateds, subways, railroad stations and many building walls and vacant properties were plastered with displays. Many were hand-painted in oil; others were posted on billboards.

Mace was convinced of the importance of such outdoor display and card advertising in trolley cars used by millions of people daily. Most of NBC's car cards and posters were conceived and executed by Mace in consultation with Green. Mace was an innovator, a believer in human interest themes and big, bold, dominating display features. He had an uncanny sense of the fitness of illustration to make a point, to sell an idea or a product.

Mace wanted those who run to be able to read. The message must be gained at a glance. This was an innovation in a period when long and ponderous advertising messages were common. The National Biscuit Company became known as the sponsor of the greatest display of permanent outdoor advertising in the world. NBC signs in all the principal cities and towns in the country became landmarks and daily reminders to millions of people that they needed a supply of NBC products. So great was the investment of the company in outdoor advertising that it was estimated that if all NBC messages on outdoor advertising were to be painted on a five-foot-high fence, that fence would be long enough to enclose the Panama Canal on either side from the Atlantic to the Pacific.

Green gave Mace full support. He himself demanded that the words "National Biscuit Company" and his favorite "Uneeda" always appear in letters of a certain type and size. Mace and Green saw eye to eye on advertising techniques.

Painters were at work somewhere every working hour of every working day on NBC signs, painting them or freshening them up. Signs on walls were painted each year. The crew started out each year at Christmas, covered the entire south, and swung back like birds of passage about the first of April.

It was conservatively estimated that some 30,000,000 people saw NBC's outdoor advertising each day of the year. One company spokesman said, "It is no exaggeration to say that the National Biscuit Company advertising is never out of sight of the American public." Millions of people also saw NBC's horse-drawn wagons, all of which bore the familiar message "Uneeda Biscuit." And Green doggedly insisted that every wagon be newly and neatly painted and well maintained—an example to the community.

Then there was a continuous flood of newspaper ads, booklets, carton slips, store cards and store hangers. The actual packages were designed to be used as an advertising medium long before this was a routine custom.

The moving picture craze opened up an important new outlet for NBC promotion. Carefully prepared slides promoted NBC products in theaters around the country. The motion pictures themselves, as well as legitimate theaters, often used NBC products as props for various scenes. This practice became so prevalent that NBC regularly listed in its house organ the names of moving pictures that featured NBC products.

Shattering further precedents at meetings of the board of directors, the energetic Mace set up exhibits of new biscuit products on a table, with a graphic chart plotting the results of advertising. This was a rare exception to Green's policy of keeping his staff separated from the board of directors. Few NBC directors were acquainted with any NBC executive except Green himself, and this was to be a source of a serious problem later.

NBC advertisements appearing in newspapers and magazines must, Green demanded, reflect care in format and phraseology. Every ad was checked not only by Green but also by Earl Babst for both legal and grammatical errors. As Babst studied each advertisement in proof, he would check on punctuation, choice of words and even typography. Once he sent a proof of a routine Nabisco Sugar Wafer ad to a friend who had been a college professor, asking him to read it for English usage. The friend, Ralph C. Ringwalt of New York City, studied the ad carefully and returned it with a long letter of criticism, pointing out nine errors in a twelve-line ad.

The company also conducted an extensive program in an effort to win friends in communities, large or small. Material was sent to representatives in the field providing assistance in organizing ladies' receptions and educating the dealer to the goals and facilities of the company. Special attention was paid to the opening of bakeries where material promoting products of the company and expounding the company's philosophy was distributed.

In its enthusiasm for winning friends and influencing people, NBC even hired a group of cultured young men to go from town to town solely to organize social teas and musicales to promote NBC products.

Of course, the National Biscuit Company was not alone in its emphasis on advertising. It was an era when new corporations throughout the country were trying to bring a positive company image as well as their products to the attention of the public. Such products as Grape Nuts, Victor Talking Machines, Corn Flakes, Ivory Soap, Heinz Baked Beans, Campbell's Tomato Soup, Royal Baking Powder, Sunmaid Raisins, Wrigley Gum and Pep-O-Mint Life Savers were all becoming widely known. But in the forefront was the National Biscuit Company, which had few equals in the art of self promotion.

Hand in hand with production, promotion and advertising came the organization of a sales department. Originally, bakery managers had the responsibility for sales as well as manufacturing. The sales departments were located alongside or within the bakeries themselves. Green had pioneered the idea of addressing the consuming public directly rather than through a middleman.

The salesman picked up his sample case each morning and went out to visit the stores, trim windows, distribute advertising material, demonstrate the company's products, put each dealer's cracker department in as excellent a condition as he could, and pass along pertinent selling suggestions. The calling list of each salesman numbered between a hundred and a hundred and fifty dealers whom he tried to visit at least once a week, sometimes more often. Reinforcing the salesman was the national NBC advertising program. Salesmen worked twelve hours a day, six days a week. There were only four holidays a year. When the salesman was not busy selling, there was always work for him to do in the bakery.

Despite hard work NBC salesmen had unusual pride in their jobs and company. They felt relatively secure. This probably stemmed from the stability of the company, which seemed less affected by economic ups and downs than some. Then, too, the company adhered traditionally to certain high standards of conduct and integrity, which made it widely respected.

When a new store opened in a community, often the first man there would be the NBC salesman.

There seemed to be a personal relationship between NBC and the people who sold their products as well as the people who bought them. Perhaps it was the nature of the products; perhaps it was the nature of the people who worked for the company; perhaps it was the nature of the company itself.

When a salesman made a sale, it was delivered by horse and wagon from the company's local selling agency. Since 1899 NBC's policy of direct selling to retailers in order to maintain control of the freshness of the product had proved an outstanding success. Wholesale selling branches or "agencies," supplied by shipment from NBC bakeries, varied in size, but all were located on a railroad siding to permit easy, economical unloading of the product.

In those days each delivery wagon carried the names of company products proudly painted on its sides. "If these wagons were to be lined up one behind another, they would be approximately four miles of wagons bearing the corporate name . . . If the horses were attached to the wagons, the procession would extend for eight miles, and it would take, roughly speaking, three hours to pass a given point," boasted the NBC magazine. It is estimated that the wagons covered some five million miles in the course of the year. Typically, the company warned its employees that "an unfavorable impression is left in the minds of the public when wagons are not painted, horses are not properly groomed, and harnesses not in best condition."

In 1908 the company bought two electric trucks, more as a novelty than as a practical step forward. Later more of these "electrics" were added. In 1914 the first gasoline truck was put into operation in Chicago. At first there was some apprehension that the fumes from gasoline-driven motors would contaminate the crackers, just as kerosene had in country-store days. But this proved not to be the case, and gradually gasoline trucks replaced the "electrics." It was not until

1923, however, that the last load of crackers was hauled by horse and wagon.

By 1915 the name "National Biscuit Company" was well established throughout the nation and much of the world. Company products—Uneeda, Lorna Doone, Oreo, Mallomar—were part of the pleasant childhood experiences of almost everyone. But a cloud—no bigger than a man's hand—hovered over the company's future. It was to grow and grow.

THIRTEEN

"A Man Must . . .
Love to Struggle"

As the life of the National Biscuit Company gained greater momentum, that of Adolphus W. Green was beginning to run down. When a newspaperman in Connecticut asked to what he attributed his success, Green repeated, "There is no royal road to success. A man must strive and strive. He must convert every obstacle in his path to a steppingstone to the end he seeks. To do this, he must love to struggle, he must love the game of life . . . Hard work is the only thing of which a man never tires. The most miserable of men are those who spend their lives seeking pleasure. They never find it."

In the usual sense, at least, Green had not spent his life seeking pleasure. With few close friends and no hobbies other than his books, his existence revolved around his home and office. At home he tended to be a recluse, spending long hours in the library of his Greenwich, Connecticut, home. He did take a fatherly interest in the development of his six children. But while Mrs. Green was understanding with the youngsters and armed with an able sense of humor, her husband was stern and impatient.

On one occasion Green presented his oldest daughter with a list of twenty books. "If you want to go to Europe this summer," he said, "you'll first have to read these." And before the young lady was permitted to make the trip, her father quizzed her thoroughly to see if she had obeyed his order.

◀ *Adolphus W. Green (center) and William H. Moore (right)*

Once, when the family was in Paris, a daughter decided to look for a job. She found one that she thought would please her father: in a book bindery. All went well until Green discovered that his daughter was called on to join a guild or union of bookbinders. He was furious. The job came to an abrupt end.

But Green's business duties, to the very end, absorbed most of his attention and time. Both at home and at work, Green's perfectionist mania for getting things done *his* way bedeviled him to his dying day. Worse, it was to endanger the growth of the organization that was his pride and love. This man was never able to adjust to the industrial revolution he had helped usher in.

One-man autocratic leadership—possible and perhaps even practical in a past era—was as outdated as the cracker barrel in the twentieth century. Although he encountered enough evidence of the fact to slow down a less determined individual, he never recognized this change.

From the beginning Green ran head on into the frustrating experience of trying to weld more than a hundred independent bakeries around the country into one united organization. Each bakery absorbed into the National Biscuit Company not only had its own formulas for baking; it also had its own traditional philosophy of doing business, its own accounting system, its own name of which it was proud, its own special products which it tended to favor over NBC nationally advertised biscuit. Furthermore, most of the old-time bakers were ill at ease with Green's methods of promoting baked goods.

The introduction of Uneeda Biscuit was a radical change. Veteran bakers shook their heads dubiously over the prospects of selling the new product. Green's demand for uniformity of production of Uneeda, as well as other products, angered and confused them. Consequently, opposition ranged from minor annoyance to outright refusal to follow orders.

Uniformity of quality. Uniformity of name. Uniformity of cleanliness. These were Green's rules. NBC products must carry NBC's brand. Local trade names must be abandoned or de-emphasized. As a result of this policy a number of veteran bakers, who had sold their interests to the National Biscuit Company, retired. Later, capitalizing on their local reputations, some established new, independent bakeries, using their old names and seeking to sell to their old customers. Green was furious when he heard of such incidents; but there was nothing he could do about it.

Then, too, there was a tendency of old-time bakers to cling to old methods of shipping biscuit in boxes and barrels. Opposition, open or secret, to the new In-er-seal packaging method was common. Whenever Green saw boxes being used and biscuit sold in bulk, he wrote angry letters or summoned meetings and demanded that the use of boxes be ended. Those who committed such offenses were summarily discharged.

Green fumed when he noticed local bakery wagons that did not prominently display the NBC name and insignia. There were the Cleveland Bakery Cracker Company wagons, Marvin's Superior Crackers wagons, Langeles Factory Crackers wagons, Miller Bakery wagons, Elliott's Bakery wagons, Dale-Care Bakery wagons. The National Biscuit Company name, if present at all, was painted inconspicuously in small letters!

In 1903 two bakers who had helped to form the federation that made up NBC, James S. Loose and John H. Wiles, left NBC to form a new merger of several companies. At the time Green felt as if members of his own family had turned against him. James Loose, a member of the original board of NBC directors, and his brother had been the owners of the factory in Kansas City which was absorbed first by the American Biscuit & Manufacturing Company and then by the National Biscuit Company.

The Loose-Wiles firm built a rival bakery in Kansas City and continued to expand, adding five more bakeries in the midwest. In 1908 it challenged NBC still further by building a bakery in Boston, and in 1912 began work on its famous "thousand window bakery" in Long Island City. At the same time Nabisco, not to be outdone, began to build an enormous bakery on 11th Avenue in Manhattan.

In his efforts to unify the company and to create loyalty to its name, Green inevitably ran into difficulty with the board of directors, made up largely of bakers who were former competitors. Insisting on undivided loyalty to the National Biscuit Company, Green increasingly resorted to authoritarian methods. Those who were slow or refused to respond to his orders were treated not as colleagues with different opinions but as bitter enemies.

Green was convinced that people needed the closest supervision in their work if they were to conform to his ideals of excellence. So, like a stern parent he attempted personally to supervise the work of the thousands of employees of a company that stretched from one end of the country to the other.

He practically lived in the *Nazu* (contraction of "National Biscuit Company" and "ZuZu"), his private railroad car, and made it a point to inspect every bakery and agency once or twice a year. He spent months rushing about the country. The car was equipped with kitchen, dining room, living room, bedrooms, even wood-burning fireplaces. Small, nervous Louis Isselhardt, the first NBC traffic manager, had the awesome responsibility of seeing that the *Nazu* was always equipped with food and fuel and in proper running order.

Isselhardt's life clearly was not an enviable one. Green insisted that his car always be on the tail end of the train, even the Twentieth Century Limited from New York to Chicago, whose famous observation car was supposed to be the rear car. Nor would Green accept explanations for mishaps or misjudgments. If ever there was a delay or a breakdown, Isselhardt would hear about it. It was practically a full-time job just keeping the *Nazu* in operating order.

In 1914, for example, the *Nazu* traveled more than eight thousand miles in twenty-one days with Green and various members of his family on board. On each trip Green would follow a similar procedure. Word would have been telegraphed ahead of his coming. A carriage or auto would await his arrival. Flowers would be presented to Green's daughters, who usually accompanied him. The local NBC manager would immediately escort Green, with much bowing and scraping, to the local NBC agency or bakery. Frequently, Green's entourage included Earl Babst or Frank Peters.

Preparations for such a visit invariably involved frantic activity: windows were cleaned, corners of the bakery were swept that had seldom seen a broom before, employees washed and dressed with special care, all equipment was shined and polished. By the time of the delegation's arrival, the local manager would be frantic. He would try to keep abreast of Green, explaining this and that as he strode through the plant. Sometimes Green confounded everyone by looking neither to the right nor to the left and rushing through the tour. On other occasions he would leisurely examine every detail. Running a white-gloved finger along the top of doors and window sills, he would bark to the ever-present Isselhardt, who habitually accompanied him at a half trot, "Make a note of that!" Or, "Be sure to remember this!"

After the nerve-racking tour was over, Green would gather members of the local management together and give them a lecture on what was wrong. Invariably, his sharp eyes and thorough understanding of the bakery business would yield valuable criticism. When Green was finally escorted to his railroad car and the train chugged off, the management of the local bakery would breathe a deep sigh of relief.

Green was not one to be liberal with his praise. On one occasion he visited an NBC plant at Milton, Massachusetts, and learned that the manager was at a racetrack. The inspection took place anyway. When the manager returned he was, of course, terrified to discover he had missed such a distinguished visitor. He wrote Green an embarrassed note of apology. Unpredictably, Green wrote back that he was glad that the manager had gone to the races since he had left his bakery in such splendid condition!

Once in Dallas, Texas, when Green fancied one of his daughters had been slighted by the manager of the local bakery, he got back into his private car and refused to inspect the bakery at all.

"We are all animated by one great ambition—to make the National Biscuit Company the ideal industrial corporation," Green told company shareholders. He sought to instill in the thousands of NBC employees the spirit of participation and loyalty that he might have sought from the young men of his law office. It was, of course, impossible. Thousands of NBC employees, many of whom were recent arrivals in America, scarcely understood the language; they did not know their employer and were inclined to be suspicious of him and his expectations.

For Green, the National Biscuit Company was "a great family." Three years after the company was founded, he had instituted a system of stock purchases for employees. The National Biscuit Company announced that "all employees would be given an opportunity to purchase the Preferred stock of the company on the most favorable terms with the view of becoming associate proprietors," *The New York Times* had reported on February 28, 1901.

Green insisted repeatedly that there be "a community of interests existing between all persons connected with the active work of the company, from the Chairman of its Board of Directors to the youngest man or woman on its payrolls." While it was an era in which child labor was legally permitted, and children as young as ten years of age worked in many industries, Green frowned upon such practices. In one report to the stockholders, he stated, "I wish also to call your attention to the fact that it is the company's fixed policy to employ no person under 16 years of age." Green also pointed out that, "In our New York plant, an employee can obtain a dinner consisting of hot meat, potatoes, bread and butter and coffee or tea for 11¢."

NBC's employee publication stated that "The movement inaugurated in this country for the better safeguarding of the health and well being of all classes of workers deserves the enthusiastic cooperation of all employers. Its importance will increase as we became more and more a manufacturing nation, and greater numbers engage in industrial pursuits."

The National Biscuit Company during the early 1900's was one of the largest employers in the nation. If not motivated primarily by humanitarian reasons, Green and his associates were certainly interested in encouraging an efficient organization. So when Earl Babst proposed to Green in the winter of 1914 that he remember his faithful family of 30,000 men and women on Christmas Day, Green thought it a good idea.

A letter was dispatched to all managers and sales agents, announcing: "On Thursday, December 24, 1914, the National Biscuit Company will give a $5 gold piece as a Christmas present to each and every one in its employ, regardless of the position occupied by the employee or whether such employee may have been in the service of the company for a number of years or for a week. This means that there will be no discrimination whatever and that each and every employee will receive as a Christmas present from the company a $5 gold piece. Accompanying this gift are the best wishes of National Biscuit Company for a Merry Christmas and a Happy New Year to you all."

Typically, Green personally arranged for a large supply of individual coin holders and personal envelopes symbolizing the Christmas spirit to be sent to all factories and agencies. Elaborate presentation meetings were organized following suggestions from the general office. There were lengthy speeches from company officers, the playing of music, testimonials, photograph-taking.

C. L. Holt, now manager of the Cambridgeport bakery, told assembled NBC employees that "No one here shares the somewhat prevalent notion that big corporations are heartless and without interest in the welfare of the individual employee. This Christmas gift, and the spirit in which it is offered you, are proof positive that the charge cannot be laid against the National Biscuit Company."

At the Chicago meeting sales agent W. A. Meehan announced that "this commendable act shall live in our thoughts and memories long after the money is spent."

In Kansas City a veteran employee, Harry Bell, rushed up to the platform after the ceremony and made a spontaneous reply on behalf of the employees in thanks for the gift. At Indianapolis factory manager B. G. Hanks, presiding at the meeting, stated, "I am sure we all agree that we are employees of the grandest company that men and women ever worked for."

Similar meetings took place in Houston, Memphis, Cincinnati, Milwaukee, Des Moines, Detroit, Pittsburgh, Zanesville, Salt Lake City, Cleveland, Baltimore, Denver, Helena, Grand Rapids, Buffalo, Milton, Mansfield, St. Joseph, Albany and Syracuse.

In New York a meeting at the 14th Street plant was presided over by Babst. A testimonial was approved stating, "6,000 persons under one roof all engaged in a mighty enterprise of producing food products of superior excellence! 6,000 persons working for a mighty corporation, which, under the leadership of a wonderful executive, has sounded the highest keynote of principle in business practice ever heard in this day and age!"

Personally appearing at the New York meeting, Green stated, "We all labor in this company, every one of us. You have only one advantage over me. With most of you when your day is over, your labor is done; but my labor for this company is never done."

It is doubtful if Green, now seventy-one years old, was aware, even vaguely, of the ground swell of skepticism and fear that accompanied these expressions of gratitude. Far from attuned to the new era in which he lived, he could scarcely be expected to understand the problems of the bakery worker. Although, for his era, something of an enlightened autocrat, Green had no contact with the world of working men and women. Such matters as low wages, long work hours, terror of losing a job, fear of starvation, mass ignorance and superstition—all were beyond his ken.

As historian Frederick Lewis Allen wrote, "The best journals and the best people concerned themselves very little with the fortunes of the average man, and very much with the fortunes of ladies and gentlemen, with the pomp and circumstances of society . . ." The theory of society, which began in England and was popularized in the United States around the turn of the century or before, was that success came to those who were able to survive the rigors of struggle. The poor were poor simply because they were less fit for struggle.

Writing at the dawn of the twentieth century, Robert Hunter pointed out that "there are probably in fairly prosperous years no less than 10,000,000 persons in poverty; that is to say, underfed, underclothed, and poorly housed. Of these, about 4,000,000 persons are public paupers. Over 2,000,000 working men are unemployed from four to six months in the year."

Industry in rare moments did recognize the change that was taking place in the social organization of a rapidly industrializing nation. At the fifth annual convention of the National Association of Manufacturers in 1900, held in Boston, the organization stated, "We have witnessed . . . a startling transformation in the methods of carrying on many of our industries. The organization of the manufacturing business, through combinations and consolidations, has created industrial conditions without precedence in history which seem to set at naught some of the time honored maxims of political economy . . ."

The baking industry was no different from industry in general throughout the United States. The average wage for men in 1910 was less than fifteen dollars a week. Working hours were from fifty-four to sixty a week, with considerable irregularity of employment. According to the United States census, two-thirds to three-quarters of the women employed in the baking industry around 1910 earned less than eight dollars a week.

In a survey of working conditions in bakeries conducted in the 1920's, Hazel Kyrk and Joseph S. Davis reported "a striking difference between the two branches of the baking industry with respect to both the average wage and the average salary. In the biscuit and cracker branch, the average salary is considerably higher than in the manufacture of bread and other products, although even in the biscuit and cracker branch, the average salary is lower than in manufacturers in general. . . . On the other hand, the average wage in the biscuit and cracker branch is less than two-thirds as large as in the bread-making branch. This is due to the fact . . . that the former [biscuit and cracker industry] employs a larger proportion of more or less unskilled women workers . . . In the biscuit and cracker branch . . . over half the wage earners and 23% of the lower salaried employees are women."

Employees in the baking industry found themselves faced with frequent layoffs. As Kyrk and Davis reported: "The growth of the industry itself would cause some variations between minimum and maximum months, and it is significant that the month of minimum employment is usually January or February; while the month of maximum employment is usually late in the year."

In NBC bakeries around the country workers were employed in

occupations ranging from the most menial position to the highest paid and most skilled work, that of the peeler.

Man and muscle, rather than machinery, were characteristic of production methods of the bakery of the early 1900's. The first job in a bakery was the receiving, handling and storage of ingredients. Flour was shipped to the bakeries in 100-pound sacks. These had to be lifted out of freight cars or trucks, stacked on wooden flats, then carried to the mixing departments when needed. Many other supplies used in baking came to the bakery in heavy barrels or sacks. Manpower moved them.

Mixing operations depended on the same source of power. All ingredients were brought to the mixers by hand. They were sorted and weighed by hand, picked up and tossed into the mixers by hand. This included seven or eight hundred pounds of flour as well as other ingredients. If the baking recipe called for eggs, they were broken and shelled, one at a time, right on the spot.

Once the dough was ready for the ovens, it had to be wheeled to the forming and cutting machines by hand. Delivered in large tubs, it was then cut into 40- or 50-pound chunks and lifted into a set of rollers, where it was reduced to sheets of the correct thickness. Machines marked out the shapes of the crackers or cookies and the freshly scored dough was brought to the door of the ovens.

There were few, if any, guards on the machines to prevent accidents. Even the flywheels on the machines had no protective devices. Bakers would lean over and stick their hands into the dough and feel its consistency even while mixing blades were in motion.

All large-scale commercial baking at that time was done on reel ovens. This type of oven, like a Ferris wheel, as previously described, was about two stories high, built of brick with the heating chamber fired with coke or oil at the very bottom. Trays were suspended from the reel, much like the seats of a Ferris wheel. Working as fast as possible, the peelers fed the oven by hand, putting cracker dough, in rectangular sheets and marked with the desired shapes, through a narrow door in the brick chamber and onto the revolving trays.

The peeler's work required experience and skill as well as muscle and coordination. He was the aristocrat of the cracker-baking industry. Nine hours a day he would wield his 30 by 40-inch wooden peel or shovel, holding it by its small handle and turning it after each load to prevent its warping out of shape from the heat of the oven. He would insert his peel under the crackers in dough form, pick them up, turn a right about face and deftly place his load on the hot oven shelf. A standard crew on a cracker oven consisted of two men to roll the dough, two peelers to peel in the oven, and two take-out men for peeling the crackers out of the oven. A seventh man, the machine captain, usually completed the crew.

Each man had his own peel. Often he had his initials burned into the handle so it would not be stolen or mislaid. Woe betide anyone who took a man's peel! The peeler gave it the best of care and kept it sharp. A dull or broken peel was thrown away, for it produced crippled crackers. A man would usually sandpaper the peel tip every morning to remove any nicks, even though continual gliding over salt on the machine apron kept a peel razor-sharp. A press, something like one used to keep a tennis racket from warping, was used to store a peel when not in use, and for the same reason. The average life of a peel was about ten weeks, for in that time, continued abrasion from salt and daily sanding out of nicks made the peel too short to be used.

A good peeler was always in demand, and journeyman peelers traveling from city to city to see the country could be fairly certain of picking up a job at the local cracker bakery.

After one revolution around the flame, the baked sheets of crackers were removed from the oven by the take-out man with his long-handled peel. Then they were stacked by hand in the trays, carried to the packing table, and placed in containers by hand.

Packaging operations were laborious. Even though small cardboard cartons and tin boxes with glass fronts replaced the old-time cracker barrel, they still had to be filled by hand. In long rows women formed the famous Peters carton, then placed the crackers and cookies inside. Sealing and wrapping were also done by hand. Many shipments were made in large wooden crates that had to be filled and nailed shut by hand. Once ready to leave the bakery, the heavy crates had to be manhandled to the trucks and freight cars.

Even with Green's advanced ideas of modern construction methods, work in a bakery was arduous and monotonous. Ventilation was primitive and in the summertime always a problem. Bakers, covered with perspiration, were coated with flour dust, creating not only a ghostly appearance, but also a menace to sanitation. Exhaust systems to draw out the gasses from coal-fired ovens, which often permeated the plant, were inadequate. Prickly heat was an occupational disease.

Heat exhaustion was common in summer. Injuries were frequent. Working hours were long, usually nine or more. The workday started early and extended to the evening.

Working conditions in NBC bakeries were no worse than in most industrial plants and better than some. Green hated the sloppy, disorganized inefficiency he found characteristic of most of the bakeries. He had a personal compulsion, whether trying a legal case or running the world's biggest baking company, to fight confusion and establish order.

Like virtually all industrialists of his day, his understanding of labor unions was limited. As Cochran and Miller expressed it, he shared with other employers of the era "an almost psychopathic fear of having to meet representatives of labor on a footing of equal authority." Consequently, his lack of understanding of the militant labor movement of the early 1900's, International Workers of the World, caused him considerable anguish.

Nor were the fears of Green ameliorated in any way by reading such warnings as that of Jack London, who proclaimed before a Yale audience, "The Capitalist Class . . . has failed in its management and its management is to be taken away from it . . . The revolution is here, now. Stop it who can!" Such sentiments were enough to throw even the most hardy capitalist of the day into a rage not unmixed with twinges of foreboding.

When a walkout of NBC wagon drivers took place in Chicago in 1905—evidently over a matter of wages—Green arbitrarily ordered all Chicago NBC bakeries closed, discharged all employees including salesmen who could not be transferred, and sold all the horses. No goods from other plants were allowed to be shipped into Chicago. For about a week NBC completely halted its business in the area.

When NBC bakeries were reopened, deliveries were made to the trade with police protection on the wagons and at the bakeries. Green also fumed when he observed changes on his board of directors indicating a trend toward control by outside financial interests rather than old-time bakers. The new members, untrained in industry, were interested largely in finance, banking and high society. In 1906 William H. Moore, who had renewed his interest in the company by purchasing a large block of NBC stock, was elected a director. For the next two decades, although from behind the scenes, he provided much of the leadership of the Biscuit Company.

Green's dedication to NBC was such that he mistrusted any

officer who had interests other than the baking industry. Green, now an old man and none too well, was in no position to do other than accept the development. Besides, other troubles were mounting.

Many were the result of his increasing eccentricities. There was, for instance, his mania for punctuality. He was himself always on time and he hated to be kept waiting. One morning a representative of an advertising agency had an 8:30 appointment to show Mr. Green a new billboard idea. The agency man was late. Green began to pace up and down his office, frequently pulling his heavy gold watch from his vest pocket, snapping it open, studying it, and then closing it ominously. Promptly at 8:31 he closed the door of his office.

A few minutes later a message was brought to him. The agency representative was ready for his appointment. "What appointment?" asked Mr. Green.

Green insisted that not only buildings and offices but executive employees be clean and neat. A slovenly person would be dismissed, often without warning. One day the company's advertising manager, Alfred Mace, appeared without his vest. After a moment of silent scrutiny, Green inquired, "Where is your vest, Mr. Mace?"

Mace murmured an apology. The next day he was dressed to conform to Green's standards.

Green did not permit his executive staff or their employees to shed their coats, no matter how hot the summer day. On one occasion Green was about to enter the office of his chief architect, A. G. Zimmermann, when he observed a young employee bending over his drafting board in his shirt sleeves.

Green glared at the young man, speechless with rage. "Tell that young man to either put on his coat," he finally instructed Zimmermann, "or else find himself a job somewhere else."

In winter, as he entered his office, Green had a habit of unbuttoning his heavy fur coat and letting it fall. If the office boy was not there to catch the coat or if he let it trail on the ground, he would be severely reprimanded. One day a young boy, new on the job, stood as he had been instructed, waiting to catch the coat. But he did not anticipate how heavy it was. When he tried to hold it, he was bowed down by its weight and it fell to the floor. He received a sharp tongue-lashing.

At the start of the work day Green would usually summon his various managers to him to brief them on the day's activities. The managers stood in line outside of his office so their president would not be kept waiting. When Green entered the elevator, any subordinates who were in the elevator stepped out and let the president ride alone as a mark of deference. Although Green continued to smoke his big black cigars, he frowned upon smoking by subordinates.

Drinking on the premises was strictly forbidden as were parties of any kind, including those around the Christmas season. Clothing had to be conservative and women were cautioned against the use of makeup.

No executive dared leave the building until Green had gone. As six o'clock approached, there would be much whispering: "Has he left yet?" "Is Mr. Green gone?"

With all his petulance, Green displayed surprising respect for others who had ability and courage. On one occasion he attended the theater with his wife. Afterward, for some reason or other, he decided to visit his office. He approached the front gate, but was stopped by the watchman.

Green indignantly exclaimed, "I'm the president of the company!"

"Is that so," the watchman replied. "Have you a pass?"

When Green said he had no pass, the watchman refused to let him in.

Next day Green ordered a raise for the watchman.

But Green's behavior—something to reckon with even in the early days—grew more intolerable with each passing year. Gradually, the men to whom he looked—if not for guidance at least for obedience—began to desert him. James H. Douglas of Cedar Rapids, Iowa, the energetic first NBC sales director, a vice president and member of the board of directors, decided not to accompany Green when the executive offices were moved to New York, and resigned. Green's bitterness increased when Douglas became a top executive of the Quaker Oats Company.

In 1906 Frank O. Lowden, always a close friend of Green's and one to whom he looked for advice, resigned from the board to become a candidate for Congress from the State of Illinois. He was elected and went on to the governorship of that state in 1917. It was a severe blow to Green, who had few friends as understanding as Lowden.

Another loss was that of tall, sandy-haired John D. Richardson, Green's original advertising manager who had been made head of the western sales department. In January 1915 Richardson resigned and later developed an interest in the Chicago Carton Company.

On September 2, 1910, Benjamin F. Crawford, first president of the company, died. Although he had retired years before, his death was a sentimental loss to Green. The passing of Crawford, however, was a minor blow compared with the death of Green's wife, Esther, in the fall of 1912. When Mrs. Green first became ill, her husband sought every possible medical assistance. Since no American doctor seemed able to find a cure, Green sent for a noted expert in the use of radium, Dr. A. Bickel, who came all the way from Vienna to attend her. It was too late.

Frank M. Peters, the office boy who had risen to become Green's law partner, inventor of the Peters carton and a vice president of the Biscuit Company since 1905, resigned in 1915. Green had considered Peters in many respects his closest friend, and had named him executor of his will.

Peters gave no reason for his resignation. Neither did George E. W. de Clercq, former manager of the supply department, now in charge of packaging. He and Green had suffered together through the early years of the launching of Uneeda Biscuit. Now he joined the Robert Gair Company of New York, pioneer paper package manufacturers. De Clercq, like several other NBC officers, was to return to NBC in later years, under a different administration. Peters never did; he joined the American Radiator Company.

Perhaps the cruelest blow of all occurred the day in 1915 that Earl D. Babst, a member of the firm of Green, Peters & Babst, legal counsel for the company and one of its most energetic administrators, announced his resignation. Green had considered Babst his natural heir to the presidency. But whether Babst became tired of Green's eccentricities or just tired of waiting, he resigned from the company to become assistant to the president of the American Sugar Refining Company. Green interpreted this as a hostile act.

By the end of 1916 there were very few people left on the board of directors or in positions of executive responsibility from the original group that had formed the company. Most of the old-time bakers were gone. David F. Bremner resigned in 1905; Louis D. Dozier died in 1915; James W. Hazen left the board in 1905; James S. Loose resigned in 1902; Cornelius Rumsey resigned in 1899; Harry Vories resigned in 1906.

William T. Baker, a colleague of Green's on the old Chicago Board of Trade and a member of the first board of directors of NBC, had died late in 1903. Norman B. Ream, member of the board of directors at its inception, died in 1915. There were few individuals left whom Green trusted. Frederick W. Waller and Roy E. Tomlinson, both vice presidents and products of Green's old law firm, remained. Tomlinson, quietly competent, filled the post of legal counsel left vacant by Babst.

"The policies which have so successfully guided the company's affairs in former years," Green reported to his stockholders in January 1917, "have proved themselves adequate to meet the demand upon our organization, equipment and resources in the year just ended. We confidently expect this will continue to be the case during the coming year."

However, Green was not destined to witness the further progress of the company. On March 8, 1917, "the creator of the modern cracker business" was found dead in his bed at his Plaza Hotel suite, the victim of pneumonia contracted on a southern tour of NBC bakeries.

The year that Green died the company, at the close of business on December 31, had assets of $73,506,453.41. Since the organization of the company on February 3, 1898, there had been paid, out of earnings, 79 consecutive quarterly dividends of 1¾ per cent on the preferred stock. On the common stock 77 dividends had been paid—30 quarterly dividends of 1 per cent, 8 quarterly dividends of 1¼ per cent, 8 quarterly dividends of 1½ per cent, 27 quarterly dividends of 1¾ per cent, 3 extra dividends of 1 per cent, and one extra dividend of 2 per cent.

The company's only indebtedness at Green's death was for those raw materials and supplies which were purchased so recently that the bills could not be adjusted before the close of the fiscal year of 1917.

The passing of Green was not totally unexpected. He was seventy-four years of age and had increasingly been showing his years. Nevertheless, the monumental contribution he had made to the industrial development of the country was recognized in many press tributes.

On March 10, 1917, NBC bakeries and agencies throughout the country closed down for an hour at 11 o'clock, the time of the Green funeral. In New York the general offices were closed for the entire day. A special train left Grand Central at 9:40 in the morning, transporting NBC employees to the funeral at St. Mary's Church in Greenwich.

Honorary pallbearers included Francis L. Hine, representative of the First National Bank who had been involved in the founding of the company; William H. Moore; Paul Moore, his son who had recently joined the NBC board; Frank M. Peters, who came from Chicago for the funeral; Henry J. Evans, T. S. Ollive, Lambert Mason, S. S. Marvin, all old-time bakers who had helped found the company; and R. E. Tomlinson, general counsel for the company and third vice president.

As the funeral train picked up speed leaving Greenwich following the interment, Judge Moore—in conversation with the thirty-nine-year-old Tomlinson—asked casually, "Mr. Tomlinson, we are thinking about suggesting your name for the presidency of National Biscuit Company. Would you be interested?"

Out of the cracker barrel and into the cracker department ▸

The general store begins to offer packaged merchandise

FOURTEEN

Young Man in a Hurry

As PRESIDENT of the National Biscuit Company, one of Roy E. Tomlinson's first official acts was to sell the *Nazu*, Green's luxurious private car, which had become a symbol of autocratic management. It marked the end of an era.

It was not the only change to take place with the coming of a new administration. Innovations under the leadership of the quiet-speaking Tomlinson and the even quieter Judge Moore were numerous. But they were a reflection of the imperatives of a new era rather than the will of individuals.

Although the baking of Fig Newtons, Lorna Doones, Uneeda Biscuits and such products remained essentially the same, it was a time of change for almost everything else. Serious new technological and economic problems demanded attention. The voice of the "Great Commoner," William Jennings Bryan, still thundered for a greater share of the nation's wealth for the underprivileged. A United States Senator from Wisconsin, Robert "Fighting Bob" La Follette, was insisting that working people and farmers were at least as important as machines. Woodrow Wilson, a progressive college professor, had risen to the Presidency on a "New Freedom" pledge to the downtrodden. It was clear that nineteenth-century methods and organization would be hard pressed to solve twentieth-century problems.

◀ *Roy E. Tomlinson*

"For the first time, the United States came face to face with the swift pace of economic change, technological innovation, and the rapidly rising standard of living . . ." wrote William Leuchtenburg in *Perils of Prosperity*. "The generation of 1914–1932 did not invent the problems with which it had to deal—it would have preferred to ignore them. Its success was less than complete, but this was the first serious attempt of Americans to make their peace with the Twentieth Century . . .

"By the end of the decade a 'managerial revolution' had occurred; plant managers and corporation executives, rather than owners, made the chief decisions. Young men no longer aimed to found their own businesses, to be Carnegies or Vanderbilts; they wanted to rise to a high position as a hired manager or a salaried executive. The businessman was less interested in risk and more in stabilizing his business."

Roy Everett Tomlinson, the man who was to help lead the National Biscuit Company through this difficult era, was born in Oak Park, Illinois on December 4, 1877, at about the time that youthful Adolphus W. Green and William H. Moore were building their law practices in Chicago. His father, Everett Seward Tomlinson, a graduate of Yale, had gone to the midwest in the latter part of the nineteenth century. He met Genevieve Rush in Champaign, Illinois, where they were married. The older Tomlinson had established a clothing business on LaSalle Street in Chicago, which did well. Four children were born to them: Roy, Ernest, Genevieve and Howard.

The oldest boy, Roy, developed into a serious young man, more inclined to listening than talk. Coming from Abraham Lincoln country, Roy was influenced by Lincoln lore from boyhood. A friend of the family, the Reverend William E. Barton, once presented him with a set of books reputedly owned by Lincoln. The gift made a lasting impression. Tomlinson's interest in Lincoln increased and it was to be, outside of business, one of the few diversions of his life.

The turn-of-the-century years offered many opportunities for lawyers, particularly in Chicago. Among the most successful were William Goudy, William H. Moore, Adolphus W. Green and Lincoln's son, Robert T. Lincoln, all widely known, respected and well rewarded financially. Legal training was a great asset in a business world where companies were combining on every hand into giant corporations.

So Roy decided to be a lawyer. In 1901 he was graduated with the degree of Bachelor of Law from the University of Wisconsin Law

School and soon admitted to the Illinois bar. A neighbor of the Tomlinsons who was associated with the National Biscuit Company suggested that Roy look into the possibility of a position there.

So, soon after graduation, Roy Tomlinson presented himself at the NBC office in the towering eight-story Home Insurance Company Building. There was no opening for a lawyer. But Tomlinson, determined to become connected with the company, accepted a position as a clerk in the treasurer's office. A few months later he was transferred to the firm of Green, Honore & Peters, then acting as the legal arm of the Biscuit Company.

Each day the gangling Tomlinson would ride the trolley car from Oak Park to the center of town and stride the distance to 205 LaSalle Street. He would then take the birdcage-like elevator to the top floor where Green's law firm and the National Biscuit Company were located. Tomlinson's work was menial: standing at a high desk, checking accounts, occasionally running errands to clients or courthouse.

Meanwhile, Earl Babst found himself harassed by more work than he could handle in both routine business of the firm as well as special NBC assignments. He had an eye open for an assistant. One day he noticed the tall solemn-faced young man at work at his desk. Babst studied young Tomlinson from afar. He noted that he was quiet, self-effacing almost to the point of shyness, yet energetic and bright. Babst tested him with small assignments and found he could take direction and instruction. What was especially important, Tomlinson seemed able to carry out orders precisely and with great attention to detail. Even-tempered, seemingly unemotional, the young lawyer appeared well equipped for the work Babst had in mind. Babst asked Adolphus Green to assign the young lawyer to him. Green agreed.

Roy Tomlinson's early chores had to do with trademark research for the many lawsuits which the National Biscuit Company was then filing against those who infringed on its products, trademarks or product names. It was humdrum work but he executed his assignments conscientiously.

In 1905 Green gave up his law practice completely to devote all his time to the leadership of the National Biscuit Company. Responsibility for the company's legal work descended upon Babst and, in a measure, his assistant. This was the year NBC's executive officers and personnel were preparing to move from Chicago to New York. Babst asked his assistant whether he would care to make the move, too. The request took young Tomlinson by surprise.

"We'd like to have you come with us to New York to help build the company's legal department," said Babst.

"Thank you, sir," replied Tomlinson. "But if you don't mind I would like to think it over."

"Any problem?" asked Babst.

"Well, sir," replied Tomlinson, "I am planning to get married and we have already rented an apartment at Oak Park."

Babst gave Tomlinson a day to think it over.

Tomlinson and his fiancée, Eleanor Parsons, a sweetheart from childhood days, decided they could get married, squeeze in a brief honeymoon, and make the move to New York. On Christmas night 1905 Roy and Eleanor were married in Oak Park and left the next day for New Orleans. When they returned to Chicago, they packed and boarded the Twentieth Century Limited for New York, where they settled in a small apartment near Columbia University.

In New York Tomlinson's work assumed a new character. Routine trademark research was now delegated to others. "I liked his modesty, the fact that he was quiet and he always listened rather than spoke," said Babst.

And indeed Tomlinson was developing a maturity that won the respect not only of Babst but, miraculously, of Adolphus W. Green. Tomlinson never presumed equality with Green or, for that matter, Babst. Among his most valued characteristics were discipline and self-control. As the years passed, Tomlinson was able to maintain his relatively cordial relations with Green and Babst, despite the fact that both men were typical of their era: autocratic, critical and demanding.

Tomlinson did well. Soon he could move his family to a New Jersey suburb which, like so many NBC executives, he found conveniently accessible to the 14th Street area just across the Hudson River where NBC dominated the Manhattan waterfront. In 1909 a daughter, Harriet, was born to the Tomlinsons, and in 1914 a son, Everett. In this same year Roy Tomlinson, only 37 years of age, was appointed assistant secretary of the company.

In the following year a minor explosion rocked the company when Earl Babst announced that he was leaving. It had been assumed that Babst would succeed Green. But perhaps the offer made by the American Sugar Refining Company was too good to turn down. In any event, when Green recovered from his fury at what he considered Babst's treachery, he looked about for a new legal counsel. The logical successor was Babst's assistant. In 1915 Tomlinson was named general counsel.

But Tomlinson's rise had just begun. A year later he was further honored by being named third vice president. He now followed in authority only Frederick W. Waller, rotund, good-natured first vice president, an associate of Green's since pre-NBC days; and Thomas S. Ollive, second vice president, one of the few veteran bakers still left in the leadership of the company.

With the death of Adolphus W. Green on March 8, 1917, there were few candidates eligible for the presidency. Because of Green's long-standing policy of dealing with his directors individually, they were only vaguely acquainted with most of the company's executives. Plainly neither Waller nor Ollive, technically next in line, were by age or temperament suited for top corporate leadership. So the attention of the directors was focused on the third vice president and general counsel, Roy E. Tomlinson.

Ever since Babst had left, Tomlinson had looked increasingly to Judge Moore for the counsel he had been accustomed to receive from Babst. It was obvious to Moore that Green's leadership in his later years no longer fitted the needs of the National Biscuit Company. But, characteristically, Moore quietly waited, seeing much and saying little. When the time came to select a new president, Moore was ready. Without delay, he put the question to Tomlinson on the train returning to New York from Green's funeral.

The answer was brief and characteristic: "Yes, sir."

The next annual meeting of NBC stockholders took place in Jersey City in March 1917. The newspapers were full of sensational reports of the sinking of American ships by German submarines. A major crisis was brewing. Within a month President Wilson was to ask for a declaration of war against Germany. The NBC meeting was followed by a session of the board of directors in New York City. Except for the election of a company president only routine business was before the board. Next day the business world was surprised to be informed that an unknown lawyer, Roy Everett Tomlinson, had been selected to succeed the late Adolphus W. Green as head of the nation's biggest baker. At the same meeting William H. Moore was elected chairman of the board, the first time this position had been filled since Green became president in 1905.

The Cracker Baker, spokesman for the industry, stated, "It is a remarkable tribute to Mr. Tomlinson that he should be selected to head the destinies of so great a concern as the National Biscuit Company, for he is young for so responsible a position. He will not be forty until next December. However, in his fifteen years' experience with the company, he has had invaluable training."

Not given to show of emotion, Tomlinson put it in more practical language: "My job, as I see it, is to keep the train on the track."

One month after Tomlinson's election, F. W. Waller resigned to give full attention to handling Green's estate. Henry J. Evans, manager of the purchasing department, replaced Waller as vice president.

Throughout the company, particularly in executive departments, there was a feeling of relief at the election of Tomlinson. There had been little room for independent action. Now, with the new atmosphere of good will, a number of former executives who had left the company during Green's last years were encouraged by Tomlinson to return. George E. W. de Clercq, the packaging expert, returned; so did Zimmermann, the talented architect; Frank Bugbee, the financial man, and John D. Richardson, first advertising manager. John G. Zeller, the able engineer who had stayed with NBC through the difficult years, was elevated to a vice presidency.

Tomlinson was a symbol of youth, enthusiasm and a fresh point of view. Evidence of the dawning new era was an unusual meeting of bakery managers held at Delmonico's restaurant in New York City on April 12, 1917.

The primary purpose of the meeting "was to enable the managers to become better acquainted with one another and exchange experiences, and to discuss problems and questions which they had in common with mutual benefit and advantage."

This *was* something new! Green had rarely gone out of his way for an exchange of experiences. During certain periods he welcomed constructive ideas and had always been interested in suggestions from people he respected. But he did not respect many people. As years passed, he virtually ceased to listen to anyone's opinions.

From all parts of the country, wherever NBC had a bakery or an agency, company executives descended upon New York City. The gathering had no formal sessions; managers came and went as they saw fit, conferring with officers of the company. The officials inspected the facilities of the New York plant; they became acquainted with one another; they reminisced about old times; they discussed problems and questions they had in common.

Dinner at Delmonico's was the climax. The guests were summoned to the great ballroom by a bugle boy in a Uneeda Biscuit Boy costume. "There was absolutely no feeling of constraint," stated an eyewitness. "It was like a happy family, each one of whom was enjoying himself to the utmost. The tables were arranged in the form of a giant letter 'U,' Mr. Tomlinson being seated at the center of the base of the 'U.' "

An orchestra played from a high balcony. A fountain gurgled merrily nearby. Between courses the members sang popular airs. As each manager spoke, an electric star on a giant map lit up to locate his branch.

When Mr. Tomlinson rose to speak after the dinner was served, a tremendous ovation greeted him. His speech, one of the few he was to make in his entire career, was brief. He paid a tribute to the memory of Adolphus W. Green. He dwelt for a moment on the momentous crisis which faced the country at the time in the form of a great world war. He closed by emphasizing the opportunities at hand and the necessity for every NBC employee "*to think, to act, to hurry up.*"

A special poem read before the gathering included the lines:

> Thrice sure thy future, oh, NBC,
> With truth, honor and unity.

"The National Biscuit Company has ever been known for its high aims and lofty ideals," the printed program stated, "but during the next decade, it shall sweep on to undreamed of pinnacles."

If Roy E. Tomlinson had any qualms about the huge responsibility that rested upon him that night, perhaps he gathered confidence from the fact that as he sat at the center of the base of the giant "U," on his left was William H. Moore, quiet, observant, powerful even in repose.

In the years ahead the team of Moore and Tomlinson was to move the company in new, untried directions.

FIFTEEN

The Indestructible
William H. Moore

If WILLIAM H. MOORE was not active in the affairs of the National Biscuit Company during the years immediately after its formation, this in no way indicated that he had not been busy. Few men in corporate affairs were busier.

After the Diamond Match disaster the Moore brothers found themselves in debt to the extent of approximately $4,000,000. For men of lesser caliber this would have been disastrous. But not for the Moores, particularly William H.

He pledged to pay off his debt without the slightest doubt in his mind (or so it seemed to his creditors) that he could do so, and in short order. According to the New York *Herald*, the Moores "showed of what stuff they were made. The crash had left their nerve as their only capital. Their enemies, even many of their friends, thought this had been so shattered that they would be for all time out of the race as financial leaders. The Moores within a year had stultified these prophets."

It was customary for the architects of the vast new corporations that were built around the turn of the century to be well rewarded for their efforts. For helping put together the enterprise that became the National Biscuit Company in February 1898, the promoters received some $6,000,000 worth of common stock, a substantial share of which went to the Moore brothers. Thus, a mere eighteen months

◄ *William H. Moore*

after the Diamond Match failure, the Moores were involved in an enterprise of notable success. The National Biscuit Company, from the beginning, earned 7 per cent on its preferred stock, 4 per cent on its common, and a good surplus besides. The stock was readily bought and in a short time advanced to par for the preferred and 50 for the common. The men whom the Moores had induced to go into the underwriting earned a profit of 50 per cent. Large trading took place in the shares, brokers earned high commissions and their clients large profits. In February 1903 NBC was officially listed on the New York Stock Exchange.

Thus, NBC helped Judge Moore win back the prestige he had lost as well as clear up his outstanding debts. Biscuits paved the way for his return to respectability in high financial circles. While he had to sell his NBC holdings to meet his obligations, he was confident that the Biscuit Company was in safe hands. Adolphus W. Green, with whom Moore had waged a relentless price war, seemed ably fitted to lead the new corporation or "biscuit trust" as some called it.

Even if the Moore brothers would have liked to exert greater influence in NBC affairs, Green was not exactly an easy man to get along with. Better that they look for new financial spheres to conquer. In December of the very year that the National Biscuit Company was founded, Judge Moore formed the American Tin Plate Company, receiving $10,000,000 of common stock for his services, the market value of which at that time was $4,800,000. This commission, according to the New York *Herald*, "added to that of the fifty-five-million-dollar Biscuit merger, brought the fortune of the brothers up to $6,800,000. They paid their debts on Diamond Match and had nearly three million dollars of their own left." With the success of the National Biscuit Company to his credit, Moore had no difficulty in receiving underwriting for Tin Plate. This company, too, went on its way to success.

Early the following year William Moore took another giant step to become the most successful financial operator in the west by putting together a new corporation called the National Steel Company. This was followed in April of the same year with the formation by the Moores of the American Steel Company.

In these bold moves the Moore brothers worked closely with several associates, especially William B. Leeds, known as the "tin plate king," and Daniel G. Reid, a former Indiana banker who became interested in the tin-plate business. Like Moore, Reid was one of the organizers of the American Tin Plate Company as well as the National Steel Company, the American Steel Hoop Company, and the American Sheet Steel Company.

The Moore brothers, together with Reid and Leeds, became known in eastern financial circles as the "four horsemen from Chicago" or the "big four from the prairie." With Judge Moore at its head, the combination went on to achieve fantastic success in the steel industry. Financial returns were almost beyond belief. According to Matthew Josephson, "the Moores paid themselves $5,000,000 and $6,000,000 respectively" for organizing the American Steel & Wire Company. Altogether the Moore brothers and their associates collected some 265 tin-plate mills into a single corporation, among other financial feats.

But Judge Moore was not a man to be satisfied with halfway measures. Why not organize the entire steel industry into one enterprise? Of all the financial operators in the nation, none knew the meaning of centralization any better than the Moore brothers. And they had the courage not only of their convictions but of their victories as well.

In 1899 the Moores actually had arranged the impossible: to buy out the holdings of the Carnegie Steel Company, taking over the great properties and issuing $100,000,000 in bonds, $250,000,000 in 6 per cent preferred stock, and $275,000,000 in common stock, a total of $625,000,000.

Andrew Carnegie had made a tremendous fortune in steel. But as he grew older, he wanted his future reputation—tarnished to an extent by certain brutalities in handling labor matters—to rest more on his philanthropies than on his profits. So he was not disinterested in a possible sale, if the proper price could be obtained.

In May Henry Clay Frick, a personal friend of Judge Moore, had come to Andrew Carnegie with an offer from the Moore brothers to buy the entire Carnegie steel empire. It was an audacious proposition. Carnegie accepted the offer, and an option payment of $1,175,000 was made, part furnished by Frick and the rest by the Moores. But the deal fell through, and the Moores coolly forfeited the option. Among the causes of the failure, it was believed, was the secret opposition of J. P. Morgan, the eastern financial titan.

In March 1901 William Moore and Indiana banker Daniel Reid put together the American Can Company, a consolidation of independent manufacturing plants, with $8,000,000 capital.

Judge Moore moved steadily ahead toward his goal of organizing a giant combination—the largest the world had ever seen—in the steel industry. But the center of the steel industry lay at the doorstep of the famous J. P. Morgan.

So Moore, whose power in the west matched Morgan's financial control of the east, decided to move from Chicago to New York, the scene of new developments in the battle for control of the steel industry. He found a suitable house, just off Fifth Avenue, in the heart of fashionable New York, surrounded by such neighbors as John D. Rockefeller, Jr., the William Rockefellers, the Joseph Harrimans, Lydia Fox, John R. Platt, Charles B. Curtis, Harold Childs and Chauncey DePew, and diagonally across Fifth Avenue from the imposing brown bulk of the University Club.

The white limestone mansion chosen by Mr. and Mrs. Moore was located at 4 East 54th Street. It was five stories high and designed by Stanford White of McKim, Mead and White. The Moores, particularly Mrs. Moore, were especially aware of White's outstanding reputation in Chicago as a result of his work at the Columbian Exhibition of 1893. The house had huge bedrooms, numerous parlors, twenty-one fireplaces, two passenger elevators, mahogany doors three inches thick, eight servants' rooms, an impressive entrance hall with fawn-colored marble columns, walls covered with green and gold cloth, a marble staircase with a cherry mahogany rail, and a conservatory on the second floor.

Judge Moore established an informal office on the first floor. The family library was on the third. Along the winding marble stairway huge display cases were built to house the Judge's numerous horse-show trophies. Four blocks uptown were the stables for Moore's hundred or more horses. Additional horses were maintained at Pride's Crossing in Massachusetts and Convent, New Jersey.

By now Moore had attained an international reputation not only as a financial promoter but also as a breeder and exhibitor of thoroughbred horses. Nearly every horse show held in this country and many of those abroad had entries in his name, and his trophies and blue ribbons were many. His stable of horses was rated with the finest anywhere.

A vigorous walker, Judge Moore presented an imposing figure striding from his home to his office, walking stick in hand. Sometimes his wife, Ada, accompanied him. She, too, in her own way, was impressive-looking—tall, erect, even-featured with very black hair. There were two sons—Paul and Edward—when they moved to New York. Both were born in Chicago; both were to attend Yale University.

While the move to New York permitted many business and social contacts impossible in the west, most important of all to Judge Moore was the close proximity to J. P. Morgan and other tycoons who had huge investments in the steel industry.

After Morgan's astonishing success in consolidating railroads, he was now turning to the steel industry. His next move was naturally looked upon with keen interest in financial circles. He was not enthusiastic about the potentialities of steel until December of 1900, when at a private dinner at the University Club he found himself seated next to Charles Schwab, a close associate of Andrew Carnegie and a fluent conversationalist.

Schwab was the only speaker, and he stirred Morgan's imagination by describing possibilities of manufacturing steel on a scale never conceived of before.

The sheer immensity of the project made even such a bold financial operator as Morgan pause. But "so contagious did the idea of combining steel companies become," according to Frederick Lewis Allen, "that it was as if a giant magnet had moved over the surface of the industry, pulling together into compact groups the innumerable separate particles of which it had previously consisted."

Morgan and the Moore brothers, working separately, accomplished several mergers in the steel industry. Inevitably, the idea of combining these giants into one mammoth corporation occurred to them. And thus was born the first billion-dollar corporation in the country—the United States Steel Company. "United States Steel was born of a war between men who have been called the Titans of finance and industry," Stewart Holbrook says in *The Age of the Moguls*. The Moores dealt with Morgan as with their other opponents in the past—with confidence and boldness. "They obtained better terms than anyone else who entered the combination," *Everybody's Magazine* reported. "The position they held in the several corporations they had organized is suggested by the fact that when calls were made for the stockholders to deposit their shares in exchange for steel corporation shares, stockholders and directors—from six to a dozen—signed for the other institutions; but in the Moores' companies, the calls were signed simply: 'W. H. and J. H. Moore.'"

The dream of consolidating steel was a reality. On February 13, 1901, the syndicate headed by Morgan reached agreement. And Judge

Moore became a member of the board of directors of the greatest steel empire in the world.

Judge Moore now moved into railroading, one of the most sought after financial plums in the country. It was not long before he and his associates had bought control of the Chicago, Rock Island & Pacific Railway, then the St. Louis & San Francisco Railway, and after that the Chicago & Alton Railway. In six years the team had transformed the Rock Island line from a local carrier to a great system, increasing the trackage from 3,619 miles in 1899 to 14,468 miles in 1905.

Wall Street was almost paralyzed by the boldness of Judge Moore and his friends, particularly in the buying of the Rock Island Railway. This deal was put through so expeditiously and silently that it seemed, as one writer put it, to have been "dashed off in an idle moment—like a spring poem."

Explaining his audacious entrance into the railroad field, Judge Moore told a friend, "Why, we looked over this railroad business and decided that we'd like it, so we went into it."

"His work is the work of the General and Chief," the magazine *The World's Work* stated in January of 1907. "He makes the policy, approves the operations, vetoes or puts into effect the great financial plans. When the system needs millions of money, he moves into the firing line. When it comes to purchasing thousands of new cars, dozens of new locomotives, he wants to know just why. In the council chamber, he is now supreme. In conflict with other powers, his is the hand that fires the train, or carries out the flag of truce. He is the arbiter of peace and war on the whole Rock Island System . . . There are three Presidents and two Chairmen in the Rock Island System, but 'the boss' is not an official at all. He is ex-Judge William H. Moore—big, quiet, retiring, but omni-present capitalist."

Fresh from his latest triumphs in the railroad industry, Judge Moore now had few new worlds to conquer. He had all the money he needed, and more. His interests in the world of horses had yielded him new renown. His wife, Ada, developed her interest in art into one of the great collections of Oriental art in the world. But Moore had a special concern for one of the companies he had helped found: the National Biscuit Company. He was shrewd enough to realize that Adolphus W. Green, brilliant and capable as he had proved, needed assistance, whether he would admit it or not.

So Moore purchased a considerable block of NBC stock, renewed his interest in the company and, late in 1906, was elected an NBC director. At the same time he became a member of the executive committee.

Moore, now financially involved once again in the bakery business, was resolved not to permit the success of the company to be endangered by Green's increasing personal eccentricities. Besides, Green was getting along in years and was not well. The company needed reinforcements for the inevitable day when Green would no longer be available. Never given to impatience, Judge Moore bided his time and, as openings occurred, cautiously added people to the board of directors who, in his estimation, would provide the kind of leadership the company needed. Many of the old-time bakers were gone; some had died, some had retired, some were not able to get along with Green. They were replaced by financial men and bankers, with a good sprinkling of Moore's friends from the world of horsemanship.

When Frank M. Peters withdrew from the board in 1915, E. R. Thomas, Lehigh Valley Railroad magnate, was appointed to succeed him. John S. Runnels, president of the Pullman Company, became a director in June 1914. J. W. Ogden, a railroad director and vice president of the National Horse Show Association, was elected a director in February 1911, and soon became a member of the NBC executive committee. Robert A. Fairbairn, a member of the New York Stock Exchange and breeder of horses and livestock, was elected a director in February 1915, and the following year joined the company's executive committee. Howard M. Hanna, Sr., brother of the late Senator Mark A. Hanna, interested in the iron and steel industry, was elected a director of NBC in February 1906. Edward F. Low, prominent in banking and investment lines, was elected a director in March 1917. James McLean, a corporate official and president of the National Horse Show Association, became a director in 1920.

Francis L. Hine, a vice president of the First National Bank, was elected to the board of directors in March 1904, replacing William T. Baker, Green's old colleague. The First National Bank of New York, of which Mr. Hine was shortly to become president, was involved in the financial affairs of the National Biscuit Company almost from the beginning. When the Biscuit Company moved its headquarters from Chicago to New York, the First National became the company's bank. Judge Moore not only served as a member of the board of directors of the Biscuit Company and the United States Steel Company but also, in 1902, joined the board of the First National Bank. Hine succeeded George F. Baker, one of the architects of the United States

Steel Company and adviser to J. P. Morgan, as president of the First National Bank.

Even though the character of the NBC board of directors gradually changed, Moore was in no hurry to exert his influence on company policy. Green was too firmly in the saddle for Moore to oppose him. With Green's passing, however, Moore met with Earl D. Babst, now president of the American Sugar Refining Company, and asked his opinion as to a successor. Babst expressed himself unequivocally. The only eligible man was Roy E. Tomlinson, his former assistant.

Judge Moore agreed. His dealings with Tomlinson had convinced him that, in directing the business of the company, the young lawyer would be amenable to suggestions from his board of directors, especially the chairman of its executive committee. As usual, Moore's judgment proved correct. The team of Moore and Tomlinson worked well together.

But less than a month after Roy E. Tomlinson was appointed, the National Biscuit Company faced an emergency that threatened its very existence.

A popular advertisement of the 1900's, painted by N. C. Wyeth, ▸
promoting Cream of Wheat, which later became part of the National Biscuit Company

SIXTEEN

World's Biggest Baker

ARMED WITH the energy of youth and steadied by the guidance of Judge Moore, Roy E. Tomlinson set out to breathe life and new ideas into the organization. Educated as a lawyer, he was now thrust into a position in which his responsibility stretched far beyond mere legal matters. "My first job was to learn how to run the business," he stated. This was soon complicated by the fact that on April 6, 1917, the nation was at war. Americans, who had believed that war in distant Europe could not possibly affect them, now found themselves involved in a struggle which touched the life of everyone. Corporations faced emergency conditions: wartime shortages, transportation difficulties, government regulation, appeals for sacrifice.

Shortly after the United States entered the war, Tomlinson addressed a letter to government officials in Washington offering the facilities of NBC in any way needed. At the suggestion of old-time bakers, who recalled Civil War rations, he indicated that the company was prepared for the production of "hard tack, or bread rations." He was curtly informed that the administration in Washington was not fighting the Civil War, but the Great War. Authorities intended to feed the American armies fresh bread, baked daily in mobile field kitchens.

But it was not long before Army officials found that baking bread in mobile kitchens was impracticable for many reasons. Among them

◀ *A famous poster proclaimed World War I ingredient restrictions* were the horrible new weapons of destruction, especially poison gas. When such gas spread into the bread-baking ovens, the bread became unfit for consumption.

The government realized that it needed to reconsider the suggestion of the National Biscuit Company. It called upon NBC, among others, to make bread rations not very different from the hardtack eaten by soldiers in the Civil War and by pilots of the early sailing vessels. NBC soon was producing some 800,000 half-pound bread rations a day, packed in metal containers impervious to gas. Some soldiers thought the hardtack was also impervious to human teeth. But it served its purpose.

Not the least wartime problem of baking companies was the rationing of basic foodstuffs. "Since the first of May, 1918," said *The Cracker Baker*, "the use of wheat flour is prohibited in the manufacture of confections, 50% only of the amount of sugar used last year is permitted for the making of candy. Concerning biscuits, not more than 80% of standard flour is allowed, with 20% of flour substitute. Only one exception is made in the case of soda biscuits, in which the proportion of wheat flour may be as high as 90%."

The complexities of feeding a nation at war resulted in a proclamation by President Wilson establishing the United States Food Administration. Herbert Hoover, its director, appointed an advisory committee from the cracker industry composed of Roy E. Tomlinson, Brooks Morgan, president of the Independent Cracker Bakers Association, and John H. Wiles, the treasurer of the Loose-Wiles Biscuit Company. "Food will win the war" became a slogan.

Tomlinson went to Washington frequently to take part in meetings which produced the first regulations dealing principally with the conservation of wheat, flour, sugar and shortening. The National Biscuit Company was still carrying on civilian production although war work occupied much of its facilities. Inevitably the company found itself faced with complex problems. Obtaining raw materials to help feed the nation was not easy, and particularly since Tomlinson insisted on unconditional adherence to Federal rationing regulations.

"An idea of how splendidly the company succeeded in its conservation work," stated the *NBC Magazine* of March 1918, "is disclosed in the fact that in March it used less than 50% of the white flour allotted to it by the government on a 70% basis. That is to say, the government allowed it to use 70% of the flour it used in March, 1917, and, notwithstanding the fact that the demand for its products in

March, 1918, was considerably in excess of the demand in March, 1917, it used only 33⅓% instead of the 70% allotted . . .

"Practically all the sweet goods of the company are now wheatless, including the wafer line, Nabisco, Anola, Lotus. In addition, these well-known packaged products are all wheatless—NBC Oatmeal Crackers, ZuZu Ginger Snaps, American Beauty Ginger Snaps, and Mallomars. The company manufactures at present about 225 varieties of crackers and cakes, of which more than half contain no wheat." (Substitute ingredients included corn and rye.)

Meanwhile, NBC employees were being enlisted in the armed forces in increasing numbers. Before the war ended, some two thousand NBC employees were in the armed forces. Others left the company to work in armament factories.

Tomlinson was particularly concerned with the war's threat to NBC's traditional high standards of quality. He was convinced that the basis of the company's success was the quality of its products. With second-grade commodities often the only kind available, there was a danger that habits of laxity and slovenliness would develop. Tomlinson knew this could prove disastrous.

Although he was just past forty years of age when faced with this critical war crisis, Tomlinson conducted himself with cool courage. "The past year has been most difficult from an operating standpoint," he told NBC stockholders in 1918. "The manufacturing facilities of the company were sufficiently elastic, however, to meet the unprecedented demands which the war imposed." Inflation also was a harassment, with the price of sugar, barley, wheat and other staple products shooting skyward.

Still another problem had to do with advertising. Since demand for products far exceeded the available supply, Tomlinson saw no need for promotional activities. N. W. Ayer, the company's advertising agency since its inception, recommended keeping the company's name before the consuming public against the day when the war would end. This difference was eventually to lead to a severance in the long-time relationship between the company and the agency.

Rather than primarily promote products, NBC ads during this period sought to further the war effort. Tomlinson instructed Alfred Mace to use company advertising to explain that NBC products were being made under government supervision on a strict win-the-war basis. In response Mace created a poster destined to become famous. Entitled "Made As He Says," it showed a dramatic drawing of a stern-faced Uncle Sam staring out at the reader, his arms filled with NBC packages.

Another highly praised NBC advertisement read:

> Uneeda Thrift Stamp!
> Uneeda War Saving Stamp!
> Uneeda Clear Conscience!
> BUY! BUY! BUY!
> National Biscuit Company
> P.S. Uneeda Biscuit!

"We commend to businessmen generally," stated an editorial in the New York *Tribune* concerning this ad, "and especially our large advertisers and their advertising writers, the remarkably fine and clever bit of advertising which now appears in the subway cars and doubtless all over the country . . . A more effective placard for the Uneeda Biscuit could hardly have been devised."

On the heels of the Armistice came the "jazz age" of the 1920's; a mad, whirling, hectic postwar era involving both unprecedented excesses and opportunities. It was a time of visible prosperity and hidden poverty, a time of great technological advance and lagging social change.

"The benefits of technological innovation were by no means evenly distributed," writes William E. Leuchtenburg. "While workers' income went up 11 percent from 1923 to 1929, corporate profits rocketed 62 percent and dividends 65 percent. Despite the high productivity of the period, there was a disturbing amount of unemployment. Factory workers in 'sick' industries like coal, leather and textiles saw little of the boom prosperity . . . In 1929, 71 percent of American families had incomes under $2,500, generally thought to be the minimum standard for a decent living."

The 1920's also introduced an unprecedented era of high-pressure advertising and salesmanship. The go-getter became the American hero. It was a period of increasing government expenses; the Lindbergh flight and the Florida boom; the revolt of youth; cynicism. The postwar generation smashed old idols and ideals, but it had nothing with which to replace them. "Here was a new generation," wrote F. Scott Fitzgerald, "grown up to find all gods dead, all wars fought, all faiths in man shaken."

New methods of communication—the high-speed newspaper press, the motion picture, the radio—revolutionized society's ability to learn and be informed, just as industrial change was revolutionizing methods of production.

War conditions resulted in some permanent changes in NBC's methods of doing business. They speeded the adoption of the motor truck, replacing the horse in the distribution department. The war was also instrumental in shifting the company's emphasis from the so-called snap line (chocolate, vanilla, ginger snaps) to other products. The bakeries found they could make much more rapid adjustments to new types of products than had been thought possible.

Now, with the emergency finally over, Tomlinson set about introducing new policies and practices. He had witnessed the disintegration of the leadership of A. W. Green, who had refused to delegate even the most trivial responsibility. Tomlinson believed that the company was too large for leadership by any *one* man. Like President Coolidge, he followed the rule of "never doing anything that someone else can do for you." He also had the example before him of Judge Moore, who had developed to a high point the art of providing absentee leadership. So, from the start, Tomlinson delegated authority and responsibility.

In 1917 many of the company's plants were leased; many more were obsolete in their construction and equipment. Carrying out suggestions of Judge Moore, Tomlinson inaugurated a policy of purchasing the leased bakeries and modernizing them, or even replacing them with new plants. Such expenses were paid for directly from the earnings of the company. Not a penny was borrowed!

The team of Tomlinson and Moore championed a new financial philosophy. It had been Green's policy to hold profits below the 10 per cent level. Under the Tomlinson administration profits were to zoom as high as 20 per cent. In 1922 NBC split its stock four to one, and issued a 75 per cent stock dividend. That year net earnings rose from $6,000,000 to $11,000,000. Dividends on common stock in 1923 rose from $3,000,000 to $6,000,000.

The financial policies of Tomlinson and Moore represented a growing trend in American corporate life: *profits first*. Stockholders of the National Biscuit Company were in a happy position. With the stock split and stock dividend in 1922, the holder of 100 shares purchased in 1898 would have received 700 shares. Taking the average for 1928, which was 177½, the market value of the 100 shares, which had cost $3,057 in 1898, would have increased to $124,250.

From 1901 to 1928 the total assets of the company increased from almost $59,000,000 to almost $121,000,000. During this period the company retired some $1,680,000 in bonds and mortgages that were assumed at the time of the company's organization. From 1898 to 1928 NBC paid the common stockholders almost $90,000,000 and the preferred stockholders $51,000,000, for a total of some $141,000,000 to all stockholders during this period.

The Wall Street Journal published a lengthy article in 1927 summarizing NBC's financial status under the heading "National Biscuit Had Record Year—Annual Net Profits Nearly Quadrupled in Past Decade." *The Review of Reviews and World's Work* reported that "The company had enjoyed annual net earnings of approximately $5,000,000 in the period from 1919 to 1921, which jumped to 12 millions in the years immediately following and grew to a high point of 22 millions in 1930."

Green had insisted that prices be kept low and profits come through increased volume. During World War I, however, increased costs of raw materials caused prices to creep steadily upward. After the war ended, the company made no move to bring prices down to previous levels. This tended to restrict volume in the face of rising competition. One of the company's most vigorous competitors, the Loose-Wiles Biscuit Company, cut prices drastically and kept a careful control on profits. By such tactics Loose-Wiles was able to draw close to the National Biscuit Company and challenge its leadership in the industry. Other competitors also appeared on the scene including the United Biscuit Company of America, which was incorporated in 1927. (In 1966 the United Biscuit Company became the Keebler Company, with headquarters in Elmhurst, Illinois.)

This increased competition created some sentiment within NBC to cut prices. But, because of the desire to maintain a favorable profit picture, high prices were maintained.

In yet another strategic area, Tomlinson also introduced a new philosophy of business. Green's policy had set a pattern in which production and advertising dominated the scene. Sales and sales personnel were regarded as performing a "service" function. Wholesalers were invited to "get out of the way." The retail trade was recognized in a perfunctory manner.

In his early years Tomlinson introduced a policy of decentralization in the sales organization. Sales executives were encouraged to spend time and money cultivating the trade. But it was years before NBC was able to achieve an improved relationship with the trade.

In small as well as large matters the Tomlinson administration thus broke sharply with the Green pattern.

There was, too, a fundamental difference in the company's approach to people generally and employees in particular. Tomlinson's leadership in the 1920's tended to be relaxed. The company was doing magnificently. There was no need for the whip-cracking of the Green era.

Green had concentrated on the manufacture of the biscuit, and wherever he could he shut down production of bread, candy and such items. Influenced by the thinking of Judge Moore, Tomlinson sought to encourage some diversification from the start. He approved the establishment of the company's first subsidiary, the National Bread Company. Whereas Green had deliberately tried to limit the number of products made by the bakeries under the company's jurisdiction, now a surge of new products was encouraged.

Symbolic of the new era in NBC was the gradual deemphasizing of the Uneeda Biscuit. Although Uneeda continued to be a prime product of the company, under Tomlinson's direction other products came to the fore and were energetically promoted. Even the sacred trademark conceived by Green went through a series of alterations. In 1918 Tomlinson had "In-er-seal" replaced by the letters "N.B.C." within the seal. Also symbolic of change was the repainting of the famous Uneeda Boy trademark. The once pensive youngster now sported a smile.

But with it all, the basic tradition of the company was maintained. The National Biscuit Company "holds undisputed leadership in the manufacture and sale of package and bulk crackers, cakes, fancy crackers, cookies, etc.," said *The Cracker Baker*.

Tomlinson's relations with Moore were cordial. He rarely acted on important matters without consulting him. After dinner in the sumptuous family mansion on East 54th Street the wives would occupy themselves while the two men were closeted in Moore's immense dark-paneled library. Neither man was loquacious. Moore would listen, his eyes fastened on a patch of the ornate ceiling, while "R. E."—erect, always dignified—would quietly tell of his latest plans for the building of a new bakery here, or the discontinuing of a line there.

As always, Moore had a knack for getting to the crux of whatever problem Tomlinson might raise.

"Will it be more profitable to buy the bakery or to rent?"

"Is it necessary to expand the advertising budget?"

When the conferences were over, the gentlemen would join the ladies. But William H. Moore was getting along in years. It was difficult to separate the "Judge" from the prospering National Biscuit Company, about to celebrate its silver anniversary. At the last board meeting he attended, NBC stock was split and the usual dividend declared.

Moore's health had been failing. A trained nurse was habitually within his call. On January 11, 1923, at the age of 75, he died peacefully while sitting in his favorite library chair and the nation lost one of its most effective financiers.

Of course, the company lost its chairman of the board. The office was discontinued and not reinstated until 1929, when Tomlinson was elected to that position. But more than that Tomlinson lost his most dependable, strongest and wisest adviser.

William H. Moore was survived by his wife, Mrs. Ada Small Moore, and two sons. Of the three sons born to William H. Moore, two played active roles as directors of the National Biscuit Company: Edward S. and Paul.

The funeral took place at the St. Thomas Episcopal Church, at which Moore was a parishioner. The church was filled. Services were conducted by the Reverend Dr. Ernest M. Stires, rector of the church.

Honorary pallbearers were Jackson E. Reynolds, president, and Francis L. Hine, chairman of the executive committee of the First National Bank, of which Mr. Moore was a director; Dr. J. Clifton Edgar, Moore's physician; Robert A. Fairbairn, an NBC director; Frederick S. Wheeler, president of the American Can Company, of which Moore was a director; Vernon C. Brown, Frederick C. Swift and R. Lorn Smith, bankers; and Roy E. Tomlinson.

Moore was reported to have left an estate of some $24,000,000.

Roy Tomlinson now stepped into the breach. Between the end of World War I and 1925, bakeries were built in Pittsburgh, Detroit, Los Angeles, on Lexington Street in Chicago, and Bethune Street in New York. A printing and carton factory was built in Beacon, New York. The new bakeries, mammoth five- or six-story red brick affairs with huge high turrets like medieval castles, increased the company's ability to transport products to the grocer and thence into the home with, as the advertisements said, "oven-freshness."

As a result of intensive production and postwar promotion efforts the country was eating more Uneeda Biscuit than ever, as well as Graham Crackers, Saratoga Flakes (twin wafers, crisply thin, with a delicate salt flavor), ZuZu Ginger Snaps, Nabisco Sugar Wafers, Tokens, National Arrowroot Biscuit, Coconut Dainties, Butter Thin Biscuits, Cameo Biscuit, Social Tea Biscuit, Fig Newton Cakes, and Five O'Clock Tea Biscuit.

The mortality of some products, however, was high. The names were legally protected and at some time in the future might reappear as an entirely different cookie. Among the many popular products whose names are forgotten today were: Unity, Dulcet, Amoret, Robena Grahams, Manor, Pondrosa, Velvia, Solara, Mirabel, Sylph, Hobbies, Momora, Trumpet, Rustics, Bedtime, Sea Foam, Sorbetto, Epinuts, Seminole Gems, Champion, Tangs, Almona, Aces, American Pride, Table Grahams, Popularity, Slim Jane, Copia, Butteroons, Cubs, and Toytown.

There had been little scientific testing of cookies or crackers. In the days of Green the company had an "experimental station" set up in the New York bakery and presided over part-time by Dr. Charles M. Chandler, head of Columbia University's chemistry department.

During Tomlinson's early administration a full-time laboratory was established under another Columbia professor, Clark E. Davis. The primary work of the laboratory was to test the quality of the millions of dollars worth of raw materials NBC purchased. The laboratory also worked out exact formulas for the company's products so that the various bakeries might achieve greater uniformity.

Traditionally, biscuit bakers had always kept formulas in their heads. Materials were used according to the whims and prejudices of the foremen at different bakeries. Only the foreman of the bakery and the chief mixer had access to these "formulas." Generally, they were reluctant to share them with newcomers on the theory that their jobs might be threatened.

Green had tried to bring about a uniformity of product. But it was not until the era of Tomlinson that scientific methods were applied to this end. Raw materials were assembled through a special department. A printed card listed all the ingredients used in a formula. The materials called for were carefully weighed and measured by assemblers according to batches, which were placed in front of the mixing machines where the mixer followed the printed instructions.

New machinery was obviously needed to keep up with the new products. The sandwich machine, an automatic traveling table, moved twenty-one biscuits at a time into position under an icing hopper, where a cream filling was stenciled from the hopper onto the biscuit or base cake. They were then moved under another biscuit hopper, where the second base cake was neatly centered on top of the filling. At about this time a new continuous cutting machine, bought from the Thomas L. Green Company of Indianapolis, was installed in the Detroit bakery. To keep the cutting machine supplied with dough an automatic rolling machine was designed by H. O. Mercier, NBC engineer.

From the earliest days, various local bakeries produced special products based on regional tastes and traditions. Mounting costs, however, made it impossible for bakers to supply such items in great quantity and—with certain stubborn exceptions—they passed out of existence.

In New England the Crown Pilot Cracker and Bent's Water Crackers remained popular, as did Kennedy Commons. The Royal Lunch has long been a Yankee favorite, as have molasses cookies such as Mary Ann. Philadelphia favored the Trenton, a browned cracker about the shape of an English walnut. For a few weeks every summer the NBC Minneapolis bakery ran off quantities of Harvest Cookies.

In the south Vanilla Wafers seemed to be perennially popular. The Uneeda Biscuit itself, once a national favorite, began to forge ahead in some regional areas. Today 80 per cent of Uneeda Biscuit is sold in New York City and other large metropolitan areas. The oyster cracker had long been fancied in the New England area. Originally the oyster cracker was square, until Dr. E. T. Oakes of the NBC laboratory, conceived the notion of presenting the Oysterette in a hexagonal shape. In certain areas of the midwest there was a strong preference for a cracker called "Premium Flake" or "Saltina," which replaced Uneeda in popularity.

The Premium Saltine, a soda cracker, had long been a favorite in certain areas of the midwest, particularly in the Missouri area where it was invented. It had won prizes as far back as 1876. Green was jealous for his favorite soda cracker, Uneeda Biscuit, and kept the Premium Saltine confined to its home ground. However, in the twenties the Saltine began to be manufactured and distributed in factories throughout the country and was soon in wide demand. The popularity of the Saltine was to increase many times over in the years ahead.

Most of the pretzels in the country were, and still are, manufactured in what is known as the "pretzel belt." Some 70 per cent of all pretzels are produced and marketed in New York, Pennsylvania, Ohio, Chicago and Milwaukee. The pretzel was originally brought to the

United States by the early German settlers. But it was not until the time of the Civil War that a small bakery in Lititz, Pennsylvania, a short distance from Lancaster, began producing pretzels commercially.

At that time they were made by hand, baked on open-hearth fires and sold in the streets. While a number of plants in the National Biscuit Company made pretzels from the start, the company did not get involved in this phase of baking to any extent until 1925, when it purchased a bakery in York, Pennsylvania, devoted entirely to the production of pretzels and pretzel specialties.

For many years, the art of "pretzel twisting" defied the machine age. It was said that the true pretzel required "the artistic touch of the pretzel twister." Trained women turned out from 10,000 to 12,000 pretzels per day. A spectator once described the scene in the York pretzel factory: "One is amazed to see the army of immaculately uniformed girls twisting dough into pretzel shapes with almost machine-like alacrity and skill . . ."

The New Yorker magazine once made one of its surveys of pretzel twisting. "The National [Biscuit] Company has seven hundred twisters, all girls—about half the output of each company seems to be hand-twisted—and they each twist about thirty-five and forty a minute. The Bronx Company—Quinlan's—claims that one of its six hundred twisters can do a pretzel a second. Holtzman's without batting an eye, told one of our researchers that they once had a girl who twisted twenty-five thousand in ten hours, or about forty-two a minute. She was back at work next day as sane as you or we."

Before the coming of the machines, pretzel manufacturers found it extremely difficult to replace pretzel experts. In Louisville, Kentucky, for example, even in the depth of the Depression, the Municipal Relief Bureau had trouble finding skilled pretzel "benders." The pretzel industry received a body blow with the introduction of Prohibition in 1919. But the blow was not as severe as was feared. NBC's advertising and promotion department, working overtime, actually broadened its appeal.

A "bite yourself an alphabet" campaign, for instance, met with wide success. "Americans like to laugh, and the National Biscuit Company is giving them a chance," reported George Oliva, successor to Mace as NBC's advertising manager. Oliva had joined the company when scarcely more than a child. The "bite yourself an alphabet" campaign was his invention. "Any man, woman or child from 6 to

60 can join," he wrote. "All you need to belong is a set of teeth . . ."

The pretzel became a family snack. Even the repeal of Prohibition did not return the pretzel to the exclusive province of the beer drinker. So great was the pretzel's popularity in those days that one NBC bakery turned out some 5,000,000 a day, twice as many as before Prohibition. In 1966 Nabisco pretzel-making facilities—including all sizes and shapes—could produce a total of some 39,000,000 pretzels in eight hours.

Another product introduced in the twenties, available for five cents in a sealed packet, was the Peanut Sandwich Packet. Soon the Sorbetto Sandwich Packet, similarly packaged, came along.

The new packages aroused considerable interest both within the company and outside. They gave NBC salesmen a natural entree into ice cream parlors, roadstands, milk bars, lunchrooms, newsstands, schools, drug and candy stores. Since sales figures showed that there was a demand for more packaged products, the sales force was enthusiastic about the possibilities of these "little business seeds."

These newcomers soon earned the right to a special name. On March 30, 1928, the company adopted and started to use the name "NAB," a derivative from the word "Nabisco." NAB quickly became one of the company's best known trademarks. Today, with the added impetus of vending machines, about a quarter of a billion NAB packets are sold each year.

As products increased in variety, the company grew in size and influence. R. E. Tomlinson took a personal interest in expanding the company's facilities in Manhattan. In 1922 NBC had purchased the American Can Company structure on West 14th Street. In the same year it acquired a property bounded by Tenth and Eleventh Avenues and 14th and 15th Streets, from Armour & Company. The floor space of the National Biscuit Company's manufacturing facilities in New York City now amounted to about thirty-five acres, and the factory employed more than six thousand people. So interested was R. E. Tomlinson in buying new property that some of his associates claimed his initials stood for "Real Estate."

Both Paul and Edward Moore, company directors and sons of the late Judge Moore, now played an increasingly influential role in the company's administration. Paul, especially, worked closely with Tomlinson, as his father had before him. The Moore brothers favored increased diversification, expansion, construction, modernization.

Expansion during the 1920's was by no means confined to New

York. Demand for NBC products in the Philadelphia area led the company to buy the bakery it had previously leased, and later it constructed an entirely new plant on the site.

An addition to the Kennedy bakery in Massachusetts was built; a bakery in Denver, previously leased, was purchased. The company built its first plant on the Pacific Coast in Los Angeles at a cost of approximately $2,000,000. A new bakery was built in Chicago. In Baltimore a four-story building was purchased; its conversion doubled the capacity of the company's facilities there. In Cleveland property that previously had been leased was purchased.

By the mid-twenties the company embarked on a policy of buying new and promising companies that had a family relationship to the specialty baking industry. On March 30, 1928, the Holland Rusk Company of Holland, Michigan, was purchased. Founded in 1895, it was built around a formula originating among the Dutch centuries ago. Originally the company had its major distribution among people of Dutch extraction. Gradually this changed as a large segment of the general public found the round toastlike biscuit to be appetizing and healthful.

In June 1925 NBC organized the National Biscuit Company Canada, Limited, as a subsidiary. Through the National Biscuit Company Canada, Ltd., a majority of the capital stock of Christie, Brown & Company, Ltd., was obtained in 1928. This company, established in Toronto (Canada) in 1853, had a long and successful record in Canada as a baker of cookies and crackers. Christie, Brown & Company had been in existence for seventy-five years when it was purchased by NBC.

The name of Christie, Brown & Company was known for excellent products practically all around the world. The company had selling branches in Montreal, Quebec; St. John, New Brunswick; and Halifax, Nova Scotia. Its founders, like the founders of the National Biscuit Company, placed quality above everything else. "Never put anything into a biscuit which you, yourself, would not eat." Christie biscuits came to be a household staple throughout Canada.

The National Bread Company was formed to take over the bread and hand-cake business of the company. The subsidiary started with seven bread bakeries, located in Albany, Syracuse, Buffalo, Cincinnati, Cleveland, Indianapolis and Pittsburgh. By the end of 1927 the National Bread Company had acquired additional bread bakeries at Birmingham, Houston, San Antonio, Charleston, Wilmington and other places.

The bread business had to be handled, because of perishability, differently from crackers and cookies. The driver of the bread truck not only delivered the bread to the retailer but acted as salesman, taking orders on the spot. This method had the advantage that two operations were performed by one man. The disadvantage of this type of distribution was that one man performing two jobs had little time to specialize in either. His ability to increase the sale of his product was limited.

In September 1928 the National Milling Company, a subsidiary of the National Biscuit Company, completed an addition to its mill in Toledo, Ohio, which increased its capacity by 1,500 barrels to 6,500 barrels of flour daily, an unheard-of quantity up to that time. Besides adding to the milling capacity, $1,000,000 was expended by the company on increasing the elevator capacity of the mill. By the 1940's NBC milled most of its own flour in three gigantic plants. The Toledo, Ohio, mill, the largest "soft" wheat flour mill in the world, was purchased in the 1920's. In 1941 another mill, in Carthage, Missouri, was procured. Two years later the Cheney plant, in the state of Washington, was purchased. (Soft wheat is a low-protein variety having characteristics best suited for cookie, cracker and cake flour).

An enterprise known as the F. H. Bennett Biscuit Company, incorporated in New York City in 1917, was succeeded by Wheatsworth, Inc., the makers of numerous varieties of crackers and cakes, cereals and flour. The company had achieved a considerable reputation nationally because, with Wheatsworth as its trademark, it had popularized the use of whole wheat or graham flour in numerous products. But what was of most interest to the National Biscuit Company was a companion product that Wheatsworth manufactured: a dog biscuit named "Milk Bone." In the various acquisitions of the National Biscuit Company during this period, the addition of a dog biscuit was one of the most far-reaching changes introduced into the business.

Milk Bone dog biscuits had been launched early in the 1900's and from the start the unique bone-shaped food was evidently as popular with dogs as with their owners. Milk Bone came in three sizes, large, medium and junior, and contained, among other ingredients, meat products, cereals, milk and food minerals in correct proportions. The bone shape of Milk Bone helped keep dogs chewing and gnawing.

NBC acquired, too, the McLaren Consolidated Cone Corporation with a main bakery in Dayton, Ohio, and branches in cities around the country. The McLaren firm was the main manufacturer of ice cream cones in the world. Origin of the cone, it is said, dated back to the St. Louis World's Fair of 1904, when the centennial of the Louisiana Purchase was celebrated. The fair was a gay place, with its palaces of art, education, machinery and electricity; its 1,240 acres of bustling people, big buildings and various sensations, including the famous Sousa's band.

In one corner of the fair's brightly lit midway a small, unassuming concession provided cakes for hungry visitors. There they could buy a flat-shaped sweet cake, baked on a griddle, something like a waffle. It so happened that right alongside of the cake baker was another concession—an ice cream vendor.

There was nothing new or special about the products sold by either merchant. Cakes of a waffle variety had been sold for countless years. Ice cream had been in existence in one form or another since Roman times, and in America it had been enjoyed by George Washington himself, who even owned two pewter "ice cream pots" at his Mount Vernon home.

What was new, however, was a practice, evidently spontaneous, of buying the cakes and taking them to the ice cream stand to combine the two foods.

The concessionaire who made the flat cakes evidently was not unaware of the possibilities latent in the situation. He rolled his cakes into cone-shaped forms while they were still hot and asked the ice cream vendor to put a scoop of ice cream into the empty mouth. The combination was delicious and proved popular. The ice cream cone business was on its way.

After the fair was over, two attachés who had observed the creation of the first ice cream cones, decided to experiment with their manufacture. Operating from Cincinnati, Ohio, they conducted a brief trial and then decided to go into the business seriously. They manufactured two styles of cones: the hand-rolled sweet sugar cone, and the pressed or molded type.

A number of companies, recognizing a good thing, began the manufacture of ice cream cones. But the new industry grew slowly until 1912, when Frederick A. Bruckman of Portland, Oregon, invented an automatic ice cream cone machine which took the business out of the hand-oven stage. Bruckman sold the rights to this machine to businessmen in various parts of the country. In the east the license to operate the Bruckman machine was purchased by Alexander Mc-Laren, a mining engineer, with his brother Walter.

So sweeping was the popularity of ice cream cones that by the early 1920's it was estimated that one-third of the entire consumption of ice cream in America was in cones. In 1925 there was a merger of various important ice cream cone manufacturers to create a centralized industry in the McLaren Consolidated Cone Corporation, which became part of NBC in 1928.

An interesting feature of McLaren cones was the "nesting ring" of extra thickness placed around the outside of the cone near the top. This permitted the packing of cones one inside the other for shipment without the previous huge percentage of breakage which plagued the industry in its early years. This ring, developed around 1919, held the cones firmly in place and prevented jarring and rough treatment from wedging the cones together. NBC today manufactures a dozen different types of cones, among them the original straight conical cone, the double-top cone to handle two scoops of ice cream, the flat-bottomed cups, the dripless cones with a protective double ring.

But perhaps the most important additions of the National Biscuit Company had to do with a brand-new type of product—a cereal—a "ready-to-eat" cereal.

At one time each pretzel was tied by hand. Today machines do it.

For
Daddy, Mother, Brother and I

'Cause its lots of food for a few penni

SERIES 307

SEVENTEEN

Shredded Wheat—
From Cereal to Supreme Court

If Adolphus W. Green had been told that some day his beloved company would be in the cereal business, he probably would have snorted incredulously. But at the very moment that Green and William H. Moore were bringing together bakeries from all over the nation, a small man with a big mustache was helping to found the ready-to-eat cereal industry that would ultimately have much to do with the future of the National Biscuit Company.

Before the turn of the century salt pork, mush, hominy grits, fried meal and other delicacies helped hold the inner man together until lunchtime. The housewife would rise before dawn to prepare the meal that would start the family's day. But a combination of events changed all this.

For one thing, increased emphasis was placed on diet as a means of building better health. Federal investigations revealed that adulteration of foodstuffs was taking place on a wide scale. This caused a stir around the country. People grew more conscious than ever of the need for pure food.

Health fads ranging from Dr. Graham's diet to vegetarianism came into vogue. It was an era of healers, health resorts and medicine men; of "miracle cures" guaranteed by almost every new type of food on the market. People were urged to chew their food one hundred

◀ *The first Shredded Wheat biscuit was produced at Niagara Falls in 1901.*

times. Not only food, but calisthenics, water therapy and mental suggestion were employed in this "help yourself to health" era.

Battle Creek, Michigan was the center of the country's health food industry. Here Dr. John H. Kellogg and his brother William worked together to create a successful business based on ready-to-eat cereals, especially those of a flaked variety. Here C. W. Post, a promotion-minded individual sensitive to the needs of the age, patented various cereal formulas which he successfully placed on the market. Over forty companies, all involved in the preparation of cereal foods and beverages, were established around the Battle Creek area. The New York *World* in 1902 announced that "Battle Creek is the greatest cereal producing city in the world."

But even before the boom at Battle Creek a middle-aged lawyer in Denver, Colorado, equipped with inventive ability and irrepressible ambition, recognized the possibilities of a precooked foodstuff which could be readily prepared for eating. The man was Henry Drushel Perky, born in Holmes County, Ohio, in 1843, a farm boy who became schoolteacher, lawyer, newspaper editor, expedition organizer, dreamer and promoter of new ideas.

Perky was approaching his fiftieth year in 1890 when he stumbled across an idea which excited him. Impulsive and given to emotional tantrums, he had not been successful enough in any of his various enterprises to provide himself and his wife and child with financial security. He was constantly looking for an idea that would change his fortunes.

Among Perky's many ideas was a machine for dehydrating corn so that it would keep for at least a year. He was fascinated by this notion. Could corn be so processed that it could remain edible even in a dehydrated condition? At that time corn was already being flaked, granulated, chopped and strained by many enterprising individuals.

Hot on the trail of his idea, Perky invited an acquaintance, William Harry Ford, in Watertown, New York, a man with a knack for machine-making, to come to Denver to talk over the situation. When the friend declined to make the trip, Perky bundled up his family and took a train east. Watertown was a sleepy village not far from the Canadian border. Ford was a designer for an air-brake company who experimented in his spare time in a little machine shop on Mechanic Street.

Perky explained his idea and together they conceived a special machine. Patented in both men's names, the machine consisted simply of a pair of rollers, one with grooves, the other smooth; a scraper was attached. When a crank was turned, the rollers would revolve against each other, pressing corn or whatever came between.

Although Ford did not share Perky's enthusiasm for their creation, the older man pushed ahead.

"One noon on returning from luncheon I noticed a basket of seed wheat in front of a feed store," Ford recalled. "I purchased a small measure of it and carried it to the little shop where Mr. Perky and I were in the habit of spending the hour before dinner in building castles and wondering how soon we could own the United States, if not the whole world . . .

"I boiled the wheat the next noon," Ford stated, "leaving it to cool until evening, when we started with Perky at the crank, myself doing the feeding. At the first appearance of the product, I reached my hand under the rolls and drew out threads over two feet long. Asking Perky to wait a minute, I looked about and finding a strip of wainscoting some four feet long, requested him to start up.

"Apparently the threads were endless, for back and forth went the stick taking up its load of thread until the hopper was entirely empty . . . Noticing a large butcher knife nearby, I seized it and proceeded to cut the dough into short pieces."

The next Ford-Perky idea was to bake the product they had created. The machine shop where the experimenting was conducted was owned by Frank Pluche, who lived nearby. Ford asked Pluche whether his wife had a hot oven. Pluche avowed she did.

"Over to the house I went with about a score of little biscuits," Ford described it.

"I remember very well when Mr. Ford came into the house from the shop with those first biscuits to bake," says Mrs. Pluche.

In about twenty minutes she announced that the biscuits were ready.

"When they were baked," said Mrs. Pluche, "Mr. Ford was so delighted with them he forgot the dish they were baked in was hot. He soon found it out because he had to nurse his fingers for some time."

Not a man to retain his calm in the face of such a stirring event, Perky was beside himself with excitement. Ford handed him a cigar in an effort to quiet him. But Perky pranced about, gesticulated, and even burst into extemporaneous song. He envisaged a future of thousands of the little shredders in bake shops, kitchens, hotels all over the country.

Ford stayed in Watertown, and Perky took his family back to Denver. There, with his brother John, Perky organized the Cereal Machine Company to manufacture a small hand machine which could make the wheat biscuits in the home.

To introduce "shredded wheat" to the public, the pair rented a small store in the Graham block opposite the Brown Palace Hotel. The front end of the room was partitioned off. Perky would invite friends, and even strangers passing in the street, to come in and listen to an explanation and see a demonstration of the shredded wheat process.

To bring news of his product to the people of Denver, Perky sent out a light covered wagon, painted white, lettered and decorated in gold, with a fine horse in a gold-mounted harness. The wagon distributed sample bags of several biscuits with printed instructions for their use. As interest grew, more wagons were taken on.

One employee said to Mr. Perky, "This looks as if the business is growing."

Perky raised his head and with a grandiose gesture of his arm exclaimed, "Sir, this is but a playhouse compared to what this business will be!"

To further promote his product, Perky opened a restaurant in the business section of the city. The restaurant had a unique feature. There was not a single article listed on the long bill of fare that did not have shredded wheat in it. Fresh shredded wheat was put into mashed potatoes, stewed tomatoes, all vegetables and sauces. All the meats were shredded and served in cups formed from wheat shreds. Shredded wheat biscuits were served with cream and sugar. There was shredded wheat in the cake as well as the ice cream and candy. Even the coffee was made from shredded wheat.

The reaction to Perky's experiment was encouraging. But Denver was merely one community. Meanwhile, word of Perky's activities had spread. In 1894 Dr. Kellogg went to Denver from Battle Creek to meet with Perky and compare notes on their respective experiments and adventures in preparing ready-to-eat cereals. Kellogg went home determined to invent a better food.

It took time for it to dawn on the Perky brothers that their real opportunity lay not in the manufacture of machines for domestic use in making shredded wheat but in making the shredded wheat biscuit itself.

In the summer of 1894 they decided to move their small shredded wheat manufacturing plant to Boston. They set up an exhibit at the World's Food Fair held in Mechanics Hall in October and served shredded wheat to all who would taste it.

In the following month the company, now called the Natural Food Company, established a plant on Ruggles Street in nearby Roxbury with eleven machines to supply the growing demand for shredded wheat. In the next year the demand continued to increase. The plant was moved to larger quarters in Worcester, where reel ovens were used for baking. The mechanization of production facilities was further increased with large evaporators and sealing machines.

Perky became popular as a speechmaker on health matters. His speeches hailed shredded wheat as one of the century's boons to better health. "From the most abject physical wreck, I have succeeded, by the use of naturally organized food, in reorganizing my body into perfectly healthy condition," he announced. "I use no other bread, nor cereal food product than shredded whole wheat biscuit, and dishes made from these biscuit. I am fifty-five years of age and feel younger than twenty years ago."

In a widely read brochure entitled *The Vital Question* Perky wrote, "In this age, the tendency towards specialty work, and the overtaxing and straining of brain, nerve and muscle, bringing about abnormal conditions, makes it necessary to take notice of the extraordinary waste of tissue incident to such special work." Advocating the use of shredded wheat for almost all ills, Perky planned menus in which shredded wheat was used in virtually every course, and in every food. There was Welsh rarebit on shredded wheat biscuit, chocolate jelly on shredded wheat biscuit, tomato salad à la shredded wheat biscuit, escalloped celery à la shredded wheat biscuit, mushrooms on shredded wheat biscuit, creamed spinach on shredded wheat biscuit, salmon chops à la shredded wheat biscuit, shredded wheat biscuit pudding, eggs en nest à la shredded wheat biscuit, Scotch woodcock à la shredded wheat, creamed oysters in biscuit baskets, shredded wheat ice cream and a special shredded wheat drink.

Perky announced daily and in countless ways that "Shredded Wheat is the perfect food." In a special appeal to mothers, the company stated, "Mothers, do you know that children crave natural food until you pervert their tastes by the use of unnatural food? Unnatural food develops unnatural and therefore strong propensities and desires in children. Like begets like—pure food, pure minds."

"Every woman should be beautiful and womanly, and she *may* be so. Every man should be strong, courageous and manly, and he *may* be so."

People by the thousands tried shredded wheat—and liked it.

But success did not dull Perky's ambition for vaster fields to conquer. Seeing a need for an institute of domestic science "to provide practical teachers of a practical science," he purchased the Oread Collegiate Institute, founded by Eli Thayer in the 1840's in Worcester, Massachusetts. The school espoused principles of equal opportunity in education for girls and boys. Perky took over this noble tradition by founding the Oread Institute of Domestic Science. The institute provided a one-year course in cooking, sewing, sanitation and the chemistry of food. He sought to attract students from all parts of the country.

Young women trained at the institute went out to demonstrate shredded wheat before women's clubs and other organizations throughout the country.

Perky preached the gospel of right eating with almost religious zeal. He was to write a book, *Wisdom vs. Foolishness*, which further expounded his theory of eating for health. But his success, primarily regional, did not satisfy him. His vision encompassed the whole nation, perhaps even the world.

In 1895 the power of Niagara Falls was first harnessed by a corporation known as the Niagara Falls Power Company. Once this dream of the engineers had become a reality, the company proceeded to attract industry to the falls to use the available power. A short time later Perky entertained a group of industrialists from Niagara Falls at his Massachusetts factory. He personally conducted them through the plant, after first taking the precaution of instructing the plant manager to be sure to keep all machinery running full time, even though orders had already been filled. The visitors were impressed. Perky, in turn, was invited to visit Niagara Falls to look over a possible factory site.

Perky had been successful in raising funds for the Worcester plant. But his vision of what he wanted to do in Niagara Falls involved far greater financing. His talent was equal to the task. He persuaded various people to invest in the company, notably Darius O. Mills, a quiet but perceptive banker and philanthropist whose financial career had begun in the California gold rush of 1848. Mills had retired from a successful banking career in the west thirty years later and returned to New York. There he continued to invest in banking, railway and industrial concerns, and also sponsored the construction of several "Mills hotels," which provided lodging and healthful meals at low cost.

In the plan to move shredded wheat to Niagara Falls, Perky saw a great opportunity to advertise the product and manufacturing process by building a "show factory"—"a temple of cleanliness to house the purest and cleanest of foods."

With this in view, Perky selected a ten-acre site on Buffalo Avenue in the choicest residential district, overlooking the falls. The people of the neighborhood were scandalized. But Perky pledged that he would build a factory which would make them proud, a factory like none they had ever seen.

He persuaded financiers in Niagara Falls, Buffalo and New York to join him in organizing a $10,000,000 stock company. Thereupon, workmen began the construction of Perky's "Palace of Light." He hired Norcross Brothers, prominent Boston builders, on a day-to-day basis. When Perky had the cash, work proceeded; when money ran out, work stopped.

When the coming of the new factory was announced, the Niagara Falls *Gazette* headline proclaimed:

CROWNING TRIUMPH FOR NIAGARA FALLS

It Sounds Like a Dream, Reads Like a Fairy Tale,
Seems Too Good to Be True

$10,000,000 COMPANY DECIDES TO LOCATE HERE

In mid-May of 1901 the first shredded wheat biscuit was produced in Niagara Falls. The new building had a floor space of about five and a half acres and the interior was finished in white enamel and hard wood. It even had its own air-conditioning system so that the windows need never be opened.

The main building was devoted to the manufacture of Shredded Whole Wheat Biscuit and Triscuit, a salted cracker made from shredded wheat. The center section contained the administration offices and educational exhibits; the grand entrance hall or foyer for visitors; the general offices; the lecture hall or auditorium, seating over a thousand for entertainment, lectures and conventions; the girls' dining room on the fifth floor overlooking the river, where a noonday meal was served free; the roof garden or observatory; and comfortably furnished "rest rooms" for men and women employees.

Thirty thousand lights of glass, one hundred thousand dollars' worth of marble and mosaic toilet and bathrooms for employees, all were used in the building. The total cost was over $2,000,000. The public throughout the United States was invited to come to the "world's finest food factory," open to visitors every day of the year except Sunday, with guides furnished free.

In an era of dirty, dark and disorderly factories, Perky's "palace" was indeed an innovation. In the honeymoon season as many as five hundred couples a day toured the premises. It was Perky's proud boast that the romantic memories of honeymoons would be combined, for thousands of couples, with remembrances of Shredded Wheat Biscuits tumbling from the production lines. In the course of a year more than 100,000 visitors inspected the vast wonders of his factory.

But Perky had more in mind than merely building a tremendous bakery for his precious product. He also "provided a beautiful place for employees to work in . . . probably the most rational scheme of social and moral betterment that may be found in any factory in this country."

Decades before the advent of the coffee break, employees were "allowed rest periods of fifteen minutes every morning and afternoon, in addition to the hour that is allowed for the noonday luncheon and recreation period . . .

"The physical and social welfare of the girls is largely in charge of a matron or 'factory mother' who is always ready with timely help and kindly suggestions to meet the troubles and perplexities peculiar to the sex . . ."

From specially constructed balconies and aisles visitors would see the Shredded Wheat Biscuit being made. The actual manufacturing process was amazingly simple. A measured quantity of the wheat grains went into a huge steam kettle with a quantity of water and was boiled a certain length of time under exactly controlled steam pressure. The cooking did not greatly alter the shape of the wheat grains, but they swelled to two or three times their original size and became much softer. The process does not permit the use of small, defective or broken grains of wheat.

The cooked wheat grains were allowed to stand or "cure" in great metal tanks where the natural changes inside the wheat kernel took place which, the company claimed, made it more readily digestible. From these tanks the grain, still looking like swollen kernels of wheat, went directly to the biscuit-making machines.

Here the grain fell into a hopper which dropped it between two steel rollers, the type that Ford—no longer associated with Perky —had originally conceived. One of the rollers was smooth, as Ford had designed, the other had finely cut grooves on its surface. As the rollers spun, the grain was squeezed between the grooves. The wheat fell from the grooves in a series of endless shreds upon a moving belt beneath.

The next pair of rollers dropped another series of shreds as did each of the twenty-nine pairs of rollers. Toward the end of the roll, one long biscuit was formed. This long biscuit was cut automatically into individual shredded wheat units.

These were transferred to a baking pan and placed in ovens. The pan traveled through the oven at a carefully determined speed. When it reached its journey's end, the biscuit had been perfectly baked.

The guest book of the Shredded Wheat Company, the company name as of 1905, read like a *Who's Who* of notables throughout the world. People wrote their signatures in many languages. An editor from London wrote, "I am greatly impressed by the cleanliness and beauty of the process, the perfect purity of the product." Mark Hanna, a famous political figure from Cleveland, Ohio, wrote, "A model establishment, and worthy of imitation." A visitor from Philadelphia wrote, "A factory that represents . . . [the] 'American ideal factory' . . . considers the comfort and welfare of the employees as well as dividends to the stockholders."

A visitor from Venice, Italy, wrote, "Charmed beyond description and gratified beyond expression with all the details of organization." The Bishop of Cloyne, Ireland, wrote, "I have seen this establishment not merely with ordinary interest, but with a feeling of wonder at the perfection of its machinery and of its management." The representative for the Hudson's Bay Company on Herschel Island, Arctic Ocean, wrote, "Always had Shredded Wheat for my breakfast shipped from San Francisco."

The testimonials came from Paris, London, New York, Greece,

India, as the promotion continued and Perky sought to spread his message to every corner of the nation and the world.

Advertisements for Shredded Wheat were widely published in periodicals and newspapers. Promotion throughout the country pointed to Shredded Wheat as a competitor of beef. It stated that ten cents' worth of Shredded Wheat Biscuits contain two and a half times more nutrition than ten cents' worth of sirloin steak. This type of advertising was especially convincing in view of the revelations that were taking place at the time regarding questionable practices in the stockyards of the nation.

Shortly after the company moved to Niagara Falls, Perky decided he wanted to establish an agricultural school in Glencoe, Maryland, a philanthropic project that he had long cherished. He sold his financial interest in the company for $150,000.

Perky believed that the Natural Food Company was well able to carry on without his personal supervision. When he retired, William B. Rankine of the Niagara Falls Power Company, a heavy investor in the company, became chairman of the executive board and M. B. Butler, formerly mayor of Niagara Falls, became the company's general manager, with Alexander J. Porter as president.

Perky did not live long after his separation from the company he founded. In June 1906, before he was able to launch his new project, he died at the age of sixty-six at Glencoe, Maryland.

After Perky departed, the company continued to enjoy prosperous years in which the name "Shredded Wheat" was carried to every section of the country and around the world. The original Shredded Wheat bakery in Niagara Falls soon became a landmark. As the business grew, other Shredded Wheat bakeries were opened —a second on Erie Avenue in Niagara Falls; another in Ontario on the Canadian side of the falls; another in Oakland, California; and still another in Welwyn Garden City, a few miles outside of London.

With the death of Darius Mills his grandson, Ogden, a lawyer and candidate for the governorship of New York who was defeated by Al Smith in 1926, became a chief stockholder of the company. Mills, a close friend of Paul Moore's, often talked with Moore about the accomplishments of the unique Shredded Wheat Company in Niagara Falls. When Paul Moore and his brother Edward finally visited the plant they were deeply impressed.

On a number of occasions the Moores discussed with Roy Tomlinson the possibilities of diversifying the National Biscuit Company's production to include cereal. Tomlinson was not enthusiastic about such a drastic step, but under the Moores' prodding he agreed. Late in the year 1928 an arrangement was made for the purchase of the Shredded Wheat Company. Some $35,000,000 in NBC stock was paid.

The purchase of the cereal company by NBC was a drastic shift of policy and a departure from tradition, not only in putting the company into the ready-to-eat cereal business, but also in bringing the company into a foreign operation in a major way. Shortly after the purchase of the Shredded Wheat Company, the company purchased the Canadian company, Christie, Brown & Company, Ltd., adding further to its international connections.

Following the announcement of the purchase of the Shredded Wheat Company in December 1928, the advertising department of Shredded Wheat, which had done such an amazing job of popularizing its product, was merged with the NBC advertising department. Truman de Weese, a health authority and advertising manager of the Shredded Wheat Company for a quarter of a century, was transferred to National Biscuit Company's office in New York.

De Weese described with some irony the reaction at NBC national headquarters to the purchase of Shredded Wheat. "One chap wanted to dip it in a chocolate bath right away; others wanted to top it with some cheese or peanut butter. But the more they examined it, the more satisfied they were that here was a baby that needed no condimental pajamas, nothing to add to its taste appeal. 'Guess we'll have to take in the little rascal just as he is,' they said . . .

"Uneeda folks learned a whole lot about Shredded Wheat—and they are still learning," wrote de Weese. "They found it favored with nearly 100% distribution in all cities, towns and villages. If you go into the most remote village or hamlet in faraway Idaho or Arizona, you will be certain to find Shredded Wheat in some of the stores— most likely in all of them—and, of course, they wouldn't carry it if people didn't eat it . . .

"Shredded Wheat didn't get this 100% distribution in a year, or in ten years. It didn't jump to popularity by leaps and bounds. Its growth was slow, steady and firm. You couldn't yell 'Shredded Wheat!' at people and expect them to eat it. It didn't have what advertising men call 'taste appeal'; yet thousands like the crisp, flavory shreds of baked wheat without any sugar, salt or seasoning of any kind."

But Shredded Wheat was heading into stormy weather. Since the time that Kellogg and Perky had exchanged ideas many years ago, the Kellogg Company and the Shredded Wheat Company had become active competitors. This situation was inherited by the National Biscuit Company. To R. E. Tomlinson, however, it appeared that his company had a legal right to exclusive use of the name "Shredded Wheat." Yet the Kellogg Company had started to use it. Tomlinson and his general counsel, Charles A. Vilas, came to the conclusion that legal action should be taken to prevent any company from utilizing the name "Shredded Wheat" or the particular type of "pillow-like" form in which the Shredded Wheat Biscuit was produced.

In the spring of 1932, after fruitless negotiations, legal action was begun by the National Biscuit Company against the Kellogg Company. NBC did not claim exclusive right to make Shredded Wheat. It claimed the right to the trade name and the shape in which Shredded Wheat was produced. It alleged unfair competition.

In April of 1937 the United States Court of Appeals rendered a favorable decision in the NBC suit, which subsequently the Supreme Court of the United States refused to review. In January of 1938 the United States District Court in Wilmington, Delaware, enjoined the Kellogg Company from the use of the name Shredded Wheat as a trademark for its whole wheat biscuit, and from advertising or selling its product in the same form and shape as the NBC biscuit.

It was an outstanding victory for the National Biscuit Company, its legal staff and particularly Roy Tomlinson, who remained a lawyer at heart. A favorable decision for NBC was also rendered in a suit brought by the Kellogg Company to cancel trademark registration of Shredded Wheat in England. The High Court of Justice, Chancery Division, in December 1937, held that the evidence established that the NBC trademark was a valid trademark and registerable. Thereupon, National Biscuit Company informed its stockholders that this decision would "aid materially in the greater development of the Shredded Wheat business in Great Britain."

Victory, however, was short-lived. Tomlinson and his legal advisers thought the wording of the decision of the United States Court of Appeals could be strengthened. They felt that an appeal to the Supreme Court could lead to an even more specifically worded decision. A lone voice was raised against such action. A young assistant legal counsel, George H. Coppers, thought the action inadvisable. But Coppers' suggestion was ignored.

NBC sought a rewording by the United States Supreme Court of the decision of the United States Court of Appeals. Lengthy hearings were held. Further testimony made much of the fact that the basic patent for Shredded Wheat had expired before 1912 and Shredded Wheat had become a patent-expired trademark. Also, that the words "shredded wheat" were actually generic. This was to be influential in the decision rendered.

By a vote of six to two, the Supreme Court overruled the lower court and held that "shredded wheat" was a descriptive term and that Kellogg had the right to its use. The testimony went deeply into shredded wheat production methods. It was the Court's feeling that there was no other word that could replace "shredded." This word became a key in the testimony given. The outstanding trial lawyer, Creighton Clark, representing the Kellogg Company, pointed out that there was no other word that aptly described the product but the word "shredded."

The Supreme Court decision was handed down in November 1938, following ten years of litigation on two continents. As a result, the name "shredded wheat" and the well-known pillow-shaped biscuit became common property. The opinion was issued by Justice Louis D. Brandeis the day after his eighty-second birthday.

Speaking for the majority, Justice Brandeis stated that "Kellogg Company is undoubtedly sharing in the good will of the article known as 'Shredded Wheat,' and thus is sharing in a market which was created by the skill and judgment of the plaintiff company's predecessor and has been widely extended by vast expenditures in advertising persistently made. But that is not unfair.

"Sharing in the good will of an article unprotected by patent or trademark is the exercise of a right possessed by all—and in the free exercise of which the consuming public is deeply interested. There is no evidence of passing off or deception on the part of the Kellogg Company, and it has taken every reasonable precaution to prevent confusion or the practice of deception in the sale of its product."

Two dissenters from the majority decision were Justices McReynolds and Butler, who held that "it seems sufficiently clear that the Kellogg Company is fraudulently seeking to appropriate to itself the benefits of a good will built up at great cost by the respondent company and its predecessors."

When the smoke of the battle cleared, it was found that the case had gone through four United States district courts, two United States circuit courts of appeals, two English courts, the King's Privy Council, the House of Lords, and finally the United States Supreme Court. While the decision was a blow to the National Biscuit Company, it was hardly to prove fatal. There seemed to be room in the country for both, particularly in view of NBC's aggressive and imaginative promotion conducted by the McCann-Erickson advertising agency, which had been recently assigned the task of promoting the cereal.

Late in 1952 the National Biscuit Company abandoned the famous "Palace of Light" in Niagara Falls for a more efficient and modern bakery located on a railroad siding in Niagara Falls. Perky's promotion of this Niagara Falls image was so potent that generations later the National Biscuit Compny still printed on the box, "The original Niagara Falls Shredded Wheat."

The popularity of Shredded Wheat continued, both in this country and throughout the world. New methods of production, packaging and promoting were introduced. In future years spoon-size Shredded Wheat—miniature pillow-shaped biscuits—was to become popular. So was a special method of individual wrapping to be called "Inner-pack."

Embarked on its career in the cereal as well as the biscuit business, the National Biscuit Company found itself pushing forward on wider fronts.

Company wagons distributed Shredded Wheat samples house-to-house.

Above, honeymooners mailed postcard greetings from Niagara Falls.

Opposite, Henry Perky

Treatment and Care of Equipment

Our Horse, Harness and Wagon Equipment represents a large expenditure of money and the cost of its maintenance increases each year, due to the higher standard for which we are continually striving. The advertising value of this equipment to the Company, where kept in proper condition, can scarcely be estimated, and you are expected to do your part to maintain this standard.

Your horse is your motive power. Abuse and carelessness will ruin any engine or piece of machinery, and a horse should be entitled to even more consideration. In other w[ords] use good, sound judgment in driving Don't forget this.

Always start at a walk and let him work for the first half hour or so.

Remember that when the weather is [ex]tremely hot or very cold, or when the r[oads] are heavy, you cannot expect to cover as m[uch] ground as you can under normal conditi[ons] and a longer time should be spent in ma[king] your deliveries.

Don't jerk or abuse your horse. Treat [him] kindly. You will get better results, displ[ay] better knowledge of horsemanship and b[etter] serve the Company's interests.

Treatment of Customers
Personal Conduct and Appearance

Be uniformly courteous to all customers at all times.

Never lose your temper or talk loudly or boisterously.

Deliverymen can frequently ascertain the cause of any dissatisfaction on the part of any customer, the prompt reporting of which may be the means of retaining both his business and good will.

If any misunderstanding with a customer arises, call up the office and ask for instructions. Do not enter into any dispute with a customer and so impair our confidence in [your] good judgment.

We expect our Deliverymen to have prid[e in] their personal appearance. Hence we fur[nish] without cost to you (except for deposit [re]quired), a handsome uniform, which ena[bles] you to make a good appearance and saves [you] the expense of wear and tear of your [own] clothes.

These uniforms must be kept in good re[pair] and cleaned and pressed once a week. M[aterials] are provided either at the branch or the st[ore] for polishing shoes.

You are required to wear your uniform w[hen] on duty, and to see that the garments [are] properly brushed and that your shoes are [pol]ished each morning before leaving the bra[nch]

EIGHTEEN

A Rag, a Razor Blade
and a Revolution

AT THE VERY HEART of NBC's business was, in addition to quality and service, the leisure and independence of women. Its slogan was "Let the National Biscuit Company do your baking for you."

World War I had brought about many changes in popular tastes. In increasing numbers people broke from their village provincialism—in what they thought, in how they acted, in what they wore, in what they ate. Women were especially influenced by the new winds ablowing. They had begun to achieve a measure of independence before the war, but the requirements of the crisis hastened their emancipation.

At first NBC advertisements appeared mostly on trolley car cards. With the coming of the automobile the company turned to highway billboards. When motion pictures became the rage in the early 1920's, special slides were flashed on the screen advertising "quality crackers at lowest prices."

As long as Henry McKinney lived, Roy Tomlinson felt an obligation to him and to the N. W. Ayer agency which had served the company so well through its founding years. However, during the war years McKinney, now an old man, was less involved in direct advertising activity. Various differences ultimately led to a series of changes in advertising representatives. In 1935 NBC turned the bulk

◄ *An NBC delivery man and the rules he lived by*

of its advertising responsibilities over to the McCann-Erickson company.

At the start of this relationship, the agency conducted a survey of the company's advertising policies, and found certain shortcomings. "Among people of middle age who were subject to your big advertising efforts before the war, there is still a strong consciousness of the *Uneeda Boy*, the name *Uneeda*, and the fact that the National Biscuit Company products are good," the agency reported. "With the younger generations, this familiarity with National Biscuit Company quality is less evident. Evidently National Biscuit Company has not been telling its story in recent years extensively enough to do justice to the character of its merchandise, especially in view of competitors' use of advertising."

Indeed, a whole new generation had grown to maturity since the launching of the Uneeda Biscuit. While there was still tremendous vitality in the name of Uneeda, the Biscuit Boy symbol and the term "Uneeda Bakers," times were changing.

New promotion media were available. By the 1930's radio penetrated every third home in America as Roxy and His Gang, the Happiness Boys, the A. & P. Gypsies, and Rudy Vallee became household favorites. The National Biscuit Company pioneered by presenting a three-hour radio program, longer than any previously presented by a single sponsor. It featured three dance bands and was broadcast from a New York studio over fifty-five stations of the National Broadcasting Company. The program aroused so much interest that more than a thousand people packed the National Broadcasting Company's biggest studio in New York to witness the opening, featuring Madame Maria Jaritza, Helen Ward, and introducing a promising young musician, Benny Goodman, and his orchestra.

About a decade later Arthur Godfrey would be broadcasting daily over 173 stations of the Columbia Broadcasting Company, telling 50,000,000 listeners of National Biscuit Company goodies.

The National Broadcasting Company not only brought biscuit promotion to the air waves, it also confronted the National Biscuit Company with a conundrum. The famous initials "NBC" were now being shared by two large corporations. Since radio was growing in popularity, it seemed inevitable that the confusion would increase. A new family name must be found for National Biscuit Company products. To make matters even more complex, the advertising agency had already turned thumbs down on the name "Uneeda" as old-fashioned.

At first the agency thought the word "National" might be a substitute for "NBC." Other ideas were considered. It was finally decided that the word "Nabisco" was the wisest choice to replace the initials "NBC" in most of the company's promotional efforts. Few recalled that in 1898, searching for a word to name his new soda cracker, A. W. Green had suggested "Nabisco." It was turned down by McKinney. Later it was adopted as the name of the company's famous sugar wafer.

Whatever its name, there was no confusion over the fact that the company was prospering. *Fortune* magazine told its readers, "When you come to the cryptic word 'Biscuit' in a headline on the financial page of your newspaper, you know it can mean only one company." In fact, the National Biscuit Company became synonymous not only with the word "biscuit" but also with profits, prosperity and dividends.

Even without the counsel of Judge Moore, Tomlinson found himself an acknowledged success as a corporate president. He had followed a calculated policy of delegating responsibility and it paid off handsomely. Increasingly, Tomlinson withdrew from personal participation in Nabisco affairs, seeing only a few select executives from time to time in his eighth-floor office. Tomlinson was described by *Time* magazine at the time of the Shredded Wheat purchase as "51, looks younger, and is so sincerely publicity-shy that even his friend, Bruce Barton, famed advertising man, author and interviewer, cannot get a story from him." (Bruce Barton was the son of the Reverend William Barton, long-time friend of the Tomlinson family in Illinois.)

Tomlinson's increasing withdrawal from active leadership ultimately led to the most serious crisis the company had ever faced.

But, in the meantime, Nabisco was—seemingly on its own momentum—rushing ahead to new and exciting accomplishments. No division of the company's organization did more to keep Nabisco prospering than its sales and delivery departments.

"Traditionally women had ruled the home," wrote Henry S. Commager in *The American Mind*, "but only in America did they design it, build it, furnish it, direct its activities and fix its standards." They demanded new foodstuffs, particularly those which did not require long hours of kitchen drudgery. There was more money available, too. The nation was becoming increasingly industrialized and the growing population demanded quality as well as quantity.

All over the country people were growing accustomed to fresh fruits and vegetables in all seasons and in ever wider variety. The supply of canned food doubled between 1914 and 1929. Even farmers stopped producing most of the food their families needed and began to depend on the grocery store, which increasingly was one of a chain.

In the five years between 1920 and 1925 the number of chain stores tripled. As a matter of fact 21,000 chain stores in 1925 were appropriating such a large share of the nation's retail food business that a vigorous movement gathered momentum to check their progress by law. In 1927 no less than thirteen state legislatures considered bills designed to limit the power of the chains.

Chain store price-cutting was resented not only by the independent grocer but by many manufacturers and wholesalers as well. However, chain stores bought in larger quantities, sold more cheaply, introduced scores of merchandising innovations. As Hampe and Wittenberg point out in *Lifeline of America*, the chains "made a significant contribution to the mass distribution of all consumer goods upon which our mass production and our standard of living depend. It was the competition of chains that spurred independent wholesalers and retailers into action that has led to greater overall efficiency in the food distribution system."

Behind much of the success of the chain store was Nabisco's packaging pioneering which helped speed along the merchandising revolution. The company also contributed new concepts in promotional techniques and personal salesmanship. From the start its deliverymen and salesmen had been a mainstay of its operation. By eliminating the jobber-middleman and going directly to the retailer, A. W. Green had placed a high priority on the well-known energy and loyalty of the company's distribution and sales force.

The company insisted that its deliverymen follow rules set forth in a carefully prepared leather-bound *Deliveryman's Manual*, designed to fit a man's pocket.

"Your horse is your motive power," the manual stated. "Abuse and carelessness will ruin any engine or piece of machinery, and a horse should be entitled to even more consideration . . . Remember that when the weather is extremely hot or very cold, or when the roads are heavy, you cannot expect to cover as much ground as you can under normal conditions . . . Don't jerk or abuse your horse. Treat him kindly. You will get better results, display a better knowledge of horsemanship and better serve the Company's interests . . . When possible, on warm days, stop in the shade while making your deliveries.

"Water your horse frequently . . . In cold weather do not fail to blanket your horse when left standing. Should your horse become sick on the road, or suddenly go lame, do not try to finish your route with the horse in this condition . . . Should your horse cast a shoe, report it promptly to the office . . . the condition of the horse's shoes should be noted daily . . ."

In the early horse-and-buggy days each man usually had a route of about a ten-mile radius. Crackers and cookies were packed in glass-front metal cans, returnable from the stores to the company when the contents was sold. A deposit of fifty cents per can was required. For each can of crackers a deliveryman took into a store, he would generally receive an empty in return.

NBC salesmen supplied a large proportion of the momentum that kept the company moving forward. One of the reasons for this was the salary plus commission compensation system which in effect permitted sales employees to do well if they worked diligently. Furthermore, NBC employees in the field worked hard because they wanted to hold on to positions with a company which seemed able to weather economic storms.

But the lot of the salesman was not easy. The early NBC salesman walked most of the time, lugging his heavy sample case with him.

Entering the grocery store, the salesman would set down his sample case and open it for everybody to see, especially customers.

This would be an invitation for Mrs. Jones to exclaim, "Oh, Mr. Brown, why don't you stock these cookies so that I can buy some?"

If a salesman ever forgot what was expected of him, he was reminded by his copy of the NBC *Salesman's Manual*, carefully drawn up by the veteran baker Albert G. Bixler. Once a farm boy who learned the bakers trade, Bixler was named sales manager by Tomlinson in 1921. On the question of overstocking, for example, salesmen were instructed to "exercise care at all times that you do not overstock a dealer with merchandise. Overstocking him is one of the quickest ways to cause dissatisfaction. Make it your business to see that he orders sufficient merchandise to carry him over until the next order you secure from him can be delivered, but do not make the inexcusable mistake of selling him an excessive quantity of goods, when you know he cannot possibly move them out of the store before your next visit and delivery.

"Take time to educate the dealer so thoroughly that he will understand and buy *quality* instead of price," the manual stated. "A merchant who buys from the National Biscuit Company knows that he is safe regarding prices, because whatever he pays for our goods, the grocer next door, or in the next town, or in the next city, or in the next state, pays the same, and we haven't prices to sell, he must buy our goods for quality."

The average salesman had from 100 to 150 dealers on his calling list, and he was expected to render similar service to each. His schedule called for a visit at least once a week, to some more often. A slogan of the company proclaimed, "Salesmen: remember you are selling the best biscuit in the world!"

Your personal appearance and conduct must at all times be beyond reproach [warned the manual]. In a great many cases you are the only representative of the company the merchant knows or with whom he comes in contact. Naturally the company is judged by your contact and the impression you make. So far as the merchant is concerned, you are the whole National Biscuit Company. Therefore, when you talk about our clean bakeries and the sanitary conditions under which our employees work, when you talk about the policy of this company, its high principles and fairness to all, it is imperative that you carry your point, not only by word of mouth, but by living example as well. . . .

Be neat in your dress, clean-shaven and make your personal appearance as presentable as possible when you visit the trade. You should not smoke in the stores or carry a partly smoked cigar or cigarette into the stores. Your sample case should be attractively arranged with clean, fresh samples and with eating samples in Japanin envelopes so that, when the case is opened, the dealer is immediately impressed with the fine appearance and perfection of our line.

It was not so much the printed word, however, as the "horseless wagon" that was ultimately to improve the efficiency of NBC salesmen. In 1922 NBC had 1,026 horse-drawn vehicles. Six years later there were 1,598 motor vehicles engaged in the company's sales distribution.

The transition from horse to machine was not easy. Doubts were raised as to whether the horseless wagon could ever replace the horse and wagon in the bakery business. Many considered the automobile unsanitary.

Gradually this opposition was overcome. As good roads were built throughout the country, NBC took the lead in equipping its selling branches with a complete line of machine-driven vehicles. By 1923 the company had retired all of its horses and for the next ten years electric trucks—which ran on batteries rather than gasoline— were used. Gradually these gave way to the gasoline motor truck.

Explaining the transition, the company stated in 1925, "The prime reason why we deliver our products in motor trucks is not that they are more economical than horses and wagons. We endeavor to deliver to the grocer who is 100 miles from our agency as soon, practically, as to the grocer next door to it, so that our product will be as fresh in one store as another, and to do this we must use motor trucks, regardless of their cost."

Soon the rectangular yellow and red NBC truck—invariably clean and shiny—became a familiar sight in almost every community in America.

The coming of the railroad had been, years before, a vital influence on the development of the baking industry. It had permitted factories to turn out goods with at least the hope that they would reach their destination fresh and unbroken. The automobile increased many times over the opportunity for efficient distribution of company products. It was possible actually to reduce the number of sales agencies or depots, to locate them farther apart, and still improve distribution facilities.

The accomplishments of NBC in distribution were so impressive that the Boston News Bureau commented in the early 1920's, "The National Biscuit Company has practically done away with the inventory problem. Turnover is so rapid and distribution so efficient that at no time is there more material on hand or on order than is necessary to meet stabilized demand." Now a new development was to increase efficiency even further.

Although In-er-seal packages were being actively promoted (in 1922 one-third of NBC sales were packaged in In-er-seal cartons), most NBC products were still sold in bulk in square metal containers with glass window panels. These cracker tins or "caddies" were a nuisance in many ways. They held eight to twelve pounds each. Each customer's purchase had to be hand packed into paper bags and individually weighed. A grocer's deposit of fifty cents was demanded for them, involving large-scale bookkeeping for the company. When the metal container was emptied, it had to be picked up and shipped back to the New York bakery, where it needed sterilizing and often repairing. The cost of freight shipments of the 6,000,000 cans over a year's time was a considerable item.

What was needed was a disposable container, strong enough to replace the can. The Interstate Commerce Commission imposed penalties for shipping goods in boxes other than wood or metal. Corrugated containers were looked upon as impractical and opposed by wooden and metal box manufacturers. Opponents of cardboard boxes described them as "flimsy substitutes."

Not until the spring of 1914 did a legal ruling open the way for the use of fiber containers for general shipping purposes. The corrugated box, more compact than the old-fashioned wooden or metal containers, and durable, too, now permitted a large number of products to be packed and shipped.

NBC specialists devised a substantial tight container of moisture-proof, grease-proof pulpboard, which was put in production at the NBC carton factory in Marseilles, Illinois. Cardboard boxes were disposable, so the huge expense of returning and processing metal boxes was no longer necessary. The asphalt-laminated cardboard box was exactly what was needed. Called a "Qu," later the name was shortened to just plain "Q." The letter "Q" had its origin, it is believed, in such words as "cubic" or "cube," which indicated a measurement of volume. Rather than call NBC units boxes or cases, the company called them Q's.

To display products in the Q, a brass-bound glass cover was supplied. Each merchant was required to pay a deposit of twenty-five cents each. When the Q was delivered to the store, the merchant would remove the laminated cover and replace it with the glass cover. Racks were also made available to the dealer with tilting shelves upon which the Q could be displayed. When the container was empty, the grocer merely discarded it and transferred the glass top to a fresh Q.

There was some doubt at first as to whether the Q could successfully replace the metal container. "I was a 'doubting Thomas,' " said one salesman at the time. "I did not express my opinion, but judging from the slipshod paper caddies which our competitors had been putting out, I thought that biscuit would not keep fresh in this 'Q' container. In the country where I live—Minnesota—there are fires in the stoves from October 15th to April 15th. In summer, the thermometer, at times, reaches 90 above, the humidity being so heavy that your fingers almost stick together.

"I was very badly mistaken. Anyone who will not admit a mistake stands in his own light. This package is practically airtight and will keep the contents well, and make a better display."

The Q was first introduced on an experimental basis to see how it would be received. Under the gleaming metal-and-glass cover housewives and children peered down at tempting cookies and crackers. In a short time the Q replaced the metal container in all areas of the country. The millions of metal containers were temporarily stored at NBC's Beacon, New York, box factory. Later they were ordered destroyed. It is estimated that the company wrote off approximately $3,000,000 when it rid itself of some 6,000,000 cracker tins.

Production of the Q was increased. "If you can imagine a strip of cartons five times encircling the world at the Equator," NBC told its employees, "you have a picture of the year's output of the carton factory."

Soon another simple cardboard device was introduced which permitted the contents of half-empty Q's to be raised so that the cookies or crackers were always near the top of the box. Thus the last remnant of the old cracker barrel was eliminated.

But introduction of the Q added a further chore to the responsibilities of the NBC sales force. Thousands of salesmen from coast to coast found it necessary—in addition to their many other services —to make certain that the Q was properly placed on a rack, its cover removed, and the metal-and-glass cover device placed so that the customer could see the crackers and cookies to their best advantage.

The wise salesman would carry a dust cloth in his sample case as part of his essential equipment. He would check each Q and its glass cover to make sure that it was clean. Another necessary tool was a razor blade. With this he could scrape off any dirt or discoloring elements that might mar the case or its glass cover.

In rural stores salesmen would often discuss with the storekeepers the inadvisability of keeping barrels of herring or containers of kerosene too close to the Q, since the odor might penetrate the boxes which were being opened and closed repeatedly.

"Your first act in greeting the dealer should be to look over the cracker department, rearrange any packaged goods that are out of place, look over the bulk goods, see that glass display covers are clean, pasteboard dividers or paper removed from Q when no longer useful or necessary—in short, refresh the general appearance of the stock," salesmen were told.

"It is your duty to look after the rack, straighten up the stock and clean the glass display covers whenever necessary, but you can appreciate that such work in each store on your district will require considerable of your time, unless you launch an educational campaign among your customers, pointing out the advantage to them of giving proper care to their cracker departments at all times, instead of depending entirely upon the services you give during your periodical visits."

By 1937 Tomlinson was to report to NBC stockholders, "Our 2,500 salesmen on an average visit every food store once each week. Orders from the salesmen are sent to the bakeries, which produce only goods which have been ordered by dealers. Over 96% of the products of our bakeries is delivered by our own trucks to retail food stores. This assures delivery of our merchandise to dealers in fresh and undamaged condition. After delivery to the stores, our salesmen cooperate with retail dealers in keeping our goods attractively displayed in order that they may be quickly sold and reach customers' tables at the peak of their freshness."

But while the men in the field were building up a momentum that was to permit Nabisco to outdistance all competitors, things were slowing down in the home office. Imperceptibly at first, then more obviously, the company was stumbling in its effort to keep up with the times.

Somehow the name "National Biscuit Company" in addition to symbolizing purity and quality also conjured up a vision of old-fashioned bakers. The company's image was associated with horse-drawn wagons and clerks with green eyeshades bending over roll-top desks.

In an economy rushing on at a breakneck pace into an era of mechanization, supermarkets and new ways of doing and thinking about almost everything, the National Biscuit Company tended to linger behind.

Roy E. Tomlinson and Alexander C. Nagle, a director ▸

NINETEEN

The Company
That Forgot to Stay Young

"THIS IS AN incredible story, and you'll just have to take our word for it—it's perfectly true, we swear," stated *The New Yorker* magazine in the Talk of the Town in 1936.

We met a gentleman at lunch the other day who told us that the National Biscuit Company has a Vice President in Charge of Fig Newtons. We rushed right back to our office and called up the National Biscuit Company (Chelsea 3-8000). To the switchboard girl who answered we said, as calmly as possible:

"The Vice President in Charge of Fig Newtons, please."

Without audible surprise, she connected us with a lady who said:

"Can I assist you, please?"

We repeated our request for the Vice President in Charge of Fig Newtons.

"Well," she said, "if you wish to speak with the Vice President in Charge of *Sales* of Fig Newtons, that's Mr. F. K. Montgomery, but if you want the Vice President in Charge of *Ingredients and Manufacture* of Fig Newtons, that's Dr. E. T. Oakes. Which one do you want?"

We said we'd think it over, and hung up.

The story reflected a situation that became, in a fast changing society, a serious corporate liability. "From the time Tomlinson became president until the depression of 1929," one company executive

◄ *In 1936 Ritz was becoming the largest-selling cracker in the world* expressed it, "there was considerable vigor displayed by the management group. We were actively coming out with new products in the 1920's. But, as an aftermath of World War I, perhaps, and the taste for profits brought about by high prices during that period, higher than normal prices were continued. As was realized later, there developed a deterioration in the National Biscuit Company's position in the industry, particularly insofar as sweet and iced merchandise was concerned. A similar gradual deterioration also took place in team effort of management."

As the company prospered, Roy Tomlinson became increasingly convinced that his prime responsibility was to interfere as little as possible with present progress. As time passed, he not only tended to discourage innovation but personally became more and more the elder statesman, available to only a few company officers and scarcely any outsiders. He wrote few letters, made no speeches, issued no public statements. Among the nation's business leaders he became a symbol —although a vague one—of the ideal corporate manager.

Personally reticent and self-effacing, Tomlinson preferred to choose reliable subordinates and let them manage. This not only appeared to work well, it also permitted Tomlinson a measure of the tranquillity that he desired. But it also restricted mobility and made change difficult.

On occasion a member of the NBC board of directors might raise a question, or a production manager might point to the need for a new method or machine. But the response to suggestions for change was usually "Let's wait and see."

The company was doing so well, change was viewed as a threat.

There were those, to be sure, who were convinced that the company should be looking overseas for additional markets. A survey was even made to see whether NBC could profitably establish a plant in South America. But this idea was dropped because South America seemed, as one executive said, "so far away." Questions were occasionally put forward such as the need for plowing back more money into company operations instead of increasing the dividend rate. The answer—expressed in one way or another—would be "Don't be in any rush."

Tomlinson had great loyalty to the men around him. He seldom interfered with the running of most departments.

The company traditionally tended to give special attention to its financial department. A. W. Green had taken the first steps toward establishing a team of dedicated men who were responsible for financial matters. The first secretary and treasurer was Frank E. Bugbee. Probably because he was unable to live with Green's personal quirks, he retired temporarily "on account of illness" in 1916, but returned after Green's death. In a sense he was the architect of the early financial structure of the company.

Following him came a succession of capable, finance-oriented executives, starting with George P. Wells, who began as a cashier in 1904 and became secretary-treasurer of the corporation. Wells built up the financial department and hired hardheaded, tough-minded assistants. He frowned upon borrowing money, paying high wages, or permitting time payments. "We don't care about romance around here," Wells was fond of saying.

Henry C. Taylor joined the company as a cashier in 1904 in Brockton, Massachusetts, and ultimately became company treasurer. Taylor extended the policies of Wells. Although able and intelligent, Taylor was conservative to the point of reprimanding his secretary for wearing jewelry while at work. His greatest dislike, next to laziness, was waste. He assumed he was hired by the company to keep its money from being spent, and for decades he worked diligently at this assignment.

Taylor insisted on a policy of cash on delivery. NBC deliverymen had to collect money *on the spot*, or else deliveries were not made, even to long-standing customers.

Similar considerations prompted the activities of accountant Charles E. Dunlap, originally hired by Wells in 1905, who rose to the position of vice president in charge of accounting. Dunlap was bright and energetic and helped modernize records and handling of inventories. His career, like Taylor's, was dedicated to protecting the company's finances.

Such men did their jobs well. Sales reached amazing, if unrevealed, heights. It was not until 1936, under a ruling of the Securities and Exchange Commission, that the company made public data about its sales, cost of sales and executive salaries. The guiding idea was to make a large profit and plow back as little as possible. The wide margin of earnings that resulted was, unfortunately, deceptive. While dividends were kept high, spending for future progress was limited.

If NBC became known for its cautious fiscal policies, it also acquired a reputation for conservatism in many small, less important areas of activity. There were, for example, the many petty rules and regulations accumulated by the company since its inception. Clothes of both men and women employees had to be of the most conservative character, no flashy sweaters or ties. There would be no loud talk or whistling within the building. Feet upon desks were strictly forbidden. Party celebrations of any kind, even for Christmas, were out.

Violation of these and other such rules was a serious matter. There were instances of dismissals without warning. All this and more helped build the NBC image of solid conservatism; but it also contributed to an atmosphere of uncertainty and fear, not only in New York but in company offices around the country.

Advertising managers had their own special problems. Superlatives were frowned upon. Advertising copy had to be sedate. Although A. W. Green had been a consistent advocate of creative advertising, his successor did not go along. "There did not seem to be a firm conviction on the part of Nabisco's top management," one executive remarked later "of any vital function of advertising in its affairs."

While it is true Nabisco's advertising budget was larger than that of its competitors, management seemed to regard it as "a reserve fund for the protection of dividends. Whenever there was the slightest threat to dividends, out came the ax and chopped the needed funds out of the advertising budget."

Such actions were not contested by members of the board of directors, most of whom were better informed on financial matters than on baking or promoting biscuits. Board of directors' meetings, held monthly, usually lasted only a few minutes and consisted of routine business transactions. Nor were the sparsely attended shareholder meetings any more inspired.

The company's failure to recognize the need for change was particularly evident in its decisions concerning capital improvements. In more than a decade only one new bakery was built. It was located in Atlanta, Georgia. Most of the other bakeries were outmoded; equipment was dated; techniques were antiquated. It was widely known in the industry that new baking machinery was being used abroad and tested by some competitors. Such machines might revolutionize the baking industry. But during World War I NBC had been able to sell all the products it could make, and following the war business remained excellent. There seemed little need to modernize. Particularly was this true with profits founded on high prices rather than volume or efficiency. Quality was not allowed to suffer, but NBC's methods of maintaining quality were costly and behind the times.

The job of checking the bakeries was largely that of one man, William L. Stewart, formerly in charge of the company's Philadelphia bakery, whose grandfather, W. L. Stewart, started as a pioneer baker in Philadelphia as far back as 1829. Stewart joined the NBC production department in 1921 as a specialist in the "sponge goods division," which produced products requiring leavening of dough. He became a roving trouble-shooter, traveling from bakery to bakery in the tradition of Adolphus W. Green.

Stewart was, in fact, a one-man quality-control mechanism. He was the highest authority within the company on cookie and cracker production. As he walked through the bakery chewing unlighted cigars, he demanded obedience and got it. His method of testing quality was simple. He would grab a handful of dough. "It doesn't look right to me," he might mutter. "Dough's too tight." Or, "Be sure to add ten more pounds of water."

"Time and Temperature Bill"—as he was referred to behind his back—believed in giving direction, but learning from others was not his strong point. So rigid were his views that he was sure new ovens being introduced by competitors could not possibly maintain high levels of quality. He took a dim view when such ovens were introduced by NBC in the newly constructed Atlanta bakery. He was not alone; many NBC bakery managers agreed with him.

There were those, however, who had more progressive attitudes. Louis Wirsching, Jr., who succeeded Albert G. Zimmermann as NBC head architect, noticed that automobile plants in Detroit, where NBC was building a multi-story bakery, were beginning to "get on the ground," not up in the air.

Automobile producers realized that production was more efficient if the production line was straightaway rather than on many stories. Wirsching felt that this was also applicable to the baking industry. He and others argued in favor of the Biscuit Company's following the motor industry's ideas and discarding the notion of more multi-story buildings. "Build in the country where we can have enough inexpensive land to build the kind of plant that we need for proper production."

But officers such as the old-time superintendent of construction,

John G. Zeller, said, "Oh, if we had a bakery like the kind you are asking, you would have to put employees on roller skates if they are going to get to work or even get around the bakery." And so the matter would end.

The machine that was to revolutionize the industry was the "band oven." Probably no single invention in the history of commercial baking equaled it in importance. This oven placed baking on a straight-line mass-production basis, increased production, and insured consistently high quality as well as bringing about important economies of operation. Frank M. Peters, in addition to his contributions in the packaging field, had experimented successfully with a type of baking oven essentially like the band oven. He patented a device as early as October 15, 1903, which contained the basic features of the band oven. But the Peters idea remained locked away in the Patent Office.

Some of these ovens were as long as a football field and capable of producing millions of crackers a day. Operation was based upon rolling the dough in a sheet of controlled thickness and feeding it into cutting machines. Crackers were cut out and stamped from a sheet of dough and entered the oven on a moving steel band. Burners extended across the top and bottom of the band for the full length of the oven. The speed at which the band moved and the intensity of the heat in each section of the oven were determined by the recipes of the particular product being baked. Some products, like Saltine Crackers, made the trip in a little less than three minutes; others, such as Vanilla Wafers, took seven minutes to travel the length of the oven.

But serious problems faced a company seeking to modernize its baking methods. The band oven required an unbroken area on a single floor or level which far surpassed the available space in most NBC bakeries. In the early years bakeries were usually built within a community near a railroad siding. As the communities grew, the bakeries were surrounded by buildings and streets; it became physically impossible to extend in any direction except upward.

The decision to convert to the band oven, in fact, required a decision to build new bakeries. Involved was a decision to spend many millions of dollars for total modernization.

John J. Toomey, a veteran peeler from the old Cambridgeport bakery in Massachusetts who rose to the position of manager of production in 1939 and vice president in charge of production five years later, was another who raised the question of the need for modernization. But caution ruled. "All those fine, fire-proof buildings that we have, John, how can we destroy them?"

It was not until 1932 that an experiment with the new ovens was tried. Two band ovens were installed on the upper floor of the New York bakery. Thick brick walls had to be torn down and replaced with steel columns and girders to make one long, continuous open space. Although costly, the experiment proved successful. The next use of the oven was in the newly designed one-floor bakery in Atlanta, Georgia.

The construction of the Atlanta bakery—containing five band ovens—was considered a gamble. It was regarded as a test of the potential value of the band oven. But the disruption caused by World War II prevented further building at the time. When a new bakery was constructed in Denver in 1941, no provision whatsoever was made for band ovens!

The company was equally timid in the field of packaging. In the early 1930's there was a trend toward the use of cellophane. Cellophane had been discovered by a Swiss chemist as far back as 1908. Jacques Brandenberger, employed by a French textile firm, coined the name "cellophane." After World War I products began to be packaged in cellophane, and the first sheet of American-made cellophane came off the casting machine in the DuPont plant in Buffalo in the spring of 1924. NBC decision makers eyed the new material suspiciously and were reluctant to spend money for experimental purposes. Competitors, however, soon had their products available in the markets wrapped in cellophane containers.

One reason for the National Biscuit Company's failure to see the importance of cellophane was that it had not yet recognized new methods of merchandising upon which the use of such packaging techniques was based. Although chain stores were the major source of its business, the company was in no position to grasp the implications of the new self-service markets. Modern merchandising was making it necessary for the product, in effect, to sell itself. And one method of achieving this was to make the product visible to the consumer.

Through these years Roy E. Tomlinson's closest associate and confidant within the company was his brother Howard, who became his assistant in 1923. Sixteen years R. E.'s junior, Howard was energetic, outgoing, full of drive and desire to bring forth new ideas. His rise in NBC was rapid. In the spring of 1926 he was elected a vice president and a year later a director. It appeared to many a desirable development for Howard ultimately to step into his brother's shoes. And, evidently, R. E. Tomlinson thought so, too.

However, such hopes were doomed. In the spring of 1929 Howard Tomlinson was rushed to a hospital in Montclair, where he lived, suffering from appendicitis. Peritonitis set in. He died shortly afterward.

Flags flew at half mast at the New York bakery. NBC leaders mourned, especially R. E. Tomlinson. To lose a thirty-six-year-old brother, one who embodied all of the attributes which R. E. fancied he himself lacked, was a cruel blow. Tired, grief-stricken, he was more desirous of solitude now than ever before. For years R. E. had nourished the dream of a contemplative retirement where he could be a senior adviser in much the same way that Judge Moore had been adviser to the youthful R. E. Tomlinson. When Howard died, these plans were shattered.

At the meeting of the board of directors on May 21, 1929, Tomlinson tendered his resignation and accompanied it with a recommendation that Frederick Beers, vice president in charge of production, be elected the new president. The vote of acceptance was reluctant but unanimous. Tomlinson agreed to serve as chairman of the board.

Beers, a small bespectacled man who had left Yale to become a "student baker" for the National Biscuit Company about a quarter of a century earlier, had been appointed manager of the production department in 1921; and, seven years later, a vice president of the company.

Actually, Beers was a product of the foresight of A. W. Green, who felt that the company needed to recruit intelligent and ambitious college men who would be willing to start at the bottom and work their way up to positions of responsibility.

Unfortunately, Frederick Beers had no more than seated himself comfortably in his newly acquired office than the Depression struck. The stock market collapsed. The nation's economy faced one of its most severe crises. Obviously, this was not the time for innovation. One of Beers's first acts was to dispatch to employees around the country a series of inspirational letters seeking ways, large and small, of maintaining NBC's sales in the face of the economic catastrophe. In one communication Beers expressed the hope "that each member of the NBC family, when making up his or her gift list this year, will keep in mind our fruit cake and our many other delicious packaged items." Beers evidently figured that if each employee were to make purchases within the company, this would in itself boost sales.

Whether it was the depressed period that made it impossible for Beers to function efficiently or whether Beers himself did not have the breadth of experience necessary for a chief executive, it is difficult to say. But in the summer of 1931 the board of directors voted that Frederick Beers be made chairman of the manufacturing committee. Frank Clifford Lowry, a neighbor of Tomlinson's in Montclair and a company director since 1926, was elected president.

Born in Philadelphia of Quaker parents, Lowry had entered the wholesale grocery industry as a young man, was active in the sugar business, and ultimately became head of the New York Coffee and Sugar Exchange. Although he had no direct knowledge of the biscuit business, he took his job seriously from the start. He started checking into details that no NBC president had bothered with for a long time. The result of such a sudden shift in policy was inevitable: friction. Within a year Tomlinson was asked by the board to return to the leadership of the National Biscuit Company. Seeing no alternative, he reluctantly agreed.

Still Tomlinson was seeking the man or combination of men to whom he could turn over the management of the company, even unofficially. As in the past, he was handicapped by his isolation; he did not actually know many people well.

A veteran lawyer, Frederick W. Bode, had succeeded Tomlinson as general counsel and had successfully contested Federal Trade Commission charges of unfair trading. In the spring of 1924 the United States Circuit Court of Appeals in New York had held that the company's discount plan was "fair in all respects as to all its competitors and customers." The decision endeared Bode to Tomlinson. But Bode, a member of the Illinois bar, did not wish to live in New York, where the company's general office was located.

He was succeeded in 1926 by Charles A. Vilas, who came from the New York law firm of Shearman and Sterling. Vilas and Tomlinson had worked as a team in the famous Shredded Wheat case.

In 1931 Clyde Stilwell, who had married the daughter of the Reverend William Barton, Tomlinson's boyhood adviser, succeeded Vilas as general counsel. None of these men, although lawyers (an unwritten qualification for NBC leadership in those days), met Tomlinson's requirements. There was only one likely person, a young man who had worked his way up from office boy to assistant general counsel under Stilwell. This man, George H. Coppers, earned Tomlinson's respect in the 1930's, when he wisely advised against further litigation in the Shredded Wheat case.

Coppers was also involved when NBC joined with other companies to challenge the validity of the Agricultural Adjustment Act before the United States Supreme Court. The suit was based on the claim that taxes were being illegally demanded under the A.A.A. The Supreme Court ruled in favor of the corporations, resulting in a refund to the Biscuit Company of $2,500,000. Tomlinson was delighted with the decision and, of course, with Coppers, who represented the company. But Coppers was too young and inexperienced to be the man Tomlinson sought.

Another company executive whom Tomlinson considered was Edward Y. Crossmore, who joined the company as a cashier in Wilkes-Barre, Pennsylvania, in 1902 and rose to become manager of the bread department. Admiring the big, burly Crossmore's ability to make decisions, Tomlinson named him his executive vice president and also made him a director, a position which he held off and on until he resigned in 1941 because of illness. Tomlinson also looked for counsel to the diminutive Alfred W. Kasten, an aggressive German-born mathematical wizard who had served the National Biscuit Company since 1915, when he became a special bookkeeper in Chicago.

But of all those who shared Tomlinson's responsibilities, there was none on whom he relied more than Frank K. Montgomery. Born in Chicago in 1884, Montgomery was employed by a wholesale grocery firm after graduating from high school. In the late spring of 1917 he became chief clerk in NBC's flour department in Chicago. There he rose to assistant manager. When the department moved to New York, Montgomery moved with it and in a few years became vice president and manager of the sales department.

Montgomery was a man of intense nervous energy. He walked fast, talked fast, and made friends easily—especially among executives of the new chain stores which were springing up like mushrooms during the 1920's and 1930's. His loyalty to the National Biscuit Company amounted to a passion. His friends remarked that he would practically salute an NBC truck if one passed him in the street. Montgomery was basically a salesman, but not in the usual mold. He never seemed to be trying to sell. He influenced people by getting to know them and establishing a bond of friendship.

The Biscuit Company needed a man like Montgomery to mend its fences in the trade. He was ideally equipped to accomplish this. Customers, such as heads of chain stores, became so fond of Montgomery that many of them would not dream of purchasing products elsewhere. It was not unusual for his friends to put competitive products under the shelf so that they could prove their loyalty to Frank Montgomery. Perceptive and convincing, Montgomery could sit with a complete stranger on a train for an hour or two and, by the time the trip was over, the stranger felt that Frank Montgomery was his closest friend. This feeling would be reinforced a few days later by the receipt of a box of cookies as a gift.

But, despite Montgomery, the National Biscuit Company was still slow to realize the significance of the supermarket. Or of self-service, which was entering the scene with a rush. As a result the Biscuit Company was at a disadvantage: clerks had to bag and weigh NBC products. And the self-service-oriented customer did not want to wait.

Montgomery, however, made important contributions in moving the company forward in its relationship to the food trade. He was aggressive, energetic and outgoing: characterizations that R. E. Tomlinson admired. As a result Montgomery—and his more phlegmatic brother, Charles—were increasingly charged with more responsibilities. Both men became vice presidents, Frank in charge of sales, Charles in charge of purchasing. To them the semi-retired Tomlinson looked increasingly to take over the responsibility of high office.

But Tomlinson's choice, while it served certain positive ends, solved no basic problems. Frank Montgomery introduced an emphasis on sales; but he had slight knowledge of the company as a whole. Nor did he provide the type of leadership that encouraged open expressions of opinion or wide participation by others. Emphasis on profits rather than corporate development increased. Dividends continued to be paid even through the Depression years.

The National Biscuit Company launched a new and permanent cracker sensation in the early 1930's. For years the company had been seeking a buttery cracker to compete with others in the field. After a long period of experimentation, a formula was produced. The new product was called "Ritz." It was a butter cracker, different from a soda cracker in that it had more shortening and no yeast. It was consequently crisper and less fluffy. A thin coat of coconut oil and a sprinkling of salt were spread over the cracker after it had gone through the oven. The recipe seemed simple. But the taste evidently had a special appeal.

Furthermore, Ritz was introduced as a prestige item with such promotional headlines as "Anytime is the right time to serve Ritz," "Tomorrow's cracker—today," and "Almost overnight, America's most popular cracker."

The Ritz cracker took the country by storm. The company baked more than 5,000,000 in the first year. In three years—aided by imaginative promotion—Ritz became the largest-selling cracker in the world with more than 29,000,000 baked daily. It became a staple in a huge number of American households and in foreign nations as well. In Europe a box of Ritz was presented to a girl friend much as a boy in America presents a box of candy.

The New Yorker pointed out in an article appearing in 1931, "Certainly it is comforting to know that the National Biscuit Company is making just as many cookies as ever; through all of the depression, production hasn't fallen off as much as a cookie, oh, maybe one Fig Newton." Nevertheless, economic uncertainties supplied additional reasons why the company should avoid new ideas of a fundamental nature and new expenditures resulting from them.

But if NBC was financially able to withstand the economic depression without distress, many of its 20,000 employees were not. With some 9,000,000 people unemployed in the nation, the average wage in the country fell from $28 a week in 1929 to $17 a week in 1932. NBC employees, like most wage earners, had several wage reductions.

There was much suffering among both the unemployed and the employed. Yet industry of the era still, for the most part, clung to the belief that individual initiative and enterprise was the cure for the troubles haunting the country. Opposed to this, President Roosevelt pledged the American people "a New Deal . . . Let us all here assembled," he said, "constitute ourselves prophets of a new order of competence and of courage. This is more than a political campaign; it is a call to arms. Give me your help, not to win votes alone, but to win in this crusade to restore America to its own people."

Such views were not well received in most managerial circles. New Deal opponents listed in *America's Sixty Families* included such familiar names as J. P. Morgan, George F. Baker, Ogden L. Mills, Philip Armour, Paul Moore and many other industrialists and financiers who had made major contributions to the nation but whose ability to analyze new economic patterns and to find solutions for new crises proved to be limited.

The National Biscuit Company traditionally sought to minister to the needs of its employees. Ever since the days of Green the company had taken a benevolent attitude toward the people who worked for it. This was expressed by *Delicatessen Merchant*, which once stated that the National Biscuit Company's "liberal pension policy seems to disprove the legal axiom that 'a corporation has no soul.'" The company was proud of its working conditions—"Equal to or better," it stated "than those existing elsewhere in the biscuit industry."

Tomlinson personally was thoughtful of those employees with whom he came in contact. One day in the late 1920's he voluntarily ordered that hours of work in the executive office be shortened and run from 9 A.M. to 4:30 P.M. for a five-day work week, an innovation in those days.

But for thousands of employees in many NBC bakeries and agencies the pressures of the depression years—insecurity, wage reductions, pressure to increase the rate of production—caused misery, starvation, demoralization and unrest. The company's policy to pay and increase dividends—even in the midst of a declining market—made it necessary to increase production and—since its employees were unorganized—cut back wages as far as possible. This was considered sound fiscal policy. The company was as cautious in embracing a modern personnel policy as it was in building new bakeries or installing new ovens.

But employees had their own way of registering dissatisfaction with the company's conservatism.

On the morning of January 8, 1935, Frederick Beers—who had returned to his post as production manager—answered a telephone call in his New York office. He listened to the strained voice of the manager of the NBC Philadelphia plant with an incredulous expression on his face. His hand shook as if the telephone receiver had suddenly grown heavy in his grasp. Unthinkable! Impossible!

Some three thousand employees of the Philadelphia bakery (who had just received a 10 per cent wage reduction) had just walked out on strike!

Then 3,000 NBC employees in the huge New York bakery, together with 1,500 more from Atlanta, Newark and York bakeries, also stopped work. It was like a bad dream. Beers rushed up to the eighth floor to break the news to R. E. Tomlinson.

Striking NBC workers were, of course, not alone in their extreme action. It was a turbulent era. Newspapermen were on strike in Newark; so were street railway workers in Los Angeles, department store employees in Boston, motor coach drivers in Chicago, aluminum employees in Pittsburgh, Chicago stockyard employees, Cleveland steelworkers, Alabama textile employees. It was estimated that in this short period almost two thousand industrial disputes took place involving more than a million employees.

For most employers of the era, strikes were nothing short of revolutionary. Trade unions were almost nonexistent in basic industries before the 1930's. Then so-called federal unions sprang up everywhere, licensed by the American Federation of Labor to represent almost any group or industry that felt the need for unionization. Such a union—Federal Labor Union #19585—had been organized in 1934 among the bakery workers in the Philadelphia, New York, Atlanta and several other NBC plants and reluctantly recognized by the company.

A new philosophy was sweeping the land. As the historian Henry S. Commager expressed it: "There is no double standard for business and for labor; each is equally free to combine and seek its end subject to the restrictions of the law . . ." But while many employees felt organization was necessary, the strike came like a stinging blow in the face to the management of the National Biscuit Company, which had assumed that its relationships with its employees had been more than fair and liberal.

What happened in the three months after the initial walkout at the Philadelphia bakery ran the full gamut of charges and countercharges, claims and counterclaims. There were appeals to the public, mass picketing, name calling, boycotts, strike breakers, injunctions, intimidations, violence, bloodshed, arrests. Police rode bakery trucks. Picketers sang, "U-Don't-Needa biscuit."

Of course, the company's position was diametrically opposed to that of the union. The idea and practice of collective bargaining were, in fact, as strange to the employees as to the employer.

By the end of April an agreement was finally signed ending the three-month stoppage and returning employees in New York, Philadelphia, Atlanta and York to their jobs. The strike was such a confusing and complicated affair that it was difficult to know, after the smoke had cleared and work had been resumed, who, if anyone, had won.

Hundreds of thousands of dollars in wages had been lost by the strikers, and wage levels were not noticeably increased by the return to work. But an era of unionism was born. In a year the Congress of Industrial Organizations, headed by John L. Lewis, had organized thousands of working people into unions. Today, while a number of different unions represent NBC employees, about 9,000 men and women, working mostly in bakeries, are affiliated with the American Bakery and Confectionery Workers' International Union (A.F.L.-C.I.O.).

The wounds of battle slowly healed. For some the strike was further evidence that a reshuffling of policy within the company was needed.

In financial circles the inability of NBC to modernize its thinking or its bakeries became a matter of increased concern. *Fortune* reported that "The National Biscuit Company has watched its income drop steadily since 1930." The magazine commented on the company's "somewhat static appearance" and stated that the company was "reluctant to spend money and bogged down with inertia that long leadership of an industry can sometimes induce."

NBC became more and more known as the "company without a future," run by individuals known as the "nine old men." (The average age of NBC's nine chief executives in 1945 was about 63.) *Investor's Reader*, a publication issued by the financial firm of Merrill Lynch, Fenner & Beane, expressed the opinion that the National Biscuit Company "needed an injection of bounce and energy. There has been criticism that the management was set in its ways and either unwilling or unable to meet changing conditions."

"Stockholders got especially upset in 1943," the publication went on to say, "when net profits tumbled to $8,658,000, the lowest in decades and less than half the $17,104,000 cleared in depressed 1932. A transfusion of new blood was called for all around."

The readers of *The Financial World* were told in March 1938 that "The earnings record of leading biscuit companies over the past five or six years have not been impressive. Of the three largest units in the field, only United Biscuit has been able to make much of a profits comeback from the levels of 1932 . . . National Biscuit has made the least favorable showing of the 'big three.' "

While the National Biscuit Company still led the field, there were signs of a wobbly future. Financially the company was in splendid shape. It had never borrowed a dollar. It had never missed a dividend. But from the point of view of those who looked beyond the dollar sign, the company was ailing. "Below the surface," said *Fortune* magazine, "it was growing aged and slow to move, slow to accept new ideas, slow to adapt itself to a rapidly changing society."

While the board of directors of the company had tended to view the payment of dividends as the thermometer on which to judge company health, it was now beginning to have other ideas. The Moore brothers, primarily financially oriented, increasingly realized the need to keep up with changing times.

What was needed, they concluded, were fresh ideas and energetic young leaders to put them into operation.

Top left, Paul Moore; top right, Frank C. Lowry; bottom left, ▶
Frederick Beers; bottom right, Frank K. Montgomery

TWENTY

Office Boy to President

***

EFFORTS TO UNEARTH new leadership for the company had to defer to a bigger crisis. The nation was again at war.

The economic emergency of World War II was for the National Biscuit Company, in many ways, a repeat performance of World War I.

Roy E. Tomlinson—whose period of leadership spanned both wars—reported to his stockholders in 1941 that the company "is producing large quantities of food for the Army and Navy. In addition to its regular line, it is producing field rations in volume . . . Our laboratory and experimental division conducted extensive experiments, which were helpful in developing the present type "C" rations, designed for use in emergencies, during maneuvers or combat . . .

"Pilots and parachute troops of the United States Army Air Corps," Tomlinson stated, "also have a new emergency field ration, the mainstay of which is a 'pemmican' biscuit, containing in condensed form virtually all the essentials of a balanced diet. Our company was requested by the Army to assist in working out a practical baking procedure and eventually all difficulties relating to formula, production and packaging were solved."

During the latter part of 1942 and the early months of 1943 all types of fats and oils—lard, hydrogenated shortening, spray oil and butter—were extremely difficult to obtain in the amounts needed to

◀ *George H. Coppers samples a cookie*

keep bakeries running. There was, too, a grave shortage of paper stock for packaging.

From the start to the finish of World War II Nabisco delivered more than $90,000,000 worth of products to the armed services. The company's knowledge of protective paper packaging provided important assistance to the Quartermaster Corps. Every section of the company was involved in working for victory. Thousands of employees served in the armed forces. Even the Milk Bone bakery made biscuit for the war dogs of the Army and the Marine Corps.

The war brought increased civilian spending as well as special GI ration orders. By 1944 the company's bakeries were operating at capacity. Housewives were known to follow the cream-and-red NBC delivery trucks down the street to the grocery store and then stand in line in the hope of being able to buy NBC products.

In spite of the war boom, the company's profits were down; dividends were being eked out and general morale was low.

For some of the nation's leading corporations the postwar era represented a time of change, a time for unprecedented technological retooling. Many corporations found themselves overwhelmed by their new requirements. Time-tested ground rules for operation of a business no longer seemed to work. Methods of leadership which had led to fantastic successes in the first half of the twentieth century seemed inadequate.

The National Biscuit Company, for example, had the cash to undertake a large-scale postwar program. But it seemed to lack the ability to adjust to new aspects of the postwar industrial world. Its equipment was aging; and so were its leaders. In 1944 there were thirty cracker bakeries, four cereal bakeries and seventeen bread bakeries; and almost all of them were antiquated. The company's one great asset was the fact that it owed nobody; and nobody owed it.

The NBC board of directors, for the most part, was not composed of men whose backgrounds could provide the guidance needed at this time. Most of the members lacked interest in company details, and so did many important stockholders. Momentum was keeping the company going. Some executives predicted that, when this momentum ran down, the situation might become critical. The sharp-tongued general manager of the New York bakery, Russell Shultz, warned that the company "was not growing. It was not getting anywhere . . . There hasn't been a new thought in forty years when it comes to handling cookies and biscuits."

Another executive wryly commented, "The company faced a dim future. All it had was money." Still another described the personnel situation succinctly: "Nobody advanced; nobody retired."

There was little outspoken criticism within the company, but much muttering over lunch tables. Inevitably, younger men, impatient with their superiors, speculated on how *they* would manage affairs if *they* had authority. One of these was George Henry Coppers, now Nabisco's general counsel. Under his clerklike appearance was a tremendous reservoir of energy and ambition. One writer later was to describe him as fairly "bursting with ideas."

George was an only child. Both of his parents, George Coppers and Letitia McGrath Coppers, were over forty years of age on November 29, 1902, when he was born in a New York apartment house on West 139th Street. Never strong physically, he showed signs of nervousness at an early age and stuttered badly.

On occasion George would stutter so that his father lost patience. "Write it! Write it! Write it!" Mr. Coppers would exclaim. This, of course, only made matters worse.

They took George to a doctor, but there was very little that could be done for the boy except to encourage him to build himself up physically. So young George went to a nearby YMCA several times a week to work with bar bells and other paraphernalia. Always bright in his studies despite his speech impediment, George graduated with high grades from grammar school and DeWitt Clinton High School. However, even though his mother worked as a secretary to add to the family income, college was out of the question. By now George was six feet tall, a good-looking boy, high strung, intelligent and eager. He went to the YMCA employment agency to find a job.

The first referral was to the New York office of the National Biscuit Company on 14th Street. Coppers was seventeen. The war was over. Times were returning to "normalcy." The company needed an office boy. On September 9, 1920, Coppers was hired with a starting salary of twelve dollars a week and promises by George Wells, NBC secretary and treasurer, that he would get an increase if things turned out well. The astute Wells liked Coppers and helped him learn his job. But the going was not easy. George's stammering was not only an embarrassment, it was a threat to his employment.

One day Coppers delivered a message orally to Frederick Bode, general counsel of the company. It was so difficult to understand what he was saying that Bode was irritated. When the boy left, Bode called Wells and asked why he had hired someone with such a handicap.

Despite such criticism Wells retained Coppers. Soon he was appointed a clerk in the accounting department and in 1923 was transferred to the legal department to assist in tax work. The boy was obviously unusually bright and able to learn.

Encouraged by some NBC officers but mainly driven by his own desire for self-improvement, Coppers began to study at night, entering the evening school of the Pace Institute of Accountancy and Business Administration in downtown New York. Working days, he attended night school for three seemingly endless years. When he finally graduated, it was with high honors.

In those three years young Coppers had been given increasing responsibility in handling tax assignments in the NBC legal department. But there was no future in it for someone not trained in law. So Coppers decided, with the encouragement of the company, to apply to Fordham University in the Bronx, not far from where he lived. He was accepted. For five more years he worked days at the National Biscuit Company and attended college and law school at night.

It seemed as if those grueling years would never end. But in June 1929 he was graduated with the degree of LL.B. *cum laude*. It was no small accomplishment. But George Coppers managed to find time for courting. A month after his graduation from Fordham he married Miss Eleanor Sherwin of Englewood, New Jersey. Early the next year, at the age of twenty-eight, Coppers was admitted to the New York State bar.

George Coppers' achievements gave him confidence in himself and his future. While unable to completely overcome his stammering, he had come a long way. Only when he was nervous or upset did his handicap recur.

In 1930 he was invited to speak at a meeting of alumni of Pace Institute. Coppers had made very few public speeches, but he accepted the invitation. When he rose to deliver his remarks before an alumni and student audience, he found himself scarcely able to say a word. He stuttered and stammered through his short speech. To make matters worse he was called upon to give a prize to an undergraduate. He was so shaken he dropped it. He and the youngster then bumped heads when they both leaned down to pick it up.

For Coppers the experience was a nightmare. He vowed to his wife that he would never again make an attempt to speak in public. But, typically, he began a long and determined effort to overcome his handicap once and for all.

If Coppers was not successful at public speaking during this early period, he was evidently eminently successful at impressing NBC officials with his other capabilities. In the summer of 1938, when he was thirty-six years old he was rewarded for his years of hard work when R. E. Tomlinson appointed him general counsel to succeed Clyde S. Stilwell, transferred to other duties. Tomlinson liked Coppers and had respected his judgment ever since the famous Agricultural Adjustment decision years earlier.

Coppers was not a gregarious man. Although he had made many friends, he was not easy to know well. Intellectual, dedicated to his work, he was rational where others might be emotional. He was rough in an argument, impatient with indecision on the part of others, quick to anger over inefficiency, not given to small talk. If he did not breed affection, he did command respect.

In the early 1940's NBC owned fifty-nine manufacturing establishments scattered all over the United States producing some two hundred varieties of products. The company made almost all its own baking machinery, at its huge block-long machine shop in Evanston, Illinois. It produced its own cartons and flour, and spent about $10,000,000 a month in the commodity markets. It employed some 29,000 people throughout the nation. It claimed all the grocery stores in the entire United States as its customers.

But beneath the rosy surface the nagging problems of development and modernization persisted. According to *Fortune* magazine, although the company had learned the economies of the band oven, "it did next to nothing about it . . . Reluctant to spend money [a band oven cost nearly four times as much as the reel oven], and bogged down with the inertia that long leadership of an industry can sometimes induce, National Biscuit as late as 1940 was still building new reel ovens."

In 1945 there were 165 known competitors with national, or more commonly, regional distribution of some cracker or cookie lines. The major national competition came from Sunshine, formerly known as Loose-Wiles, and the United Biscuit Company. Both companies had more advanced equipment in proportion to their total plant than did the National Biscuit Company. The Sunshine Company, for example, had about 50 per cent converted to band ovens.

On at least one occasion Alexander C. Nagle, president of the First National Bank and an NBC director, raised aspects of the issue with Paul Moore. Like his father before him, Paul Moore served a leading role on the company's strategic executive committee.

"The National Biscuit Company," Nagle said once, "doesn't seem to attract as many young men to it as it should."

Moore thought for a moment and replied, "There is nothing dynamic about the company."

With criticism mounting in financial circles, the necessity for the company to make a change—or many changes—became a matter of concern to both Paul and his brother, Edward, directors and owners of large blocks of stock. It was also apparent to Edward S. Moore, Jr., a huge lumbering young man who came east from Wyoming in 1945 to fill a position in the company's executive offices. Young Eddie was casual in his manner and obviously disdainful of NBC's tradition of quiet dignity and gentility. He strode about coatless (many thought deliberately), collar and tie askew, often laughing uproariously. In his office his feet were as likely to be on his desk as under it.

There was a method in Eddie's behavior. He was trying to bring some life into an overly staid and venerable institution. More than that, he was trying to figure out what needed doing to bring the company up to date.

Exactly how much influence young Eddie Moore had on his father and uncle is not known; but it may well have hastened the coming of change. One day in the summer of 1945 Paul Moore, chatting with Roy Tomlinson at the Links Club in New York, posed the question as to whether there was younger leadership available in the company.

In his quiet, contained manner, as if discussing the weather, Tomlinson replied, "We have such a man, I think. His name is George Coppers."

It was not a complete surprise to Coppers that he was being considered for the presidency. Ever since he had been named general counsel, he had been considered a man who was going places. This was based not only upon Coppers' obvious ability, but also on the fact that he was a lawyer and—traditionally—being a lawyer appeared to be a prerequisite for company leadership.

But it was one thing to offer the name of George Coppers for the presidency; it was another to convince him to accept it. When Paul Moore discussed the possibility with Coppers, the answer was clear and to the point: "If I take this job," said Coppers, "there will have to be some changes."

"We understand that," replied Moore.

"If you want me to run the company," continued Coppers, "I'll do it. But I want control. I want to call the shots as I see them."

The directors knew their man. They agreed that Coppers could write his own ticket. The final plans were worked out and on September 24, 1945, the board of directors officially elected George H. Coppers, age forty-three, president of the National Biscuit Company as well as a director and a member of the executive committee. The sixty-eight-year-old Roy E. Tomlinson, who had served the company as president and chief executive for twenty-eight years, was elected chairman of the board.

Within the company's inner circle the naming of Coppers was not a surprise. But he was almost unknown outside New York. Actually, Coppers had little personal experience with the biscuit business as a whole, but he was to prove he knew how to pick people and work with them. Furthermore, he brought with him a driving energy, a fresh point of view and an impatience with old ways of doing things that was what the company needed above all.

One of Tomlinson's rare public speeches was made at a company dinner following his retirement from the presidency. Rising to his feet in the full dignity of his seventy years, Tomlinson responded characteristically to various eulogies:

"My reputation is secure as far as this company is concerned," he said, "because if I did nothing else, I did pick George Coppers for president."

Within twenty-four hours after his election Coppers went into action. His first act was to make drastic changes in the top executive echelon that ran the affairs of the corporation. Moving with precision, he held discussions behind closed doors with a number of the company's leading officers.

One of the first was Frank K. Montgomery, the executive vice president who had organized the company's sales department into such an efficient machine. Through the years the hard-driving Montgomery had become, in effect, acting president. Also interviewed were Charles T. Montgomery, vice president in charge of purchasing;

Frederick Beers, who had remained a vice president since vacating the presidency years before; Clyde S. Stilwell, vice president and former general counsel who had been Coppers' immediate superior for a number of years; Ernest B. Tomlinson, R. E.'s brother, a vice president serving in the Chicago office; Charles Dunlap, vice president and comptroller.

The average age of these key officials, including R. E. Tomlinson, was sixty-four years. On September 25, the day after Coppers became president, the company announced the retirement of five of its vice presidents. Two more retired within the following year.

"Many of the senior officers have expressed their desire to be relieved of active duties," Coppers stated. "And in the immediate future, sales, production and purchasing departments, among others, will be headed by young men with many active years before them."

Prior to this time, the company had no regular pension plan. When pensions were granted, it was on a hit-or-miss basis. Coppers changed this by instituting, as fast as he was able to have it drawn up, a program wherein executives who had given years of service to the company could retire with a proper pension.

For long it had been evident that the company required such changes. R. E. Tomlinson was well aware of it. Why had he not done something about it? The fact of the matter is that most of the people occupying top administrative positions were his close friends. Many were his neighbors in New Jersey, others were related by blood or marriage. He felt that he could not make changes without violating his deep loyalties to these associates. "I couldn't have done what Coppers did," he said later.

Under Coppers' presidency net profits advanced to $19,655,000 in 1946 and to $22,902,000 in 1947. But this postwar spurt was not actually the result of any change of policy. It was too soon for that. It was the result, rather, of the repeal of excess profits taxes, the end of the Office of Price Administration (OPA), and inventory profits in the rising commodity markets of 1946–47. Actual proof of whether or not the leadership of Coppers was to set the company out on a new and consistently profitable career was to require much more planning, preparation and hard work than had yet been done.

Disturbingly new ideas were everywhere, and it was the wise corporate leader who was able to learn from them.

The changing status of business, for example, was one such concept. Osborn Elliott wrote in *Men at the Top*, "Half a century ago, the cognoscenti of Boston chuckled when President Lowell of Harvard, in composing a citation for the degree offered by Harvard's new Graduate School of Business Administration, described business as 'the oldest of the arts and the youngest of the professions.'

"Many people thought the idea preposterous. Business a profession! What an innocent notion! Business was a rough and tumble battle between men whose first concern was to look out for Number One, and the very idea," as Elliott points out, "of professors being able to prepare men for it was nonsense. As a matter of fact, many a tough fibered tycoon of those days was dubious even about employing college graduates!"

But the idea was gathering strength that business was a profession and that it was necessary to learn to run a business in a more organized way than the school of hard knocks provided. For example, from 1900 to 1910 hundreds of books were published on business management. In 1908 the Harvard Graduate School of Business Administration was founded. With the years its prestige in business circles increased. It was, it is true, difficult for tough-minded, pragmatic old-timers to admit that anything learned at a school like Harvard could conceivably make a contribution to the financial success of their enterprises. Nevertheless, the idea was slowly accepted that one could learn from those who had made a study of business administration.

George Coppers was not a man to shy away from ideas or formal learning. He had turned to the advanced management program at the Harvard Graduate School of Business Administration even during his busiest days as corporation counsel.

The Advanced Management Program was an intensive schedule of weekend education designed for business executives who had reached or closely approached the general policy-making levels of their organizations. Courses available at the institution included corporate strategy and business policy, financial analysis, accounting policy, marketing, labor relations, human behavior in organizations, international business, and the relationship of business to the world society, as well as other subjects. It was quite a dose! And every Monday morning Coppers was back at his desk in New York.

For about a dozen weekends George Coppers went to school. The opportunity to meet other corporate executives and to learn from the organized curriculum of the institute was a revelation. He soaked up information as a sponge does water.

But perhaps the most influential part of Coppers' Harvard education came from Philip Cabot, a small, frail professor who had a profound conviction that business was a profession. No puller of punches, Cabot advised, "Declare a sham a sham and a fraud a fraud, and the great ones of the earth shall bow down to do you homage."

He also said, "I state bluntly my belief that much of the alleged failure of our business and industrial leaders has been because the society of which they are the servants has given them the wrong orders or no orders at all. I go further and suggest that it has practically forgotten what orders it gave them, and has issued contradictory orders . . ."

Such a philosophy appealed to the outspoken, straight-talking George Coppers.

Professor Cabot would warm up to his subject: "Setting aside the cases of individual depravity, which are no more common among businessmen than among teachers, lawyers, doctors, politicians, or accountants, I believe it can be proved that an overwhelming majority of businessmen have labored honestly to carry out the orders which they understood they had received from the nation.

"Most competent observers will agree, I believe, that during the century which closed with the panic of 1929, the businessmen of this country were the major group to which the nation looked for leadership. During an earlier period, the leadership of the nation was in the hands of the ministers, the lawyers and the doctors . . . Personally, I have no question that our business leaders did fail to lead, in the sense that they failed to see the direction in which the life of the society which we call the United States of America was moving, and failed to adjust themselves to the rapid changes which have occurred . . ."

For Coppers, as well as for most of the business executives who attended the Cabot lectures, this was little short of revolutionary. "If you will bear in mind," Professor Cabot stated "that businessmen are merely servants of society, this proposition hardly requires argument, for if they do not serve society faithfully and skillfully, they will be discharged. Our modern industrial society is far more complex than it was fifty years ago. The methods of business administration which were then adequate are now inadequate, and if businessmen are to regain the position of leadership which they once held, they must adjust themselves to modern conditions. Fifty years ago, it may well have been true that businessmen could do their full duty to society by devoting themselves to economic problems with a single mind. But that is not true today."

Throughout the lecture series Professor Cabot, as well as his teaching associates, stressed the various categories in which modern corporate leadership operates. There were economic problems, social problems, and political problems.

"The business administrator of my generation," said Cabot, "did not regard sociological problems . . . as any of his business. If he thought about them at all, he would have said that 'they were problems for the professors.'

"But the businessman today cannot shrug his shoulders and leave these problems of social evolution to the professors, because he cannot possibly evade the obvious fact that it is the impact of industry upon society that is the most important cause of the changes which distress us . . ."

On the subject of labor organization, Professor Cabot shocked some and surprised others: "Why cannot enlightened management and large-scale industry deal directly with its own people whom it understands?" he inquired. Referring to labor unions, he said, "The important point, I think, is that these great organizations are *here*. They are a part of the environment in which we live. It is not our business to try to change these institutions in accordance with our ideas of how things ought to be, but to accept them as matters of fact and adjust ourselves to them . . .

"Stating a personal opinion, namely, that in the present condition of our society we had better accept these great labor organizations which are supported by a Federal statute as a matter of fact, and concentrate our attention on making the necessary adjustments to them. If we adopt this course, and succeed in establishing sound working relations between labor and management organizations, I think I can see tangible achievements of great importance which these organizations can accomplish working together, but not separately . . .

"To put it bluntly, this problem of social reorganization of industry is a problem for businessmen . . . I agree that the dominant social obligation of the business executive is to make the business profitable, but I suggest that he cannot afford to focus his whole attention on economic problems . . . What I am urging on you is the necessity in large-scale enterprises of understanding 'the society' or 'social structure in all its works!' "

George Coppers applied many of the ideas he learned at Harvard to revitalize the National Biscuit Company.

The first need was for *policy*, the second for *people*. Both must be forceful and youthful to meet the requirements of the present—and of the future.

Fair Lawn, New Jersey, bakery ▸

"We Can't Afford to Sit Still."

Not long after he became president, George H. Coppers sat down at his desk to formulate a statement of his views. Before the statement was drawn up to his satisfaction, it went through no fewer than five drafts.

One morning all supervisory employees throughout the company received a communication entitled *Company Policy* signed by George H. Coppers:

On occasions which have now become too numerous, when I have asked one of our people, "Why don't we do this?" or "Why don't we say that?" I have been told, "That is against our 'Company Policy.'" Who originated that particular policy, when, or why, has long since been forgotten, but our people go on following the so-called "policy" sometimes blindly and without question.

Maybe the "policy" was adopted as a wartime measure or to meet some other temporary situation. When the reason for it no longer existed, maybe the person who issued it forgot to recall it. All too often our people have gone on following it, and no one has stuck his neck out and said, "Why are we still doing this?" And all too often people have availed themselves of "Company Policy" to avoid taking responsibility and making decisions themselves. Or they have used it as an explanation or excuse for their failure to do some perfectly obvious thing.

And so now I say to you that there is no "Company Policy" except such as is dictated by your common sense, sound judgment, observance

◀ *George Coppers lunches at Chicago bakery with Roy C. Gasser and Charles C. Auchincloss, directors; Edward S. Moore, Jr., executive vice president; and George A. Mitchell (foreground), vice president, finance.*

of the law and the dictates of your conscience. Company policy will be made from *here on*. And when it is made be sure you understand the reason for it, exactly what situations it covers and how long it is to last. And if you don't understand these things, ask about them.

You will, of course, continue to observe all written instructions contained in departmental circulars, etc.

The statement raised a furor. It was the subject of lunchtime discussion within the company wherever there was a branch or bakery. Paragraphs were clipped out and tacked on bulletin boards and walls.

But it was not merely by such proclamations of formal policy that George Coppers began to establish a new approach to almost everything. Other, even more definitive, statements were to come. But it was in the area of selecting executives that Coppers even more emphatically revealed his prejudices and preferences. It was one thing to retire a number of executives who had seen their best days. It was another to find energetic, youthful, capable replacements. Like his predecessor, Coppers believed in delegating authority. But he had an advantage. Having served in the ranks for so many years, he had developed an almost uncanny skill at estimating the talents and limitations of his colleagues.

Once Coppers was asked how he judged men. "I don't know," he answered in the crisp, almost brusque way he had of responding to questions. "It's just the way I read a guy."

On another occasion someone pessimistically told Coppers, "No one man can change the thinking of this company."

Coppers' response was typical: "All a guy can do is try."

The *Nabisco* magazine stated in March 1946, "One thing is clear —our company is just starting a new and inspiring chapter in its long and successful history. Vigorous younger men are at the helm. Forward-looking policies are being adopted—modern, progressive plans of all kinds are on foot. In the executive office, there is an atmosphere of action—prompt and decisive action—to meet the new and different problems of this troubled period. Avenues of promotion are being cleared, so that the capable young men of Nabisco can rise faster and with more certainty than ever before."

Among the capable men whom Coppers selected to give leadership to the company were some who had served long apprenticeships in the ranks; others were relative newcomers; still others—but not many—were from outside the company altogether.

There were some Nabisco men, capable and loyal, who seemed to have reached a point of no return in their forward progress. Some became discouraged or demoralized. Some left. Others were aware of their latent powers and had confidence that their day would come—and prepared for it. Such a man was George A. Mitchell, born in Jersey City in 1900. Mitchell's schooling was limited by the need to earn a living, and at fifteen years of age he applied for a clerk's job with the Jersey City sales branch of the National Biscuit Company. He was hired. He soon showed an ability at figures which led to a series of promotions: cashier in Jersey City; then in Wheeling, West Virginia; then Grand Rapids, Michigan. By 1924 Mitchell was recognized by the company as a man who could enter a new situation, put his finger on a financial problem, and help solve it. It was a talent of immense value to Charles Dunlap under whom Mitchell worked for fifteen years.

In 1928, when the company acquired the Iten Biscuit Company with headquarters in Omaha, Nebraska, Mitchell was elected its assistant treasurer. Acting as financial trouble shooter, Mitchell traveled around the country during the 20's when the company was absorbing various bakeries, many of them, like Iten, in the west. Part of his responsibility was to assist in integrating new acquisitions into NBC's financial organization. His rise was steady: auditor in 1924, assistant treasurer in 1928, comptroller in 1939.

But Mitchell's distinguishing characteristic was not only a head for figures, honesty and efficiency. Nor was it even his dedication to his work. The special ingredient that marked him for George Coppers' attention was in a different area. During the years when the company was pinching pennies rather than investing in the future, Mitchell developed his own ideas as to how things should be. "To anticipate difficulties before they happen," he once said, "is the most difficult and important function. We should all strive and prepare ourselves for growth." And that is exactly what Mitchell did.

Thus, when Coppers looked about for an adviser on financial matters, Mitchell was his man. He was that rare financially oriented executive whose knowledge of company functions was total. He saw beyond the dollar sign. In 1948 he became Nabisco's vice president in charge of the auditing, comptroller and treasury departments.

Another man to whom Coppers looked for assistance was his friend of many years, Russell M. Shultz, who visited the company in 1926 when he was twenty-four years old to discuss a job offer and, as he said, caught, "that gorgeous aroma of vanilla wafers." He had stayed with the company ever since. Shultz had originally hoped to become a physician and was preparing to enter Johns Hopkins University. But the Depression was on and money was short. Instead he became a chemist for the National Biscuit Company in New York and served as manager of various bakeries around the country. Later he became general manager of the Chicago bakery, and after that, general manager of the bakery in New York.

Shultz was, through the years, sharply critical of company policy. Very little was immune from his scrutiny. He blasted "negative thinking." "Time after time," he said, "I have seen when something new is proposed, a great deal more time is spent on figuring out why that particular thing will *not* work than would have been spent on it had everybody knuckled down and made it work. It has always been my experience that the things that you worry about very seldom cause you any great difficulty—it is those things you do not think about and do not worry about that very often cause you your trouble."

When Coppers asked Shultz in 1946 to take charge of his research department, Shultz hesitated. As he said later, he "wanted no part of research in the National Biscuit Company because I had serious doubts whether any one individual could change the thinking in an organization which so long had been practicing conservative tactics." Before he accepted the position, he specified three qualifications: that he have but one boss, that the research director have the final say on the amount of money that he wished to spend, and that there be no cut in research and money spent in depression years, because "then, if ever, you need research."

As Shultz recalls it, Coppers "never batted an eye." The answer was an unqualified yes on all three conditions. Shultz became a vice president in charge of production, engineering and research.

Another member of the Coppers administration was Harry T. Eggert, who had risen from junior clerk in 1916 to manager of the company's insurance department. A close personal friend of Coppers', Eggert had exchanged many an idea with him as to how they would run the company if they were ever given the chance. Aside from a brief interval during the 1934 strike when Clyde Stilwell had been in charge of personnel, the company had never had anyone directly in charge of employee relations. Now Coppers, recognizing Eggert's long experience in the field, appointed him vice president in charge of personnel. The first of many innovations was the immediate establishment of a formal pension plan.

Still another man to whom Coppers now turned was Alfred W. Kasten, who had joined the company at the age of 19 as a student cashier. He had taken a hand in building almost every department from sales to finance.

A bantam rooster type, cocky and aggressive, Kasten was one of the few men who made the transition from a high rank in the Tomlinson board of strategy to the Coppers administration. In the fall of 1945 he was appointed assistant to president Coppers. However, three years later he became ill and in a week was dead at the age of fifty-three.

With the passing of Kasten, Coppers looked about for someone else to become his executive assistant. This time his choice was the son of the Nabisco director and grandson of Judge Moore, Edward S. Moore, Jr.

Eddie Moore had attended Princeton University but left (like his grandfather before him) to go west for his health. He operated a Wyoming cattle ranch and, for a time, helped publish a daily newspaper before returning east to join Nabisco in 1945 as a vice president and member of the board of directors. While Moore knew little about the baking business, his rough-and-ready intelligence seemed to fit into the Coppers scheme of things.

There were, of course, other men whom Coppers gathered about him. There was Warren S. Warner, vice president of sales, merchandising and advertising; and Howard B. Cunningham, vice president in charge of purchasing. But perhaps the most important—and in many ways the most colorful—one of all was Lee S. Bickmore, a young salesman from Pocatello, Idaho, overflowing with energy and enthusiasm.

From such people as these Coppers set out to fashion a team to lead the company along new and daring paths. The Coppers philosophy, as expressed in his special statement, had been warmly welcomed. A renaissance spirit was in the air.

People had been brought from the field before, but generally the "field" was considered to be New York and New Jersey. The rest of the country tended to be ignored. Now employees began to feel that they had a chance for promotion, wherever they lived and whatever their particular assignment. There was a stirring toward rebuilding the company in little ways and big, and not only structurally but philosophically and psychologically as well.

For the first time a suggestion system was put into operation. People were encouraged to express their ideas no matter how critical.

This state of mind even pervaded meetings of the board of directors. They lasted longer. More questions were asked and answered. The number of people participating in the annual shareholders' meetings increased noticeably. By 1958 all attendance records were broken at such meetings with more than 78 per cent of the total number of shares represented either in person or by proxy.

Whereas previously the company had paid little attention to public opinion, now it began to be concerned about its image before its customers, suppliers, and even the general public. "We in the food business have more than the usual businessman's obligation to the public," Coppers stated in a speech before the American Bakers Association. "In a sense, we have in our hands for safe keeping and improvement the condition of the public health."

Press relations improved, releases were issued, interviews were granted. In the past, few company officers had appeared in public to speak or grant interviews. Now Coppers, overcoming his speech impediment with courage, made frequent speeches. *Fortune* said of him, "His management has a Youngish Turk tone that is not entirely concealed by the careful speech of a lawyer and C.P.A."

Employees were encouraged to take part in community affairs. Coppers here, too, set the example. He became involved in a growing number of outside activities, ranging from the American Red Cross to the YMCA. He even accepted an invitation, not without some trepidation, to serve for a year as chairman of the New York Chamber of Commerce, a position that involved considerable public speaking.

Even the arena of financial expenditures was not beyond experiment. Company engineers were invited to "ignore costs" in preliminary experiments concerning various phases of the company's operation, including the bulk handling of materials. The time-honored notion that the company must hoard its money received short shrift from Coppers, whose philosophy, as he expressed it, was "You have to spend money to make money."

A flexible budget was introduced which permitted money to be apportioned where it was needed most, at any given time. This caused much head-shaking among the old-timers. But Coppers was not deterred. Not that he did not worry. By nature Coppers was a worrier. He worried incessantly about the company and his role in it.

Nothing caused him more concern than the attitudes and conditions of Nabisco employees, ranging from top executives to the most recently hired bakery worker.

"People just will not be abstractions," Coppers would declare. "We must recognize the fact that people spend the greatest part of their waking hours at their jobs and it is a large part of their life . . . The social and economic problems are interwoven."

Coppers was particularly critical when confronted by dehumanized charts and slick presentations. "We have all seen organizational charts," said Coppers. "Some are very beautiful. The president sits on top, and under him sit all the vice presidents, under them the various department managers, and so on down the line. You can see the whole thing very clearly as you look down at it. But what does it look like when you are looking up at it? Believe me, if it is going to work, the image must be just as clear looking up as looking down. And just as beautiful!"

Though Coppers was not effusive or easy to approach, he did not allow this to prevent rapport with his colleagues. He wanted people to have ready access to him, and he vowed that he would be available at all times. But when air conditioners were installed in his office because of his rose fever, it became necessary for his door to be closed. To solve this problem a special door was made with the upper part of glass so that people would not get the impression that they were being shut out when the door was closed. When he saw somebody peering through the glass, he would often leave his desk and invite them in.

Communication among company employees on all levels was a matter which engaged much of Coppers' attention. A new system was developed wherein heads of departments reported directly to the president. Coppers insisted upon this, not only in order to add his own talents and thinking to the total available brains, but also to keep him in touch with developments within the company. But Coppers did not give directions or make decisions on all matters. "I don't know much about this thing," he might tell a vice president. "I'll ask about it and let you know tomorrow."

Coppers also insisted that top leadership work as a team, exchanging ideas and supplementing one another. He wanted every division to operate with full information about the problems and accomplishments of the company as a whole.

"I am not the least bit hesitant in saying that the most important problem facing supervisors . . . is the challenge of leadership," Coppers told a convention of Nabisco executives. "There is a steady demand to do a better job, to turn out a better product. If we don't recognize this, we will find that the market is slipping away from us . . . But make no mistake about this, the people in any organization are the whole organization. No group or company is bigger or better than the people in it—and it won't go any further than its people take it. A supervisor who offers intelligent leadership and understanding, who can successfully inspire enthusiasm and loyalty, will enjoy a good year."

On all levels of operation Coppers took care to select men with the special qualities needed for the job. He was haunted by the feeling that the company was not doing an effective job in the field of human relations. "The relationship today between an employer and thousands or tens of thousands of employees is without parallel in history," he wrote in *Nabisco*, the company magazine.

"The most important tools we businessmen have to work with are people. If our people feel the same way we do, and are just as anxious for the effort to succeed as we are, we will have the benefit of a thousand heads, in addition to 2,000 hands . . . Industry is merely a part of society. When you try to separate the parts, the whole thing breaks down. I read just recently that there are two good ways of going out of business today. One is to mess up the economic end of your business—your buying, selling and merchandising. The other way is to mess up your employee relations . . .

"Company policy is a screen behind which people hide when they don't know the answers, or when they fear to try something new or different. In our company we threw it out . . . We got tired of having people use 'company policy' as a drunk uses a lamppost—for support rather than light . . .

"Our job is to develop techniques which will permit us to deal with thousands of people, not as abstractions but as *individuals*."

In pursuit of this goal, Coppers made various innovations, many of which were being tried in other corporations. Some were complicated, costly programs. Others were small, simple gestures in the direction of building better relationships.

Coppers guaranteed that whenever possible, promotions would take place from within. "Every employee must have sound incentive for doing a good job," he said. "Among the most important of these is the hope for advancement in his organization.

"As I get around and meet employees, I realize that Nabisco is rich in people. There is a loyalty and esprit de corps about Nabisco people that is not easily matched. There are long service records that speak well for our general satisfaction with our jobs."

This was a postwar era of unrest and militant demands by employees for a greater share in the nation's wealth. Corporations throughout the country were engaged in expanding benefits and providing employees with greater security. Nabisco had lingered behind. Now Coppers sought to catch up with the trend, if not surpass it.

In announcing the company's new pension plan in the spring of 1946, Coppers told Nabisco employees that "For almost two years prior to my election as president, I worked with a committee of department heads to formulate the plan best suited to the needs of the employees and the business. Various types of plans were considered, many of them calling for employee contributions. We felt that the company should assume the full expense of the plan.

"The plan which we adopted involved a substantial increase in the company's annual pension costs. From a present annual cost of about $450,000, it is estimated that the new pension plan will eventually cost about $1,670,000."

The pension plan was the first in a series of benefits provided, including hospital, medical and surgical benefits, major medical assistance, vacations with pay, holidays with pay, group life insurance, improved working conditions, and a system whereby suggestions from employees received various awards, depending upon their value to the company.

Coppers was no less conscious of the need for improved mechanical facilities. Much of the company's plant and equipment was outmoded; the organization had engaged in little or no research for future expansion or greater efficiency; little attention was given to product diversification.

Competitors had been installing band ovens for many years. This was one reason why production had improved and, with it, profits. It seemed impossible for Nabisco to maintain its leadership in the baking industry unless it found ways of modernizing plants and equipment.

"We know that we can't afford to sit still," said Coppers. "An ever-changing market demands a steady flow of new products and the development of improved marketing and distribution techniques." As usual, when involved in an area beyond his immediate experience, he sought advice. During his first years Coppers spent $180,000 for the counsel of various management consultants. The conclusion was unavoidable. The company would have to spend some of its financial resources for a huge modernization program. This meant first and foremost the replacement of the old-fashioned Ferris wheel-like reel ovens—still in operation in most of the company plants—with modern straightaway band ovens whose production capacities were so much more speedy, efficient and profitable.

Most of the Nabisco bakeries were located in the middle of urban areas where any great extension of factory footage was impossible. Since the band oven could not operate vertically, there was no alternative if the company was to modernize—but to declare the old factories obsolete, buy land outside the city (or within it if sufficient area was available), and build a new type of bakery.

An entirely new philosophy was needed to justify spending many millions of dollars. Coppers was just the man to face realities when he saw them. "We plan on spending $15,000,000 to $20,000,000 [this sum was to go beyond $200,000,000 before the program was concluded] on expansion and modernization as fast as we can," Coppers told *Investor's Reader* in an interview.

But mechanization was not only a matter of the band oven, important as that was. A variety of other mechanical contrivances used in the baking of cookies and crackers had not been updated for years. There was a need for a new look at mechanical innovations for dough feeders, packers, weighers, bundlers and other devices.

Coppers called upon Russell Shultz to get a program organized and under way. Shultz had serious doubts about whether "any one individual could change the thinking of an organization which so long had been practicing conservative tactics." But with the help of experienced men like John J. Toomey, former vice president for production, he accepted the assignment. Shultz also undertook a study of improvements in bulk handling of the vast quantity of raw materials which the company used in bakeries all over the nation. By 1948 one bakery—located in New York—was beginning to pump shortening direct from railroad tank cars into bulk storage, thus eliminating the handling of the old-fashioned lard barrel or drum.

Stainless steel or glass-lined cars, especially designed for Nabisco, were tested and used. Everything was done to encourage experimentation in new ways of doing things. There were experiments in the bulk handling of flour with an eye to the potential application of the results to sugar, starch and cocoa. Two pilot cars were built for this purpose.

For years flour had been shipped to bakeries in 100-pound sacks loaded into cars with an 80,000-pound capacity. New cars now could handle more than 100,000 pounds and were emptied by pneumatic piping. Continuous mix equipment began to be used in the production line in various bakeries.

One of the problems of mechanization was the fact that, in the words of Shultz, "We had no research and we did not know the fundamental things that we should have known. We have had to find these out by long and tedious work. We have had to run down all of the so-called baking art to find out what was true and what was not true."

Aided by what research and development were discovering, and propelled by the obvious need, Nabisco began constructing new bakeries equipped with band ovens. In a decade more than $150,000,-000 was spent on new plants in Houston, Portland, Ore., Chicago, Philadelphia, Toronto and Montreal, as well as major renovations in Pittsburgh, Denver, St. Louis and elsewhere.

The staggering amount of detail involved in such radical changes demanded a coordination unprecedented in the company's history. Then what had seemed impossible happened: the building or renovation of one huge bakery after another, and the replacement of obsolete equipment with modern mechanical baking machinery.

The plant rebuilding program was not confined to the cracker business. New bread bakeries were built at Plattsburg in 1949, Cleveland in 1950, Elmira in 1950, Rochester in 1951, Toronto in 1952. Another Albany bread bakery was opened. A new pretzel bakery was built in Chicago.

When Coppers became president, the company already had at Toledo the largest soft-wheat mill in the world, with a storage capacity of 6,400,000 bushels. Other mills were located at Carthage, Missouri, and Cheney, Washington. Its own mills supplied the company with 80 per cent of its flour. Now these operations were expanded to keep abreast of the needs of the new baking machines.

A large building and modernization program took place in the printing and carton operations at Beacon, New York, and Marseilles, Illinois, and at Nabisco Foods, Ltd., in Welwyn Garden City, England, where Shredded Wheat was made.

The image of the National Biscuit Company began to change physically as well as psychologically. Instead of the old multistoried red brick feudal-looking bakeries within the city limits, low, streamlined, bright-looking modern bakery buildings appeared of which any community could be proud. Employees were pleased to work in buildings which provided adequate parking facilities, good lighting, improved ventilation, air conditioning in cafeterias, offices and locker rooms.

There had been considerable muttering in some circles about the Coppers spending policy. Questions were raised at numerous annual shareholder meetings.

"What caused Nabisco profits to drop?" a shareholder asked.

"What do you believe the future holds for the company and employees?" another wanted to know.

Nabisco, the company employee publication, listed frequent questions under the heading "Why are profits down, Mr. Coppers?"

Coppers explained that because of the vast expenditures, "the rate of profits in relation to sales has declined. Also, the need for expansion made it desirable to reinvest a larger portion of profits in the business, and this has held down dividend payments. In the long run, however, we believe that this policy is in the best interest of the stockholders and benefits other team members as well."

The construction of an eight-oven biscuit and cracker bakery in Fair Lawn, New Jersey, some twenty miles northwest of New York City, was the climax of the multimillion-dollar reconstruction program. On October 27, 1958, the new bakery, which was claimed to be the finest plant of its kind in the world, was officially opened.

This marked the completion of a twelve-year expansion program. According to Coppers, "We're not through with expansion and modernization, but we have accomplished what we set out to do."

For more than half a century the company's New York bakeries had provided it with the largest production unit in the country. It was claimed that the complex of buildings making up the 14th Street bakery, laboratory and executive offices, comprised the largest bakery in the world. The closing of the Manhattan plant, in operation since the days of the New York Biscuit Company before the turn of the century, brought back nostalgic memories. Sentimental old-timers eyed the red brick multistoried buildings sadly as they were sold for use by smaller industries.

The dedication ceremonies at the Fair Lawn bakery and laboratory were impressive. With George Coppers at the formal dedication ceremony were New Jersey's governor, Robert B. Meyner, and Fair Lawn's mayor, Richard J. Vander Plaat. During the first week some 19,000 people visited the plant, including Nabisco employees and their families, customers, suppliers and the company's new neighbors in Fair Lawn.

Many employees who had worked in the New York bakeries now shifted to New Jersey. Many already lived in the state, since it was convenient to the New York bakery.

The new bakery was—and remains—an impressive sight. Occupying forty acres in the Fair Lawn Industrial Park, it embodied all of the scientific and practical knowledge acquired by company engineers and production experts since Coppers had launched his vast program a dozen years earlier, and before. The most advanced materials-handling, production, and packaging techniques and equipment devised to date were utilized to the fullest. The plant was geared to produce 177,000,000 pounds of crackers and cookies a year, a total which has been steadily increased.

It took three years for the Fair Lawn plant to be constructed. Its modern mechanical equipment included a huge master control console, sometimes referred to as an electronic brain, used for directing the automatic delivery of ingredients in sequence from the storage facilities to any one of sixteen mixing machines.

Within a short distance of the bakery was Nabisco's ultra-modern and fully equipped research center, housing the company's laboratory, the mechanical development department, and experimental baking division. It was the first time that these three important phases of the company's research had been located under one roof.

Here were facilities for expanding the company's line of products and developing the most modern production methods known in the industry. Whether a new product or ingredient, a new method of processing or packaging, a new piece of equipment, the origin and testing ground could now be the new Nabisco Research Center.

The research laboratory had several divisions involved in scientific research and quality control.

The analytical division was organized to work mostly on raw materials, analyzing them to make sure they met the company's quality specifications. Sub-laboratories located in the individual bakeries around the country analyzed raw materials at the scene of delivery and tested finished products for quality. Under the direct supervision of the production department, they were guided in their activities by the analytical division. The final function of the analytical division was to help other divisions by doing chemical analyses for them upon request.

Work in the process and products division of the Fair Lawn laboratory covered a wide range of activities from basic research to trouble shooting for other departments. Studies ranged from analyzing new types of icings to ideas in the processing of dog food.

The packaging control function of the laboratory measured the physical properties of packaging materials to insure freshness in various climates, ranging from hot, muggy weather to freezing or below-zero temperatures.

In its mechanical development department machines could now be conceived which were unavailable anywhere in the world. The department was equipped to carry a new piece of equipment from the design and drawing-board stages right through to building the first production unit.

An outstanding example of such new ideas was what is known as the "stack pack," first used in packaging Premium Saltines. In this pioneer method of packaging, the crackers were lined up on their edges, then a specific number sealed in wax paper. This permitted the consumer to open one pack at a time, remove the crackers, and then close the pack until the next time. This packaging was soon used for a variety of other products.

Experimental baking could be carried on at the laboratory in a complete pilot bakery. All mixing, baking and icing facilities were provided. The purpose of the experimental baking section, of course, was to develop and test-run new products so that the company could know exactly how a particular variety would bake when actually in production in its many bakeries. The oven in the experimental bakery was built exactly like band ovens, but it was only one-quarter as long.

George Coppers stood before the assembled gathering at the dedication exercises at the Fair Lawn bakery—visiting dignitaries, executives, directors and employees. The job that so many people had said could not be done had been accomplished. Fair Lawn was a symbol of this. The Coppers program had extended to almost all the operations of the company; but the major portion had been devoted to improving the company's position in biscuit and cracker production, the basic and largest part of the business. The company had spent more than $200,000,000, financed entirely from earnings. This mammoth modernization program had been successfully carried out without borrowing a single penny!

When it was his turn to say a few words, Coppers described some of the problems attached to the Nabisco modernization program. "Perhaps the biggest problem . . . is that of slim profit margins," he said. "The gains we have made in production efficiency, impressive as they have been, have not kept pace with increasing labor and material costs. A reduction in the cost of doing business is a primary aim in our own program and we are undertaking a continuing survey of production and distribution expenses.

"We feel the surest path to satisfactory earnings lies in our own ability to improve the efficiency of our operations. If we can make headway in this direction, National Biscuit should do well . . .

"We have learned that our most important asset does not appear on the balance sheet. It is the people, the employees who make the thing click . . .

"We are presently completing a twelve-year building program which gives us what we believe to be the most modern production set-up in our industry. Yet, we know that we can't afford to sit still. An ever-changing market demands a steady flow of new products and the development of improved marketing and distribution techniques."

As George H. Coppers looked over the audience and described the various facilities they were about to see on their tour of the new bakery and its adjoining laboratory, his words emerged in sharp, clipped, lawyer-like phrases. As he spoke, his voice had a resonant, confident ring.

He did not hesitate or stammer. His eyes were on the future. His job was, in many ways, just beginning.

Quality-control testing at Research Center, Fair Lawn, New Jersey

"Tenderness tester" checks cracker strength and crispness ▸

Food chemist explores ingredient reactions.

The central control panel of modern Nabisco bakeries electronically directs the flow of ingredients

Railroad cars of wheat are tipped and emptied at Toledo mill.
Automatic machines ease stack packs into Ritz Cracker cartons.

300-foot band ovens in the Chicago bakery ▸
A battery of cookie mixers

TWENTY-TWO

Cookies,
Crackers and Coppers

IF ONE WORD could characterize the leadership of George H. Coppers, that word was "change." For example, if ever a product was a reliable profit maker year in and out, it was Barnum's Animal Crackers. They were not only popular at home, they were exported to some seventy countries around the world with more than five million pounds sold annually. Yet Coppers refused to let success stand in the way of critical examination.

Encouraged by this attitude, a youthful scientist spent long hours in the Fair Lawn laboratory studying ways of improving the efficiency of baking animal crackers. The method had been unchanged for decades. But the scientist had a new idea. He experimented. Finally he made his report. His idea was simple.

When a child opens the gaily colored cardboard "cage" with its ribbon handle, he encounters a variety of creatures. These might include tigers, elephants in different poses, a bear, a hippopotamus, a rhinoceros, a polar bear, a horse, a sheep, a dog, a lion, a jaguar, a bison, a bull.

The proposal was that animal crackers be produced in a new way. A different type of die, it was explained, could make the animals more identifiable.

The proposal was accepted. Animal crackers became more recognizable. Their appeal was increased—and also their sale.

◀ *Chairman George H. Coppers and President Lee S. Bickmore enter the board room.*

Improvements in form, formula, production methods, appearance, packaging and promotion were made on scores of other Nabisco products. Sometimes changes were small and subtle, scarcely detectable. Others were more obvious. Sometimes products—long part of the American way of life—were discontinued, judged to be outdated in taste, lacking in promotional sales potential, or of doubtful profit potential.

In bread baking, too, there were changes. Coppers thought bread could be made profitable. The bread division, a stepchild since the days of A. W. Green, now began to receive a surprising measure of attention. For the first time a vice president was put in charge.

At one time the company had operated some eighteen bread bakeries, located from Burlington, Vermont, to Houston, Texas, producing bread, rolls, cake, doughnuts, pies. The division actually was an industry within an industry. However, the bread business did not prosper. By the 1950's there were just a dozen or so bakeries left in the company.

Although bread, crackers and cookies are all part of the baking industry, nevertheless, the baking of bread is different in many important respects from that of biscuits. Because bread was more perishable than cookies or crackers, it needed faster handling and direct distribution from the salesman to the storekeeper.

One of the problems in the past had been that the baking and distribution of bread had not been given specialized attention. Such special consideration was required because bread baking—seemingly identical with biscuit production—was in fact a different industry. It had its own special production and distribution methods, its own trucks, its own staff. It was not advisable (or even possible) to administer the bread division in the same manner as other divisions of the company.

Coppers realized that if very little had been done to modernize the manufacture of crackers and cookies, even less had been done in the bread division. He was resolved to introduce modern techniques here as he had elsewhere.

By 1960 the Syracuse bread bakery was utilizing a continuous method of producing white bread. It succeeded in increasing the popularity of the company's bread throughout Ohio, Pennsylvania, and various parts of New York. The Cleveland premiere of "miracle mix" bread was the result of an extensive testing program conducted at the Nabisco plant in Syracuse. As a result of such efforts the company developed four continuous-mix plants to supply its markets, with other plants specializing in other related products such as rolls and pastries.

About this time Nabisco formally opened its Albany bread bakery, at that time the newest and best equipped company bread-making facility. Millbrook, a quality loaf of enriched bread, was originally introduced by the National Biscuit Company at its bakeries in Pittsburgh, Burlington and Wilmington, N.C. The company made the product available throughout the upper New York State area accompanied by wide-scale advertising and promotional activities.*

To test, to experiment—not to be satisfied with success—this philosophy led to taking a new look even at Nabisco's popular dog food, Milk-Bone.

As far back as 1908 Milk-Bone had been one of the largest-selling dog biscuits in the country. When the Milk-Bone operation was obtained by Nabisco in 1931 from the F. H. Bennett Biscuit Company, the acquisition at first was considered of small value contrasted with other items that the Bennett Company manufactured. These included the well-established Wheatsworth line of products. However, as years passed, Wheatsworth disappeared from the scene and Milk-Bone remained.

Milk-Bone achieved its popularity as a dog's "dessert." Nabisco advertisements described it as "an additional food for the dog, helping to keep his teeth clean, giving him something to chew on, helping cleanse his breath." In effect, Milk-Bone was a "nourishing snack for canines."

Until 1955 Milk-Bone had been produced in New York. However, the bakery could not manufacture enough to meet the increasing demand. So the Nabisco bakery in Buffalo was converted into a Milk-Bone manufacturing plant, with various new production methods used to make production speedier and more efficient. The same sanitary and quality-control procedures were practiced as with other Nabisco products. Band ovens were introduced, basically similar to those used in biscuit baking but somewhat wider and shorter.

Today the use of dog biscuits carrying the Milk-Bone trademark

* In 1968 NBC decided to discontinue its bread business and sold its entire division to the Interstate Bakery Corporation. Nabisco explained that "a company of our size should have everything on national distribution and we could not go nationwide in the bread business so there was no reason to stay in it."

has expanded considerably since the early beginning days in a corner of F. H. Bennett's Lower East Side bakery in New York. In recent years a new dog biscuit called "Flavor Snacks," consisting of six individual flavors and colors, has been added. In any given year over three billion Milk-Bone brand bone-shaped dog biscuits are devoured by millions of bone-hungry dogs.

Special attention was now given to the company's complex purchasing operation. The function of the company's purchasing department had been from the start to buy to the best advantage the materials and equipment needed to conduct the company's business. The department has had three major areas of responsibility: purchasing wheat, flour and grain products, which involves the running of three flour mills; purchasing raw materials and equipment, which includes everything from automobile parts to butter; and purchasing materials for Nabisco's packaging requirements, which includes operating a paperboard mill and printing plants located at Beacon, New York, and Marseilles, Illinois.

As Nabisco entered the second half of the twentieth century, its purchasing experts were buying over 4,000,000 pounds of cheese a year, 40,000,000 pounds of cocoa-bean products, 2,000,000 pounds of butter, 17,000,000 pounds of corn syrups, 7,500,000 pounds of eggs, 12,000,000 pounds of figs, 4,000,000 pounds of honey, 8,500,-000 pounds of sodium bicarbonate, 6,500,000 pounds of peanut butter, 23,000,000 pounds of salt, and 10,000,000 cwt. (hundredweight or hundred pounds) of flour of all kinds.

"From Zanzibar, East Africa, we get our cloves," a purchasing department circular explained. "Mace comes from the West Indies. Figs are gathered in California and in the groves of Turkey, Spain and Portugal. Many green acres of California yield their supply of currants. Cinnamon is gathered from Indonesia in the East Indies; ginger roots from Jamaica in the West Indies. From Jamaica also is gathered the allspice. Citron comes from Puerto Rico. From California come the oils of lemon and orange. California, too, yields almonds and walnut meats. Grated pineapple from the Hawaiian Islands. Caraway seeds come from Holland, coconut oil from Ceylon and the Philippines."

Encouraged by Coppers, production, traffic and research executives accelerated the installation of methods for bulk handling of raw materials. As early as March 1935 the company had explored the possibility of handling flour in bulk cars. The purpose was to do away with costs of transporting flour in 100-pound bags both at the mill and in the bakery. The unsanitary aspects of using and reusing flour bags were always a problem, and the danger of foreign substances such as bag tags and strings getting into the dough was always present. The war prevented any real progress until the mid 1940's.

After the war various Nabisco departments worked with railroad companies to bring about bulk deliveries of almost all ingredients. Installations were made in new bakeries for the receipt of bulk flour.

Most major ingredients, previously received in small units, were now handled in bulk. All this made it necessary to enlarge the containers in which they were stored. Gone was the familiar scene of manual handling of flour and sugar in cartons or paper sacks. Gone, too, were the broken sacks, high wastes, shrinkage, dust, and high accident potential.

The old-fashioned barrel which, together with the sack, was one of the major means of supplying raw materials to the bakery in past years, virtually disappeared. Barrels were a nuisance, a time consumer, an expense and a threat to health. They had to be emptied and cleaned. Foreign substances were a constant worry. They were difficult to move, and a chronic problem that harassed the baking industry for many years.

Bulk handling was responsible for changing the entire concept of "warehousing" raw materials. In most industries warehousing takes place *after* the product has been produced or packaged. It is then kept in storage until distributed and sold. Dealing for the most part in perishable products, Nabisco does its warehousing *before* the product is manufactured. By storing raw materials before they are put on the production line, a gigantic never-ending backlog of commodities is made available.

The introduction of giant tank cars, carrying all kinds of liquid products from syrup to shortening, permits such warehousing to take place on a huge scale. Liquid products are pumped out of tank cars. Flour is brought to the bakeries in mammoth plastic-lined railroad cars direct from the flour mill and sucked up pneumatically by gigantic vacuum equipment at the rate of some twenty tons an hour. Tank cars of sugar roll into the bakeries, where they are also unloaded mechanically.

The only major commodity that arrives in the old-fashioned way is salt. When salt is improperly stored, it tends to absorb moisture and become lumpy. It must be free-flowing to be used as topping for crackers. So it is transported in 100-pound paper bags in the traditional manner. An average carload of salt is about 70,000 pounds.

Part of the Coppers "revolution" was the emphasis placed on effective market research and carefully researched programs of merchandising. Impatient as usual with hit-or-miss methods, Coppers would grow red around the neck—always an alarming sign to his subordinates—when unscientific or sloppy methods were employed to "guess" which products would succeed or what marketing methods should be employed. As one former advertising executive pointed out, "When Coppers was elected president . . . research facilities were at a minimum and no real advertising policy existed. Coppers had the courage not only to launch an extensive plant modernization program but to establish an adequate research facility. He backed his belief in merchandising and advertising with the establishment of a consistent, effective policy that continues to be maintained."

A series of major innovations in the organizational structure of the company were taken, which contributed greatly to its future progress.

A new division was established in the fall of 1954 called the "special products division," designed to handle the sales of such products as cereal and dog food varieties. Heretofore, these items had been sold and delivered directly to retail stores together with biscuit and cracker products. Now they were to be sold and delivered through wholesale channels.

The special products division was originally set up to serve only the Pacific Coast. It gradually moved eastward until it covered the entire country. "We are enthusiastic about the formation of the special products division," Coppers told shareholders. "It places a responsibility for the promotion and sales of our cereal and dog food items with an organization specifically designed for the purpose. It will enable us more readily to add to our line new products which do not require store-door distribution and it leaves the company's regular sales organization free to concentrate its full efforts on our extensive cookie and cracker line."

The new division proved particularly useful as the company began to diversify its products. Nabisco entered the cake-mix business when it purchased Hills Brothers, makers of the famous Dromedary line of prepared baking mixes, dates and candied fruits, one of the oldest fruit companies in the country, dating back to 1871. Later the company purchased Ranger Joe, processors of the presweetened cereals Wheat Honeys and Rice Honeys.

"For our own protection," Coppers told shareholders, "it was important that we enter these fields . . . We set up the special products division to distribute cereals and dog foods through wholesalers and chain store warehouses . . . The average shelf life of most of our products is about 30 days, although improved packaging is extending that. Cereals and pet foods have a much longer life and it was expensive to market them through our regular sales division. So, to make them more competitive, we instituted the special products division."

Although Coppers was not trained in advertising, he recognized the need for stepping up the company's advertising program. "Our experience . . . gives ample testimony that consistent advertising is the most successful method of promoting volume sales," he stated. "This makes possible more economies in mass production manufacture and distribution. Such an advertising program, carefully planned and administered, takes the story of Nabisco products to millions of people in the most effective possible way. As the front line of our selling effort year after year, our advertising builds consumer acceptance, sales and profits."

The rise of the supermarket had, more than ever, left the choice of product brands to the consumer. The grocery clerk, traditionally available to recommend a product or a brand to the consumer, was no longer a store fixture. Advertising replaced him. Clear brand preferences became more important than ever. By 1952 Nabisco's expenditures for advertising were over $9,000,000 or about 2.6 per cent of total sales.

But Coppers was not satisfied with the progress made. He realized that a new era was demanding much more in the way of new ideas. This new era looming before the National Biscuit Company featured self-service, attractive packaging, impulse buying, vending machine salesmanship, widespread use of transparent cellophane permitting the consumer to see what he was buying before he took the package from the shelf. Intensive national brand advertising also placed a heavy responsibility on the science of market research.

Consumer preferences and prejudices, regional buying habits, became a sphere of merchandising which Nabisco leaders had to know and understand. Salesmen now had to be experts on distribution and display. They had to do more than merely provide general service; they had to become professionals in visual problems and the science of space utilization.

There was scarcely a corner of the company's huge domain that was not invaded by the philosophy of "change." Even the company insignia, which A. W. Green had conceived and so jealously protected, was not above critical study in light of new selling conditions and shopping methods.

For a long time the company and its various agencies had been looking for a visual emblem that could give its products a more conspicuous family identity. The Nabisco reputation and image were so highly respected, it was thought that this identification should be made as prominent and at the same time aesthetically satisfying as possible.

Particularly was such identification needed with the coming of the supermarket. Nabisco products had to be quickly identified. The package on the shelf, as well as the advertising, had to speak for itself. And the most important message it could deliver, the company believed, was "This is a Nabisco product."

In the spring of 1952, therefore, the company announced that a bright red triangular seal had been designed which incorporated the famous Nabisco trademark, and it would be placed on the upper left hand corner of an increasing number of the company's packages.

The red triangle was a product of joint thinking of Nabisco's advertising people, advertising agencies and design consultants. Even when the triangle clashed with the design of the package, it was felt it served a valuable merchandising function.

The first Nabisco advertisement carrying the triangle appeared in *Life* magazine in January 1953: "So you can always be sure you're getting only the finest, freshest, most flavorful crackers and cookies . . . so you and millions of American homemakers will not be misled into accepting substitutes . . . this famous Red Seal you know you can trust is on the easy-to-see upper left hand corner of every NABISCO package. Look for it when you buy!"

To Coppers and the men around him each package had to be examined not so much for design as for its attraction for the housewife. Appearance must be evaluated not on how a product looked on an executive's desk, but how it demanded attention on the supermarket shelf. Matters of color, shape, typography, the visual illustration of the product within and the use of transparent cellophane now emerged as urgent considerations.

Production facilities, while always demanding careful attention, were no longer the problem they had once been. Miracles of modern mechanization saw to that. Now the need was for merchandising and marketing aids. The need particularly was for packaging that sold itself. The package was no longer a mere container. Each package must be a visible advertisement for the product within it and for the company behind it. The image of the company was not only reflected and created by contents, but by the exterior package as well.

In many ways the pioneering of A. W. Green was coming to fruition. In the words of Vernon L. Fladager in *The Selling Power of Packaging*, the package was "a potent new weapon for the business strategist, an amazingly versatile new mechanism to project automation out of the factory and field into the outermost periphery of the marketing territory, a super self-salesman, an advertising medium, and a public relations representative at the grass roots level of 'point of use'!"

One of the problems which constantly harassed package designers was the use of available machinery in the creation of new package ideas. Sometimes a completely new package concept would evolve, differing in size or shape from any Nabisco package previously used. While such a creation might provide a promising sales possibility, it might be discovered that there was no available machinery that could produce the product in the form or size or manner called for by the new package proposed.

Thus the designer had to discipline his creative ideas by what was practical from the point of view of available machines. And this was not always easy.

Occasionally there were packaging ideas of such assured potential sales value that new machinery would be designed and constructed at considerable cost to make them possible. But this was rare, and usually the discipline of designing packaging for available machinery was necessary.

Packaging was also being subjected to a test in a new distribution system. In the early 1960's *Fortune* hazarded the guess that the use of vending machines "may be extended enormously as the result of the recent perfection by two separate companies of machines capable of handling paper money as well as coins. [According to *Vend Magazine*, retail sales through vending machines reached a total of approximately $3,500,000,000 in 1964.] Vending machines are already being used extensively for mass feeding operations—quite important, since restaurants employ roughly 1,500,000 workers. General Electric, for example, has converted the main cafeteria of its Lynn, Massachusetts, plant, where it employed some 13,500 men and women, to vending operation, and the company has added sixteen vending stations for light snacks . . . American Motors feeds 10,000 employees from vending machines in its Kenosha, Wisconsin, plant . . ."

It was estimated in 1964 that every 24 hours Americans drop about 83,000,000 coins into merchandise-vending devices.

While corporations everywhere were beginning to use automated machines for dispensing products ranging from hosiery to hot coffee, the National Biscuit Company had not fully recognized this potentiality. As far back as 1938 the company had launched its NAB products, which were small packets of some of its most popular crackers and cookies. The manufacture of NABs permitted Nabisco salesmen not only to increase their income from sales to large stores, but supplied good reason for getting in touch with smaller establishments throughout the country which had not previously been National Biscuit Company customers. NABs also provided a valuable sales potential in the restaurant trade. During the 1940's special early vending machines called "NAB Diners" were placed in many plants and offices throughout the country. But their success was limited and their use was not widespread.

In their careful scrutiny of the popular appeal of Nabisco products, Coppers and his staff noted that NAB seemed to be slackening in sales and popularity. And this was taking place in an era when self-service, special packaging and vending were moving forward aggressively and taking with them products of all types, including ready-to-eat crackers and cookies.

It was not until the 1950's that Nabisco established a special automatic merchandising division and halted the downward trend of its NAB sales. One of the duties of employees of this division was to call on vending operators and to make a special effort to place NAB merchandise in vending machines that were appearing by the thousands throughout the country.

Integrating NAB into the vending-machine boom was easier to say than do. A great amount of research and market study was necessary. Faster packaging machinery had to be improvised so that NABs could be produced in quantities necessary to keep up with vending-machine requirements. Because of the special size requirements of the machines, it was necessary to provide NABs in a variety of sizes, heights and types of cookies and crackers.

In 1965 there were over 700,000 confection-vending machines in use in America, of which about half displayed NAB merchandise regularly. The most popular NAB product sold in vending machines has been the cheese-peanut butter sandwich, closely followed by Oreo Creme Sandwich, Fig Newton cakes, Lorna Doone shortbread, cheese-on-rye sandwich, and Cheese-Tid-Bits crackers. NAB packets are sold in many parts of the world, including Germany, England, France, Italy, Turkey, Japan, Korea, Okinawa.

So great had been the expansion of Nabisco enterprises in the sales, advertising and marketing field that, on both the national and the international front, there was need for a department to coordinate these activities. As a result a new "general advertising department" was created in the winter of 1959. Included was Nabisco's famous test kitchen, which developed consumer promotional material and assisted in product research. A year later the company further extended its communications facilities by establishing its first official public relations department.

Earlier Coppers had turned his attention to establishing a Nabisco sanitation department, a suggestion made by his successor, E. Wheeler Barto, general counsel. While the company had from the start emphasized purity and quality, it had lagged in establishing a formal department. Following the end of World War II, Coppers characteristically not only helped establish a special department but specified that its manager report directly to him. Recognizing the similarity between public health problems and the company's, Coppers staffed the new division with people trained in public health work.

Nor did the wave of change stop there. A division previously known as "corporate development" now became the "new products division," which, said Coppers, "will have the jurisdiction over the development of new products and varieties. This will include the search for and development of ideas for new products and supervision of their market research and consumer and sales testing."

Its formation was based on the conviction that the development of new products was so important to Nabisco's future that a group of highly trained administrators should be free to concentrate on them exclusively. The company had been slow to recognize this. Not enough ideas for new products were put forward. When they were, there was often difficulty in obtaining approval. When the company's laboratory would propose a new cracker or cookie, there were always some who were confident it could not succeed. Coppers wanted to change this by introducing a department with the specific responsibility of examining all ideas and putting them to a fair test.

All of these experiments cost money. Lots of it. During the late 1940's and early 1950's some Nabisco directors and shareholders had doubts about the wisdom of Coppers' program of spending. But such doubts were offset by the fact that Nabisco continued to realize healthy profits. In 1945, when Coppers became president, the price of Nabisco common stock on the market ranged from 23½ to 34½. In the ensuing years the prices, naturally, fluctuated. However, by 1953 the low was 34 and the high was 38 and as Coppers approached the end of his term of leadership, the low was 49¾ and the high was 77⅞. By 1961 the low was 70½ and the high was 94½.

Sales increased from $220,000,000 in 1946 to over $450,000,000 in 1960. By 1960 Nabisco was distributing the greatest quantity of baked goods ever produced by a single company. A special system of sales discounts and promotional advertising allowances extended to dealers resulted in improving relations with the trade and an increase in Nabisco's share of the market.

In 1960 many of the nation's top business and financial executives were asked by *Dun's Review* and *Modern Industry* to name the twenty best-managed companies in the United States. The magazine asked the panel members to look over the nation's manufacturing concerns and make their choice. The National Biscuit Company was named as one of the select twenty. The group of executives who made up the "jury" stated further that among the reasons for the selection were such characteristics as "concentration on developing a good supply of aggressive, intelligent executives; strength in long range planning and emphasis on research and development."

The company was obviously moving ahead—and growing younger as it did so. With the moving of the Nabisco bakeries from 14th Street in Manhattan to Fair Lawn, New Jersey, it was inevitable that the executive offices of the company—located alongside the bakery in New York for so many years—also would be located elsewhere. But where?

There were those within the company who felt that the general offices of Nabisco should be located near the company's bakery, a precedent that had been established over the years. But, again, traditional practices had to bow to change. It was finally decided that the company executive departments would achieve the maximum efficiency if they remained within the city, where it would be much easier to obtain clerical and secretarial assistance and other services required by the executive branch of the company.

So on February 2, 1957, Nabisco's general offices were moved from the site they had owned and occupied for more than fifty years on the Lower West Side of New York City (there had been two sites: 85 Ninth Avenue and 449 West 14th Street) to six floors in a thirty-story midtown skyscraper located on Park Avenue between 55th and 56th Streets.

Over 100 men and eight vans, working round the clock, moved 500 tons of equipment—over 1,400 pounds per employee—uptown to the new headquarters. The job took the better part of a weekend.

"The warmly attractive offices are but one indication of the changes taking place at National Biscuit," stated *Investor's Reader*, a publication of Merrill Lynch, Pierce, Fenner & Beane. (It was the same publication some years before that had so sharply criticized the National Biscuit Company for failing to show signs of progress.) "Late this year or early in 1958 the eight ovens in its new plant in Fair Lawn, New Jersey, will be ready for biscuit baking. This will mark completion of a 12 year expansion program of the nation's #1 cracker baker."

The move to Park Avenue marked a culmination of the Coppers program. In his last report to shareholders in 1959 Coppers pointed out that the company had had "the finest year in its corporate history . . . Both sales and earnings showed substantial gains and in each case reached record levels."

The reshaping of Nabisco's policy and program in a relatively short span of years had not, of course, been due solely to Coppers' leadership. He would have been the first to share credit with the team he had built. And among those on his team none had impressed more favorably than the dynamic, personable executive vice president, Lee Bickmore.

Sophisticated in the ways of the industrial world, Coppers was concerned for some time about Bickmore. Coppers feared that Bickmore might be lured away by other corporations in need of a man of his special talents.

"We will lose him if we don't do something about him," Coppers once confided to a company director. "Lee Bickmore is the best marketing man we have. And they are hard to come by."

On April 25, 1960, George Coppers recommended to the board of directors that he continue his leadership as chief executive officer and chairman of the board, and that Lee Bickmore assume the responsibilities of the presidency. The board agreed.

But George H. Coppers did not live out the year. On December 28, 1960, he passed away in his sleep at the age of fifty-eight at his home in Englewood, New Jersey.

Funeral services were held in Englewood on Friday, December 30. In lieu of flowers the family requested donations to the American Heart Fund, the American Red Cross or the YMCA.

A few years before his death a leading periodical had sent George Coppers a questionnaire which included the question "What three personal characteristics do you feel are most needed by the president?"

Coppers answered in order of importance: "Objectivity, patience, and understanding."

"What personal quality or lack in yourself which might be considered a liability in executive jobs," the periodical asked, "have you had to struggle with most during your rise to the top?"

Coppers answered: "Patience."

"What personal philosophy or maxim has given you the most courage in living through business crises?"

Wrote Coppers: "This will look different tomorrow."

Despite his efforts to build a leadership team, the death of George H. Coppers was a severe loss to the company that he had helped almost reconstruct in scarcely more than a decade. But there were other losses, too.

On September 26, 1948, Edward S. Moore had died. Son of William H. (Judge) Moore, Edward had served as a director for twenty-eight years. Now on October 23, 1959, Edward S. Moore, Jr., his son, who had served as executive vice president, died prematurely at the age of fifty-three. Two months later Paul Moore, the second son of Judge Moore, died after forty-two years as director. With these losses and subsequent sale of company stock holdings, the Moore family ceased to play a dominant role in Nabisco affairs. Company leadership at this point passed more completely into the hands of modern professional managers. William H. Moore, son of Paul Moore, was elected a Nabisco director in 1959. He was chairman of the board of Bankers Trust Company, New York.

Mourning the passing of Coppers, the company stated, "National Biscuit Company suffered a grievous loss in the sudden death of Chairman George H. Coppers. Mr. Coppers made tremendous contributions during the 15 years he led the company. Perhaps the greatest of these was the development of a team of capable associates who occupy key positions throughout the company."

Of all of the "capable associates" whom Coppers had developed, none was to show greater capabilities for leadership and imagination —for seeing into the future and acting in advance of events—than the salesman from Pocatello, Idaho, Lee Bickmore.

TWENTY-THREE

Salesman in the Saddle

"THERE ARE three ways to succeed in business," a college professor once said as he introduced Lee Smith Bickmore to his class. "The first way is to be the boss's son. Now, of course, that isn't always possible. The second way to succeed in business is to marry the boss's daughter. The third way is to work as Lee S. Bickmore has worked."

To understand how "Lee S. Bickmore has worked," it is necessary to go back more than a century and look to the Mormon country which was once Indian territory.

Paradise was a tiny valley town in northern Utah, not visible on most maps. Among its several hundred inhabitants were Danforth and Jane Bickmore, a Mormon couple whose ancestors had crossed the plains from New England decades before. On June 5, 1908—just a dozen years after Utah was admitted to the Union—a third son was born to them, Lee Smith Bickmore.

There were to be four brothers in all and two sisters before Mrs. Bickmore died in the influenza epidemic of 1918. Following the remarriage of Danforth Bickmore, two more sisters and one brother were added to the family.

Danforth McArthur Bickmore, whose ancestors reached back into Scotland, was a man of strong opinions about most matters, including obedience in children, the need for education, and the importance of hard work. A graduate of Brigham Young College when

◀ *Lee S. Bickmore with Nabisco varieties from overseas*

it was located in nearby Logan, Utah, Mr. Bickmore became principal of the Paradise elementary school. He loved the soil and distrusted urban living. He thought even a hamlet the size of Paradise was no place to rear children. So, early in Lee Bickmore's life the family moved to a farm on the outskirts of town where the boy learned to milk cows, ride and rope, as well as his three R's in elementary school.

Young Lee showed signs of being bright and determined to advance himself. His father observed this, and approved. Occasionally Danforth Bickmore would take his children to Salt Lake City in the family automobile, about a four-hour drive away. Visiting such a large metropolis from the tiny village of Paradise was a treat for the children. The capital of Utah and of the Mormon Church, Salt Lake City was a tree-lined community—the first of many Utah towns laid out by the Mormons foursquare with the compass.

Lee did well in high school. At first he thought he might be a physician. But money was scarce, so he went to Utah State University at Logan, about twelve miles north of Paradise near the Idaho border.* The college, founded in 1888, was dedicated to the principles of Brigham Young, who had urged the teaching of scientific agriculture in Utah.

Lee Bickmore was an alert dark-haired, well-built youth with a frequent smile and an apparently limitless supply of energy. As a young man Bickmore debated in high school, college and as a member of the church, in which there are no paid ministers. As a result he found that he was able to speak in public with confidence, a facility that served him well in the future.

Although he was a good athlete, he had little time for sports. After school hours and in summers he worked at the J. C. Penney store in Logan as a shipping clerk.

When Bickmore graduated in 1931 with a degree in business administration, the nation was suffering its worst economic depression. He was able to keep his job at the J. C. Penney store, but there did not seem much future there. Rulon Bickmore, Lee's older brother, appeared to be making better progress working as a salesman for the

---

* In later years the name was changed to the State University of Agriculture and Applied Science. When Lee Bickmore became an officer of the National Biscuit Company, he applied for membership in the University Club of New York City. There was some question as to Bickmore's eligibility because the officers of the club had never heard of Utah State University.

National Biscuit Company. So when Rulon suggested that Lee apply at Nabisco, it seemed an idea worth trying.

Although most companies were laying off rather than hiring, Nabisco did not appear to be hard hit. People seemed to buy crackers even under the most adverse conditions. So young Bickmore applied for a job as a salesman and, early in 1933, was hired and assigned a Wyoming sales territory. Elated, he borrowed money to purchase an automobile and started to learn the fundamentals of his new job.

However, as the full impact of the economic crisis struck, the National Biscuit Company now also suffered from its effects. An order was issued from New York to Nabisco branches to cut the staff, dismissing the most recently hired employees first. Bickmore was out.

A suspicion lurked in young Bickmore's mind that he had been fired because he had failed to measure up. He decided that he would somehow get his job back and prove, if only to himself, that he could handle it.

In the meantime, he returned to his old position at J. C. Penney's. Depression wages made it necessary to hold two jobs, so he sold shoes on the side. Even so, his earnings were far too meager to permit him to keep his car. However, giving it up meant giving up hope of returning to Nabisco. This was the time when the banks had declared a moratorium on the payment of debts. If the banks could declare a moratorium, Bickmore reasoned, why couldn't the General Motors Acceptance Corporation? He proposed the idea in a letter. His proposition was accepted and he was permitted to keep the car until he could meet the payments.

In the summer of 1933 he was rehired by Nabisco, not as a salesman this time, but as a shipping porter at the Pocatello, Idaho, branch for fifteen dollars a week. He said goodbye to his parents and set off for the town of Pocatello.

Pocatello, located in a mountain valley not far from the famous Snake River, was for many years the center of the Union Pacific Railway. A remarkably picturesque community with an elevation of over 4,000 feet, Pocatello was surrounded by mountains on three sides and distinguished by the fact that it had an equable climate.

When Lee Bickmore drove up for his first visit, he was interested in neither the scenery nor the climate. His mind was on holding his job with the National Biscuit Company. For twelve months he worked days as a shipping porter, unloading boxes of cookies and crackers from various bakeries; nights he swept out the agency building. By September he was promoted to shipping clerk with a three-dollar-a-week raise. After a year he received another raise, this time of two dollars, making his total income twenty dollars a week.

Bickmore was able to get home regularly to see his father and step-mother, sisters and brothers, and he was in Mormon country, where he felt very much at home.

He did not stay long in Pocatello. Bickmore showed a combination of intense dedication to his work and personal consideration for others which was rare. So it was no surprise that after serving as a porter and clerk for two years he should be promoted to a full-fledged salesman once again, working in Wyoming and then in Boise, Idaho.

Three years later, in 1938, he was transferred to the important Salt Lake City area in Utah. This not only gave him an opportunity to increase his earnings but also, in 1939, to marry Ellen McMinn, a girl he had known in Pocatello and later at Boise, where she was secretary to the secretary of state. The marriage took place at Logan, approximately midway between Paradise, where the Bickmore family lived, and Pocatello, the home of the McMinns. Two years later Beverlee was born, and in four more years, another daughter, Kay.

The year after his marriage Bickmore was named special salesman at Salt Lake City in charge of training other salesmen. Three years after that he was reassigned to Pocatello, this time as branch manager.

These were years of invaluable education. America's sales methods were undergoing fundamental changes. Industry, especially the food industry, was passing through rapid evolution. Formerly, a grocer who was friendly to one of the companies whose goods he sold could be very helpful in promoting that company's products. Now this same company found its merchandise indiscriminately stacked on the shelves alongside the packages of its competitors, where it had to vie for sales in a silent face-to-face showdown.

As the grip of the depression in the 1930's tightened men's belts [state Hampe and Wittenberg in *The Lifeline of America*], it also strengthened their determination to break the grip. The belt-tightening created intense competition among food stores as consumers were forced to reduce their buying. As their will to survive grew stronger, many retailers sought less costly ways of doing business and more successful ways of attracting customers. Several changes were working on the side of these determined retailers.

The growing acceptance of the automobile as a necessity and the rapid spread of paved roads hastened the spreading of urban life and ended the farmers' dependence on small crossroads stores. America was on the go; the automobile had become a way of life.

The supermarket took advantage of the changes wrought by the automobile. It recognized the consumers' demand for more variety, and it correctly gauged the consumers' readiness for a break with retailing in the traditional way. . . .

The supermarket took advantage of the fact that people with larger incomes were willing to buy more—substantially more—if they were shown more. The supermarket went a step further than the early chains had gone in basing profits on volume rather than markup.

Bickmore was one of those in the front line of the battle being waged for consumer patronage. He saw firsthand the coming of the supermarket and the vast almost overnight changes in sales tactics.

There has been a decided increase in one-stop shopping preference [Frank Charvat states in *Supermarketing*]. Women shoppers first go to stores they believe will give them the best opportunity of making all their purchases. This desire has led to the diversified lines of merchandise handled by supers.

Visits to the food store have become less frequent. The average seems to be about three times per week. There is a decided increase in the number of people who shop once a week. There has been a substantial increase in the use of the automobile for shopping. People tend to travel farther to shop than they did prior to the supermarket development. Impulse buying has become a significant factor in food shopping. Display techniques and ability of the buyer to wander through the store have resulted in the purchase of a significant number of items that the customer had not intended to buy upon entering the store.

Such advances did not leave Bickmore behind. He was alert to their possibilities and continued to build an excellent sales record. It did appear that the company was somewhat slow to adjust to changing sales techniques. But Pocatello was a long way from New York.

One day in the fall of 1944 a letter arrived at the tiny six-man Pocatello office of Nabisco addressed to Bickmore. It was a form letter from the company's New York sales division, evidently sent to all of the five hundred branch managers and special salesmen in the country.

The purpose of the letter was to solicit ideas for a postwar salesmen's training program and sales manual. Bickmore read and reread the communication. Then he sat down at his typewriter and with his hunt-and-peck typing system composed a reply.

After the others went home, he toiled over many drafts. The final letter was a five-page single-spaced document which contained most of the ideas that had often occurred to him in the decade he had been working for the National Biscuit Company.

The invitation to present his views was like the opening of a dam, letting loose a torrent of suggestions for advancing the level of sales efficiency for the company. But it was a disciplined and carefully directed torrent.

About three hundred replies were received in Nabisco's New York office. Some were long, others short; some were full of stimulating ideas, others just repeated what was already known. One letter stood out: Bickmore's.

The Bickmore letter went from hand to hand. It was read by the sales training staff. It was shown to Frank Montgomery, the head of the sales department; George Mitchell, controller; and Russell Shultz, head of the New York bakery who had been talking about the need for new ideas for years.

Beyond question the letter was the best composed, most carefully conceived, most sensible letter of all. Here was no listing of generalities or vague exhortation. It was a virtual blueprint of what needed to be done, not merely for a distant western region, but for the entire corporate organization. There was, too, a certain enthusiasm and energetic quality—not too common—that transformed what might have been a business communication into something of a call to action.

"I was completely thrilled with your letter . . . regarding a postwar sales training program and the publication of a sales manual for our sales organization," Bickmore began. "To me it meant that Nabisco was looking actively ahead so as to be adequately prepared for the future. Our position as leaders in the baking industry was to be maintained. It meant that we are taking the first big step, namely, a recognition for the need for an intensive postwar sales training program and a sales manual. Personally, I have been surprised that an organization as large and well qualified as ours did not long before recognize this need and take steps to remedy the situation."

With bouncy candor the letter went on to list in numerical order suggestions for raising the level of the sales apparatus and accomplishing necessary gains over competitors.

First: select only those men as future salesmen who have real sales qualities, such as: size, appearance, health, training, education and personality. To get this type it may be necessary to step up our wage schedule so as to appeal to a higher type, better qualified individual.

Second: once we have the men to train, then we should have a thorough sales training program in effect to properly prepare these men for sales work. This course will probably take six months' time to develop. The trainee should be told that he is on probation and that whether or not he is retained as a permanent employee depends on his development during the training period. . . .

Bickmore provided specific information that he felt salesmen should be taught:

Orientation—The history of the baking industry, the history of the National Biscuit Company, the policies of the National Biscuit Company.

Terminology—All terms applying to the baking industry should be explained and their use denoted. This would include a knowledge of the various packs of merchandise, count per pound and package as well as price and ingredients. A thorough trip or trips through the bakery at this point would be advantageous. The proper method of writing orders, making up expense vouchers, collection vouchers and preparing pickup slips and sales promotion reports would be taught and demonstrated.

At the end of this period, which would take about a month, a thorough examination should be given covering all material presented up to this point. This examination would be a combination oral and written examination. This would permit observation of the trainee's ability to write as well as think while verbally explaining certain policies and practices of the National Biscuit Company.

The letter went into detail as to the sales presentation, the approach, the introduction, the body of the sales talk, the closing. What amazed its readers was the writer's evident familiarity with some of the most difficult sales techniques. Here was an unknown, far from New York City, giving sensible instruction to top management!

Who was this fellow, Bickmore?

When a job opened in the advertising department, it was suggested that Bickmore be invited to visit the New York general office. At that time he could be considered for possible reassignment.

Not only had Bickmore's letter aroused the curiosity of Nabisco officials, his unusual sales record in an unpromising far-western territory had also attracted attention.

In the spring of 1945 Lee Bickmore made his first visit to New York. It was a long trip—more than two and a half days by train. On a bright April morning he presented himself at the Nabisco office. He was introduced to company officers, many of whom had read his letter and were interested in meeting him. Bickmore made a favorable impression.

But when the young salesman packed his suitcase and took the train back to Pocatello, he had not received an offer of a new job. The opening in advertising had, in the meantime, been filled by someone else. His trip, however, was not in vain.

A few months later he received a long-distance telephone call inquiring whether he would care to accept a position with the company in New York City. The answer was that he would. Much as he and his family liked living in the West, Bickmore realized that if he was to advance within the company he had to move East. So a few days after Christmas 1945 Lee Bickmore arrived in New York. When he finally located an apartment in Brooklyn, his wife joined him with their two young daughters.

For a time Bickmore served as assistant to the Nabisco manager of merchandising. It was familiar work, and he made valuable contributions to it. But problems in nearby Newark, New Jersey, caused his transfer. At thirty-eight Bickmore became the youngest district sales manager in the Nabisco organization.

Industry was entering an era of unprecedented emphasis on salesmanship. Of all the Nabisco men he had met, Lee Bickmore impressed Coppers most with his practical comprehension of marketing and sales tactics.

So in 1949 Coppers asked Bickmore to return to the general office as administrative assistant to the vice president for sales, marketing and merchandising. Bickmore agreed. A year later, as Coppers may have foreseen, the chronic poor health of the vice president compelled his retirement. Bickmore replaced him. It had been a rapid rise.

Lee Bickmore and George Coppers worked well together, but they were opposites in many ways. Coppers was tense, tough, legally oriented. Bickmore was dynamic, pleasant, trained in salesmanship. Coppers tended to introspection; words came to him with anything but fluency. Bickmore was an extrovert who remembered first names; he spoke easily and well.

But the two men saw eye to eye on many things. In one of his earlier statements Coppers had pointed out that "If we can convince each salesman that he is supposed and expected to understand the problems of his customers in his territory better than anybody in the New York office, then we on 14th Street stand to learn something from him, because he is in the grocery stores every day and is in a position to know the problems of the food industry. Our job is to get it out of him."

Bickmore was just the man to "get it out of him," because he himself had been in the grocery stores for so many years. The salesman from Pocatello, in a position of leadership, was able to contribute an invaluable down-to-earth understanding of sales and merchandising problems. It was Bickmore who pushed for a special division to handle special products, who saw the need for a special division to handle new products, who turned the eyes of the company—for the first time since A. W. Green—in the direction of the consumer.

As a result Nabisco developed its first really serious market research program. It put more emphasis on the tie-in type of promotion. It began to reassert the importance of new products and the intensification of the entire marketing program. It began to make greater use of the company's new research center at Fair Lawn, where the development of new products could be speeded and the investigation of new baking methods and techniques was part of the day's routine.

In 1950 Bickmore appeared as a speaker before his first convention of Nabisco's national supervisory staff in Chicago. He did not believe in planned speeches. Instead, he had a habit of sitting in an audience, listening to others, and scribbling notes on the back of an envelope. Whether making a sale to a corner grocer in Pocatello or addressing a Congressional committee, Bickmore was poised, articulate and informal. At the Chicago convention it was obvious that Bickmore was a man who satisfied important needs of the company entering a new era.

With the rise of Bickmore, Coppers was now in a position to create the formal top management team to which he had given so much thought. It was to consist of George Mitchell, fifty-six, the financially oriented executive whose unusual grasp of virtually every phase of Nabisco's operation was a constant source of assistance to Coppers; Russell Shultz, fifty-seven, in charge of production and research, who had remained alert to the needs of the company during an era when many executives found it safer to adjust themselves to inactivity; Lee Bickmore, forty-nine, whose new marketing techniques were to open a new era in Nabisco development; and Edward S. Moore, Jr., fifty-one, who was to become Coppers' executive assistant and later executive vice president. These men became, with Coppers, members of Nabisco's executive department.

Years before, Coppers had declared, "Training his successor is the most important single job any manager or executive has." Even then the astute Coppers may have suspected that his physical ailments were to increase rather than abate. Nevertheless, the team he had put together must have given him confidence in Nabisco's future. In 1960 when the board of directors elected Bickmore president, Coppers credited him with performing "major surgery on the company" without which the company might have died.

When Bickmore succeeded to the presidency, he was fifty-one years old and had been with the company twenty-seven years. Unlike the occasion fifteen years earlier, when Coppers himself had become president, the change in Nabisco leadership was not a traumatic one, because Bickmore had already won wide respect and considerable affection.

While Bickmore was a dynamic follower of the policies of George Coppers, he had many ideas of his own. One of these was the need for diversification of Nabisco products.

Increasingly, leaders of the business world turned toward diversification of products and services. Specialization—once the key to success—no longer was the corporate virtue. Advancing technology had permitted many manufacturers to become efficient producers.

It was inevitable that Bickmore should seek to influence Nabisco toward greater diversity. One result was expansion of Nabisco's interest in the cereal market. Just a year and one-half after Bickmore became president Nabisco acquired the Cream of Wheat Corporation, famous sixty-six-year-old Minneapolis hot-cereal manufacturer. Various ready-to-eat cereal products were also added to the Nabisco cereal line.

Snacks also provided a promising area for greater diversity. The company, of course, did not have to diversify radically to enter this market. Its NAB's, pretzels, and products such as Premium Saltines and Ritz crackers were used as snacks long before snacking came into vogue. Nabisco already had an array of specially flavored crackers to satisfy the snack demand.

The company also explored such areas as vending-machine products, frozen foods, spreads, "adult" cookies, flake cereals, candy and many more.

Bickmore's impatient quest for new ideas, new products, new processes was not confined to the boundaries of the United States. The world was to become Nabisco's market place.

But Nabisco was slow to move into foreign areas on a broad scale. Not until it was approached by a Venezuelan bakery, La Favorita, did it give serious consideration to the possibility of starting a manufacturing operation on Latin American soil, which it did in 1950.

Both George Coppers and his aggressive associate Lee Bickmore grew increasingly convinced of the importance of the foreign market. Especially Bickmore. He believed that exporting American made products was not sufficient to satisfy international needs.

While the export of cookies, crackers and cereals had been booming, particularly after World War II, complications in connection with exporting were increasing. Tariffs and licensing tended to drive prices up and create distribution barriers. Also, products designed primarily for American tastes and eating habits did not always fit the requirements of foreign markets.

Bickmore was aware of the increasing number of important American corporations that were looking overseas for new business opportunities, and who were not merely seeking markets for exports. They were actively engaged in establishing manufacturing facilities where goods could be produced without involvement in the costly problems of transportation and tariffs.

"Why don't we move into this situation?" Bickmore had inquired of his fellow officers. "Why can't we find opportunities to manufacture our products in other countries?"

"Let's not rush into anything, Lee," he was told. "There is a risk involved in foreign operations. Why gamble?"

But Bickmore was stubborn as well as genial. "It's time we took a gamble," he answered. "I think our international operations could grow as important as any of our divisions except perhaps biscuit."

By 1955 George Coppers was in a position to report to his stockholders, "Our results in the foreign field have been most encouraging and our share of profits being realized through foreign operations over the past ten years has increased."

In 1953 Nabisco established its second subsidiary in Latin America, this time in Mexico. A 51 per cent interest was purchased in the holdings of the plant of the Fabricas Modernas, S.A., to be known as Nabisco Famosa. In 1960, the year Bickmore succeeded Coppers to the presidency, Nabisco acquired the Purina Grain Foods Pty., Ltd., of Melbourne, Australia, which became Nabisco Pty., Ltd.

Under Bickmore's prodding, the pace of international expansion quickened. Company officers now rushed off to a conference in a foreign country as they might to a meeting on another floor of the Nabisco office building. Bickmore himself became known in some circles as the "flying president," and thought nothing of visiting a nation thousands of miles away for a conference only to be back at his desk the next day.

In the spring of 1961 Nabisco acquired Arbona Hermanos, Inc., in Mayaguez, Puerto Rico. In the same year Nabisco opened a sales branch in San Juan, Puerto Rico, similar to the United States locations from which sales calls and deliveries were made.

A year later Nabisco acquired another bakery in England—Frears, Ltd., at Woodgate, Leicester, about a hundred miles north of London. In the same year they purchased the largest biscuit and cracker manufacturer in the New Zealand area, Griffin & Sons, Ltd.

The company's next acquisition was Biscuits Belin at Chateau-Thierry and Paris, France. In the spring of 1964 Nabisco acquired Harry Trueller GmbH, the fourth largest biscuit and confection-ery manufacturer in West Germany, originally established in 1891. Its founder, Harry Trueller, was credited with having created zwie-back, which was for many years the company's only product.

Three more important acquisitions were made in 1965: In May Saiwa, S.p.A., in Genoa, Italy, was purchased. In November a rela-tionship was established with Galletas Artiach, S.A., located in Bilbao, Spain. One month later the company purchased a 60 per cent owner-ship in Industrias Nabisco Cristal, S.A., in Managua, Nicaragua.

"We recognize the entire world as our market," stated Bickmore. "We draw the line nowhere. And we look upon our role not only as making a profit for our shareholders but also making a contribution to the area where we may locate . . .

"Values are different abroad from those at home. The stereotype of the American company coming into a foreign nation, buying a company and discharging all local employees and bringing in Amer-icans, disturbs corporation leaders abroad. Before they sell, they often ask guarantees that this will not happen. In our own country a dollar is a dollar. There, we find corporation representatives concerned about the dollar, too. But even after financial affairs are agreed, there is a deep concern for other matters. For one thing, many bakeries overseas are family owned. The owner often has developed a strong feeling of loyalty towards his employees. He doesn't want to let them down."

"We have learned to start off our discussions," a Nabisco executive states, "by explaining to our foreign friends that we are the kind of company that keeps its word. When we make assurances that we will make no changes, we mean this. But sometimes company officials are not acquainted with our record.

"We then seek to use the experiences of various companies that we already have acquired: in Canada, England, France, Italy, South America, Australia, New Zealand. We go down the list and show how local managements have been retained as well as local employees. We admit frankly that we act selfishly when we keep the status quo. We have more to gain keeping local people if they are efficient people."

There are often similarities between today's foreign baking companies and American bakeries in 1898, when the National Biscuit Company was organized. There is the same pride of local company name and product, the same reluctance to merge identity with the mother company. Gradually, however, such hesitations are overcome as confidence is created.

One point that particularly impresses foreign managements is the length of service of many Nabisco employees and executives. They feel that a company that keeps so many employees for ten, twenty, thirty years and longer, must treat people with respect. Also impressive has been Lee Bickmore's rise to president of a great American company from lowly stock clerk.

To reinforce their verbal discussions Nabisco officials have invited foreign industrialists to visit Nabisco in America and find out more about how the company operates and how it lives up to its reputation for integrity, reliability and quality.

Not the least of the company's considerations in the international scene are the millions of hungry people throughout the world. "Living in quite prosperous countries as we do," the *Biscuit and Cracker Baker* stated in September 1965, "it is hard for us to realize that there are many countries in which the vast majority of the people have no money now, and have no idea when or where they are going to get any."

The National Biscuit Company, like other food processing firms in the United States, has been conscious of the fact that, as the *United States News and World Report* put it in their January 6, 1964, issue, "Hunger is to emerge as the Number One problem in the world in the years immediately ahead." Unless a way soon is found to control the problem of world-wide population explosion, it was stated, starvation will take over as a partial solution to the problem.

The third world's food survey conducted by the Food and Agricultural Organization of the United Nations stated that one-half of the world's population is ill-fed, underfed or both.

The National Biscuit Company has interested itself in the problem of world hunger ever since it seriously turned its attention to the international market. Most of the Nabisco subsidiaries, as well as its export trade, have tended to reach those in the more affluent strata of the various countries serviced by Nabisco. An exception to this has been the use of the soda cracker as a bread substitute by large numbers of people in various nations.

The hungry people of the world have little or no money to purchase even the most inexpensive Nabisco product themselves. If the food manufacturing abilities of companies such as Nabisco are to be harnessed to help alleviate hunger, it is plain that the governments of other nations must be involved.

Nabisco took a constructive step in this direction when it cooperated with UNICEF of the United Nations in 1962 in a joint effort to develop a low-cost nutritive high protein cookie for use primarily in developing countries.

Food manufacturers, however, have encountered the problem of realizing a return on their investment in seeking to service such a vast but poverty-stricken market. Nabisco has assigned specialists to study the problem and work out a program whereby Nabisco may play its role in helping alleviate the food problem of the world.

Whether at home or abroad, Bickmore preached the gospel of creative marketing. He believed that company executives, whether located on New York's Park Avenue or the most distant branch office, must have a close, day-to-day acquaintance with the habits and changing tastes of the consuming public—particularly the housewife.

"We believe, very strongly, that the sensible reason we are in business is to earn the right to make a profit," he stated before a Congressional committee looking into packaging problems. "We earn this right only by giving consumers the best values possible. Nabisco is very much aware it can succeed as a company only to the degree that it can succeed in satisfying the needs and wants of American consumers.

"As a consumer goods company, we are acutely conscious of consumer needs and preferences. We study them. We go to consumers for this information. We believe that in our business, we must start with the housewife and then work back, gearing our selling, distribution, packaging and production practices to those methods best fitted to meeting her requirements . . .

"Mrs. Consumer is the boss," he stated. "The question is: How can we most effectively please these Mrs. Consumers of America? In our shop we believe this can be done most effectively when advertising, marketing and sales are thoroughly correlated, coordinated and synchronized in their thinking, planning and execution . . ."

"These three departments we firmly believe are a means to an end and not an end in themselves. They are interdependent on each other. We think these three facets are the cutting edge of the saw—the diamond point of the drill. Why? Because they are nearest to the consumer, and our basic approach is to satisfy the wants of Mrs. Consumers of America."

The foundation built by Coppers served Bickmore well. The task he faced was to try to satisfy the needs of a new era. And, among these needs the most important was people.

TWENTY-FOUR

The Human Mix

"EVERY COMPANY has an image," Lee Bickmore once stated. "It may not be the image that the company thought it had or would like to have. But it has an image, just as every person has an image. It probably has a different image to different people.

"A company image is made up of many factors. The three most important in many companies are: first, products; second, advertising; and third, employees."

In order to achieve a favorable image in these three departments, according to Bickmore, a company has to "decide what share of the market it is after, what economic level of clientele it should appeal to, what channels of distribution it should adopt, what ratio of profits to sales and investment it should strive for, whether it should be a high quality, medium quality or low quality house. . . .

"The consumer shopping the supermarkets sees the same merchandise, the same display fixtures, the same lighting effects, the same store layout, the same price for most of the merchandise. Even, in some cases, the employees in their store uniforms seem to be the same. In addition, actual experiments show that the big advertising spreads in the newspapers by these stores are so similar that if you left off the name, even the store manager couldn't tell which ad was his. Sameness, sameness, sameness. Imagine the confusion of the consumers.

◄ *Three scientists at Research Center*

Uniqueness must be sought in the establishment of a corporate image."

But above all other considerations, Bickmore emphasized, is the importance of organization. "There isn't another problem that is of so much importance as developing an organization . . . The future of any business depends more upon the development of people than on any other element. This is more important than developing new products, more important than going out and getting a larger share of the market on your present products. The development of people is more important than building new factories . . ."

At the turn of the century, when many of the nation's large companies were born, there was a blatant lack of concern about human welfare. Perhaps the least important ingredient in the corporate organization was people.

First of all, human beings were in abundant supply, thanks to the steady flow of immigrants to American shores. Furthermore, a series of unemployment crises created vast reservoirs of men, women and even children who desperately needed jobs. They were eager to enter the new factories at almost any wage and willing to work under almost any conditions.

The morality—or even the long range practicality—of exploiting the poor was forgotten in the daily exigencies of running a company at a profit. Corporation officers, who were uninterested in the plight of their workers, were equally lacking in concern for the public. "The public be damned" was not an unusual corporate point of view. And that public included employees, retailers and consumers, too.

It took years and no small amount of strife before corporations accepted the fact that they had obligations to people whom they hired, and to people whom they served.

"A company in the modern era," Bickmore said, "must be a good citizen as well as successful in business, if it is to survive, prosper and attract the best people to its ranks.

"The National Biscuit Company is a constructive corporate member of society. It helps in the education of its people, in community activity, tries to become one of the ingredients of a dynamic society—a dynamic company in a virile dynamic society."

In the mid-1960's Nabisco's human orbit included approximately 36,000 employees, 80,000 shareholders, 10,000 suppliers, over 300,000 domestic merchants who sold Nabisco products, and literally the entire nation as its consuming public, spreading out into lands around the world.

"For more than a decade now, modern managers have been warned that they must face up to the problems of technological and human obsolescence," Bickmore wrote in *Dun's Review* and *Modern Industry* in April 1966.

The headlines have carried the news of special programs designed to either re-train or up-grade workers whose skills have been made obsolete by the development of new machines and production techniques.

One group of men, however, has been largely overlooked in this entire matter of human obsolescence. These are the nation's business executives. The pressures and complexities of modern business have taken a very real toll of them, and created an ill that much of industry has not yet become aware of. I call it the problem of the "executive drop out."

In his own way, the executive drop out is more burdensome to his company than the school drop out is to the educational system. He does not leave. For all intents and purposes, he has taken early retirement, but he does not retire; he arrives each morning, meets with associates, transfers papers from the "in" box to the "out" box. Yet he has ceased to function as a mover, innovator, or distributor or contributor to the forward thrust of the company.

Bickmore went on to spell out what he termed "the problem of the executive drop out." "The problem eats at the very vitals of the company, the promise of its future. It is a problem that is very much the responsibility of top management." Bickmore claimed that the industrial drop out wants "most of all to maintain conditions as they were when he was doing his best work; he wants to stay with the safe ideas and techniques of by-gone days. The past is comforting and secure; he is afraid of new ideas and people and products.

"The result of this attitude is a tendency to be negative. He frowns upon a new approach to a problem, basing his disapproval on his experience. 'We tried something like that back in the thirties,' he will say. 'It didn't work then, and it won't work now.' Or he may dismiss a new idea with the comment: 'We're doing fine as it is; don't want to stir things up.' "

Bickmore claimed that such weaknesses at the executive level resulted in an unusually large loss of young men, that departments run under such a philosophy became static. However, Bickmore stated his belief that the executive drop out can be stimulated into a more constructive role. That is, depending upon "the man and upon the effort that management is willing to make."

"At the National Biscuit Company," said Bickmore, "we have instituted a program intended to accomplish two major goals: to diagnose incipient cases of executive drop out quickly and to prevent such cases from occurring."

Among activities which Bickmore pointed to as helping raise the level of executive performance were regular staff meetings at which all participate; keeping channels of communication open; knowing the men one is working with, their idiosyncrasies, strengths and shortcomings; maintaining a sense of challenge and excitement among executives by some form of incentive compensation.

Bickmore stated that in order to "attract and hold top men . . . a company needs a well thought out program that starts with the new employee and carries through for all the years he remains with the firm."

Influenced by such thinking, the National Biscuit Company took a fresh look at its complete corporate organization, including its board of directors. Meetings of the Nabisco board of directors in the 1960's stood out in sharp contrast to meetings of the board held decades earlier. Under Bickmore's aggressive leadership, members participated as they seldom did before. Reports were submitted by the various heads of departments. Questions asked by members of the board were a matter of routine: How is a cereal progressing? Are we going into full production on a new biscuit? Is there a certain cracker being made in our British plant? A decade or two before, such reports and such questioning would have been considered revolutionary.

There was a shift in the makeup of the board membership itself. Bickmore had stated his ultimate desire of having the board represent a "mix" of various points of view and backgrounds, and the board was composed of businessmen with connections outside the company, supplemented by directors who were company executives. This was a far cry from the first board in 1898, which was almost entirely made up of directors who were bakers, and from the boards of a few decades later, which had little or no interest in the detailed functioning of the company. In the 1960's most of the directors were seasoned, successful men from the world of business, banking, law and education.

As a further symbol of changing times, in 1966 Roy E. Tomlinson, now eighty-nine years of age, officially retired, after sixty-four years of service with the company, with the title of "director emeritus."

The Nabisco board in many ways placed emphasis on fuller participation in company affairs—especially by youth. No person who had passed his seventy-second birthday could serve as a board director.

In the spring of 1968 Lee S. Bickmore was elected chairman of the board of directors, while continuing as chief executive officer. Robert M. Schaeberle, forty-five-year-old Dartmouth graduate and former company controller, was elected president, with Val B. Diehl, fifty-one-year-old former head of the company's international division, elected executive vice president.

Whereas once the company discouraged large attendance at its shareholders' meetings, this was reversed. The company sought big turnouts even to the extent of giving away free cookies to those present.

Like the directors' sessions, the shareholders' annual meetings were marked by a participation, extensive in contrast with how it used to be. Mailed greetings to new shareholders urged them from the start to "Please feel free to make suggestions or ask any questions that you may have about your company."

This approach was also demonstrated in connection with Nabisco employees. Although the chance of a Lee Bickmore catapulting his way from lowly clerk to company president was less likely in the 1960's than it once was, nevertheless Bickmore encouraged conditions that would permit employees to move onward and upward in accordance with their talents.

Like other large corporations, Nabisco's personnel policies were guided by practical business considerations rather than philanthropy. However, in the case of Nabisco, such policies were reinforced by Bickmore's oft repeated conviction that the progressive image of a company is influenced primarily by "the products the company makes, the advertising the company creates, and the people the company hires."

The company's aim—as far as its employees are concerned—has been defined by one official as spanning "a wide range of human relationships—developing and administering plans affecting employment and training, transfers both domestic and international, health and safety, insurance, pension and benefit programs, employee communications, fair and equitable compensation, all the way to the intangible goal of more harmonious relationships with those labor unions who represent some of our people."

Personnel relations were not officially recognized by most companies until World War I, when, according to *Business Week* in its June 26, 1965, issue, "scientific management burst on the business world . . . Most of the founding fathers of big United States businesses had their hands too full of production problems, or their heads too full of financial worries, to become innovators in the personnel field."

Nabisco was relatively slow to move forward in this field; it was not until the coming of George Coppers to the presidency that a personnel department was officially established. In the 1960's the company had a large department doing business as an accepted routine with labor unions representing employees. The company sought to maintain levels of wages and other economic benefits equal to or better than the industry as a whole.

Nabisco placed emphasis on keeping lines of communication open between management and employees. One way was through the employees' magazine, *Nabisco,* one of the oldest in the nation, as well as plant newspapers published in two bakeries. Another was through its "suggestion system," started by George Coppers in 1946, which attracted from 5,000 to 10,000 employee suggestions each year.

Training of employees was considered an important matter. The company divided its training programs into short-range "job-oriented training" and long-range "individual-oriented development." Each trainee in such areas as chemistry, food technology, finance or plant engineering underwent a twelve-month training period with emphasis on well-rounded rather than specialized experience. The company's 1,200 sales executives were involved in special development courses, 500 plant supervisory people were taking courses in preparation for advancement, and most of the company's financial employees acquired special training at various business schools in the country. Almost all top company executives have attended the Advanced Management Program of the Harvard Business School.

One of the major problems of the company, as with most, was attracting the "right additional people" to its ranks. "Our need becomes greater each year," one Nabisco officer stated, "for well-rounded people who understand the business and who not only have the ability, but also the vision and vigor to carry our company forward. As we analyze this responsibility, it becomes apparent, with few exceptions, that the best way to obtain such people is to train and develop them within our own organization."

"It is Nabisco's policy to promote from within," the company told its engineering trainees. "Nabisco is erecting new plants, modernizing existing plants, and installing greater automation. There is, therefore, ample opportunity for a graduate engineer to advance to a responsible position in management. Performance and progress reviews are made periodically and promotions are made on the basis of these reviews with considerations being given to all-around ability."

In discussing the opportunities which it provided, the company stated, "The food industry is noted for its stability. Normal cyclical variations in the economy have only a minor effect on sales and employment. Nabisco continues an unbroken dividend record, which began in 1899. Nabisco is considered a good place to work by its personnel as shown by its unusually low turnover rate. As a result, 60 per cent of all salaried personnel have at least ten years of service, and 29 per cent have more than 20 years."

"We often ask what kind of people are we seeking for training and development," Nabisco's director of personnel stated before the company's first global conference. "For my part, we are not seeking the person who has as his slogan, I came, I saw, I concurred. In my book, 'the conformist man,' better known in the New Deal and New Frontier circles as the 'common man' is obsolescent. We are seeking the uncommon man . . .

"After all, if our company is to adapt quickly to changing conditions and is to meet the competition of the market place, it must have a constant flow of creative, new ideas.

"We need the contribution of people who can escape the bonds of conformity and recognize emerging new problems and be ready to offer fresh, sound solutions." In seeking employees who would bring a creative approach to their work, the company sought to reevaluate critically its traditional hiring policies. The company cooperated with the Plans for Progress program of the United States Committee on Equal Opportunity, under which equal opportunity to all persons employed at Nabisco or seeking employment there was assured. Lee Bickmore issued directives to divisional officials, encouraging the hiring of women in positions of executive responsibility—something which was unknown in the past.

Later in the 1960's the company also sought to encourage new and creative approaches to people generally and to the consumer in particular. This encouraged an exchange of communications between consumers and the company.

Nabisco receives thousands of letters each month from consumers all over the country, suggesting ideas for cookies, for packaging, for advertising; offering new recipes, and asking questions about products long discontinued. The company receives letters signed with the names of dogs praising Milk-Bone, testimonials from children as to Animal Crackers, suggestions by husbands who are masters of the kitchen, and thousands of letters from housewives who do most of the buying of crackers, cookies and biscuits.

In 1969 Mary Ellen Baker, the mythical character who, on behalf of the company, ministered to the cooking needs of a large section of American housewives, received approximately 3,000 letters each month.

The original Mary Ellen Baker came into being in 1941 to help prepare recipes, menus and articles for publication in newspapers and magazines. Since that time there has been a succession of technically trained women who administered test kitchens maintained to be of service to Nabisco consumers.

The company prided itself on responding to every such communication it received, whether it was a product suggestion, a testimonial, a comment about packaging, or a question: "Why can't I buy such and such a cracker?"

Considering the vast quantity of goods that the company produced, there was a relatively small incidence of overbaked cookies or crackers that crumbled in transit. In response to letters pointing out such problems, the company had a strict requirement that the individual writing the letter be personally visited by a Nabisco representative in whatever part of the country he or she was located. At that time the person is given an explanation as to why the incident occurred.

The effort to emphasize the human aspects of company operation also extended to the area of research and development. In seeking to encourage a creative approach in the research laboratory in Fair Lawn, Bickmore proposed that the people working there be "permitted to see the end results of their total work rather than a detail in which no personal pride is involved or even knowledge of the final product."

The food industry in the past spent relatively little—less than one-half of 1 per cent of its sales dollar—on research. Under Bickmore's prodding, the Nabisco laboratory added men and equipment and expanded its resources.

In 1969 Nabisco's laboratory looked upon its assignment as one of creating new products for the shelves of stores and supermarkets all over America. It also viewed its task as planning for the future, trying to predict where the company would like to be two or five or twenty-five years ahead. When Bickmore was asked whether the future of the company would be restricted by its traditional emphasis on crackers and cookies, he replied, "I don't view the future of the National Biscuit Company as necessarily restricted by its success in the biscuit industry. This, of course, will continue. However, our competitors need not necessarily be limited to bakers. They may extend into many other fields."

Company scientists worked with equal concentration on ideas for feeding the housewife patronizing the corner supermarket and the astronaut in space.

The technology of food preservation, the utilization of such nutritious, low cost materials as fish protein concentrate as a means of helping reduce starvation; the possibility of using infra-red systems in food processing; the use of micro-wave heating for uses ranging from baking in ovens to soil sterilization—all held out exciting possibilities for the future.

"The way we see it," stated one Nabisco officer, "the future of the world will be decided by bullets or calories. We like to think that it will be the latter."

"Our sole responsibility," Bickmore said, "is not dollars or services. As people we can only go so far as *all* of us go. Business in general is beginning to reach the conclusion that the responsibility of business is also to help others. This is good business—necessary business—for corporations in the last half of the twentieth century."

In support of such a conviction, *Newsweek* magazine reported in its April 11, 1966, issue, "The fact is that social responsibility has become more than a window dressing slogan. In the past few years, growing numbers of businessmen have been peeping from behind their balance sheets at the world outside their factory gates and taking an active part in what goes on there."

It was clear that the big question mark confronting companies in 1969—as other institutions—was a human one.

The accelerated pace of the decade demanded more and more

progress, and at an even faster rate. The arena for action extended from the executive drop out to the most unskilled employee. It even extended beyond labor unions with whom management had, more often than not, learned to live in good, practical relationships. Now corporations had a responsibility to learn to live with humanity around the world, to find within their vast productive and distribution organizations the know-how for doing business in a world changing so fast that even daily newspapers could not keep abreast of it.

How to set about accepting such responsibilities? Lee Bickmore stated that "first a company must start with its own organization. Our leading officers are constantly planning ahead in such vital areas as production, finances, and marketing. . . . Having placed our own house in order, the company must start to reach out into areas of need, wherever they are. I don't mean by this 'big brother' activities. I don't mean obligating people.

"But I do mean helping people to qualify to obtain a greater share of the earth's wealth, to help them achieve productive capacities, which means equality for them." As a necessary condition for this, Bickmore placed emphasis on the need for independent exchange of views in a world in which opinions of every group needed not only expression but consideration.

These, then, are the ingredients—as one important corporation sees them—for creating the right recipe for the "human mix" of the future.

Nabisco salesman stocks grocer's shelves ▸

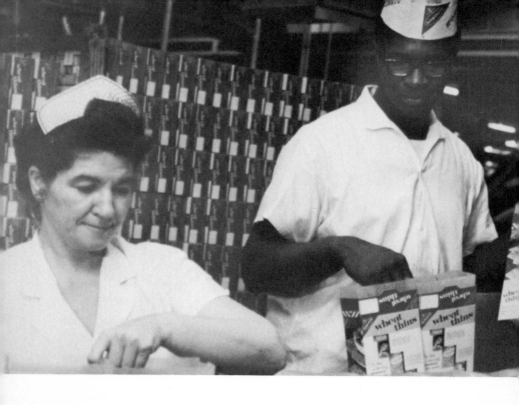

People are the most important ingredient.

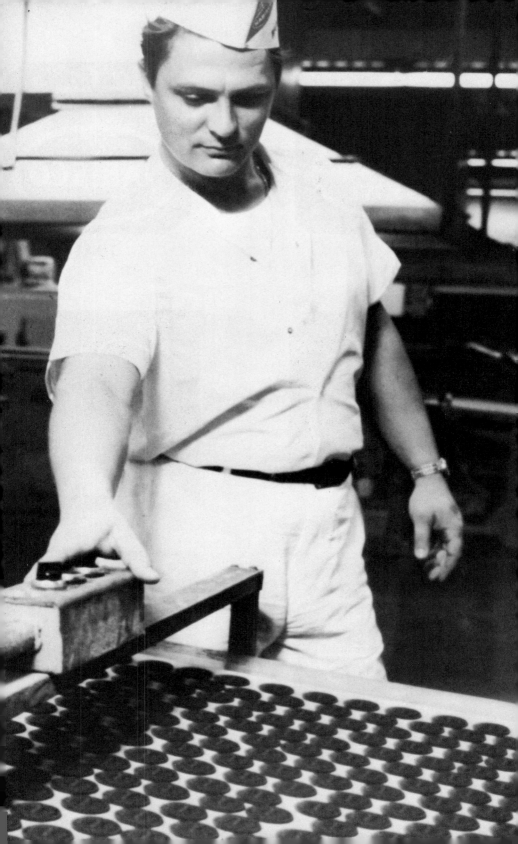

1900

1941

1918

1952

1923

1958

TWENTY-FIVE

The Shape
of Things to Come?

FROM AN INSTITUTION traditionally conservative and reluctant to become involved in the affairs of the industry of which it was part, or the community which it served, or the world in which it existed, the National Biscuit Company has been transformed in recent years into an enthusiastic participant in all three.

Nabisco has moved from introvert to extrovert. "A modern corporation has a responsibility to come forth and be heard on issues and matters affecting the common good," the company has stated.

Without sacrificing standards of quality and integrity, it envisions bolder, more imaginative, more creative arenas of action. There is renewed stress on diversification: both of products and geographical location.

As for products, there is still a magic in the name "biscuit." But the company excludes no product compatible with its marketing structure. Cookies and crackers are the starting point rather than the end of the company's product plans for the future.

The company's business outside of the United States has grown to an annual volume in excess of $150,000,000. This is more than the total sales of the entire company in the 1940's. The international division has become its fastest growing and second largest division.

Equally important in the shape of things to come is diversification of interest in people. Nabisco's image has traditionally been built

◀ *The development of the Nabisco trademark*

by its products, but its future will increasingly be influenced by people: consumers, employees, shareholders, suppliers, distributors and, generally, the community at local, state and national levels.

Lee S. Bickmore once stated that people must be included in all corporate considerations. "It is common practice today for corporations to engage in 'long range planning.' As a matter of fact they are incessantly talking about planning in terms of share-of-market goals, profit goals, sales goals. I ask the question: What about people goals? The company that places its relationship to people first is the company that has the best long range planning."

Both at home and abroad, the company works at becoming "people oriented." It contends: "We have to spend more time on the people problem. Conditions today are different from what they were. Young people ask questions; they seek motivation of a new kind."

Among "people problems" the company includes: population expansion, human rights, poverty, hunger. "The people of Nabisco realize that we, as individuals and as a corporation, live among people," the 1968 annual report stated. "What takes place in the Common Market of Europe, in Vietnam, in outer space, on Park Avenue or in the ghettos, affects us all. We recognize and accept our social responsibility as individuals and as a corporation.

"The solution of these problems will require all of the ingenuity we can muster from all segments of the economy, both public and private, if we are to survive at all," the company states. "Therefore, the corporation of today, both international and domestic, faces a world responsibility in helping to solve the problems of survival. As an international company which operates around the world, this condition becomes more evident to us every day. Those of us in the position to do so should actively seek to assist the governments of the world in the handling of the situation which could, if it is left unchecked, over the long term, destroy the civilization as we know it today."

"It has become increasingly difficult for major corporations to ignore the needs and pressures of the society in which they function," Bickmore wrote in an article in *Pace* magazine. ". . . Where major reforms are needed, as in the cases of air and water pollution, ghetto poverty and inadequate educational opportunities, vigorous corporate support may prove invaluable as a means of turning apathy into action. This support should consist of more than 'lip service' . . .

"Responsible corporate behavior isn't necessarily motivated by altruism or a desire to 'build good will,' although these factors may have some bearing. It is simply good business. Because the corporation is a citizen of the state, it cannot expect to function efficiently in an unhealthy environment. An ailing society eventually will infect the corporation, too. A corporation which lends a hand toward weeding out the ills and cultivating the growth of its surrounding society can only hope to benefit. I think we can call it a long-term investment of continuing importance."

There could scarcely be a more dramatic change in philosophy from the decades of Adolphus W. Green's leadership. Green was far ahead of his time in his insistence on corporate unity, in his intuitive understanding of promotional techniques, in his insistent demand for high standards of quality and service. But he gave little thought to people. When they were considered at all, it was merely with a gesture of paternalism. As for sharing authority, Green looked upon delegation of responsibility as at best a nuisance, and at worst a liability.

Inevitably, such a philosophy had to run afoul of changing times. Roy E. Tomlinson tried, with some success, to maintain the best features of his predecessor—to keep, as he put it, the "train running on the track." At the same time, he sought to discard the residue of Green's eccentricities and unwillingness to delegate authority.

But methods of corporate leadership, effective in one era, are often inadequate in another. As a result, George H. Coppers inherited from Tomlinson not only a highly successful corporation but one starting to lag dangerously behind, both technologically and ideologically. Representative of a new breed of corporate managers, Coppers set about to free the company from its traditional reluctance to move boldly in new directions. Under his leadership, bakeries were built, machines installed, encouragement given to employees to think new thoughts. Coppers laid the groundwork for the construction of what amounted to a brand-new company. And Lee S. Bickmore took over where Coppers left off.

Ever since its formation in 1898, the National Biscuit Company has been the leader of the biscuit and cracker industry. The size of the company's operations has always been impressive. The good name of the company and the quality of its products are unexcelled, both in the nation and the world. The fact that it has never missed a dividend and had impressive profits as well as a reputation for integrity and reliability contributed to its unrivaled prestige.

But despite this, Nabisco is impatient with past or even present success. It wants to press forward to new frontiers.

Many years ago Nabisco took the cracker out of the cracker barrel, trimmed its edges, boxed it, renamed it, promoted it—and thus helped satisfy the appetite of a growing America.

Perhaps history, on a larger scale, will repeat itself. One day, perhaps, there will not be an adult anywhere on earth who is unacquainted with a Premium Saltine, or a youngster whose face does not brighten at the sight of an Oreo.

If this should happen, the National Biscuit Company hopes that it will also have lived up to its other responsibilities in a world in which the welfare of people is becoming everybody's business.

Animal crackers by the billion ▸

Oreos are cut individually; Fig Newtons go on forever.

Sources and Acknowledgments

Any true history of a large American corporation whose life spans many decades is so interwoven with the development of our nation as to have significance far beyond itself. People, ideas, techniques and machines involved in the functioning of such corporations have exerted an influence not only on the company and its industry but on the nation.

To determine how, or whether, such influences will continue requires knowledge of how the corporation came into being and how it functions. This is why documentary corporate histories, such as this strives to be, are reservoirs of valuable information for us today.

The National Biscuit Company was something of a model company to examine for this purpose. Its history was available, its purpose has been uncomplicated, its leaders have often been men of individualism, its products have been discernible as well as appealing, its accomplishments considerable.

This is not to say that this history was easily put together. For reasons of size alone, such a company is difficult to encompass. Its records tend to overflow the space designed for them. Then, too, the dynamic quality of its recent leadership created news for the journalist but problems for the historian.

In unraveling the story of Nabisco, hundreds of sources were used: libraries, historical societies and industrial organizations. People by the score were interviewed, from peelers to corporation presidents. Bakers, controllers, directors, secretaries, advertising men, laboratory technicians, pensioners, trainees—all made their contributions. So did seemingly endless records, documents, clippings, speeches, books, articles.

Among the many publications and authors contributing to this work, I am especially grateful to *Fortune* magazine, whose two studies of the National Biscuit Company (April 1935 and June 1948) were particularly help-ful; *The New Yorker* magazine for its reports on the company's past; the many studies listed in the bibliography—especially *Lifeline of America* by Edward C. Hampe, Jr., and Merle Wittenberg, *Supermarketing* by Frank J. Charvat, *The Selling Power of Packaging* by Vernon L. Fladager, *Perils of Prosperity* by William E. Leuchtenburg, *The Great Pierpont Morgan* by Frederick Lewis Allen, *The Old Country Store* by Gerald Carson, *The American Mind* by Henry Steele Commager, *Men at the Top* by Osborn Elliott, *Morgan the Magnificent* by John K. Winkler, *Baking in America* by William G. Panchar (Vol. 1) and Charles C. Slater (Vol. 2)—and more.

I am indebted to all those who helped and wish there were room to have included more of the information volunteered as well as the names of those who contributed special assistance in one way or another. Some of those most helpful were: Eilleen Reilly, Harry F. Schroeter, John J. Too-mey, Mary McFeely, Roy E. Tomlinson, Glenn Craig, George A. Mitchell, Mary Hoban, Mrs. Faith C. Pigors, William H. Moore, Arthur L. Thomas, Robert Blauner, Louis Wirsching, Jr., Lee Bickmore, Morris Matthew, Prof. William T. Hutchenson, Harry L. Wuerth and many more.

Thanks are also due to the varied artists and photographers whose work, much of it of obscure origin, brightens these pages. These include Brown Brothers (pages 23 and 52), *Good Housekeeping* (page 24), Lewis W. Hine, Library of Congress (pages 168-69), Photo-Art Commercial Studios (page 256), and Robert Fuhring (page 324).

Much of the research was from seldom examined sources permitting the narrative to provide important accounts of industrial history pre-viously not readily available.

Of course with all projects of this dimension, there were problems of time and patience with family and friends. But the author had an unusual advantage. A box of Fig Newton cakes here or a Fruit Cake there, tended to soothe when the going was rough. If you have to write the history of a company my advice is to pick one that makes cookies and crackers.

Bibliography

ALLEN, FREDERICK LEWIS, *The Big Change*. New York, Harper, 1952.

———, *The Great Pierpont Morgan*. New York, Harper, 1948.

———, *Lords of Creation*. New York, Harper, 1935.

ALSBERG, CARL L., *Combination in the American Bread Baking Industry*. Stanford, Cal., Stanford University Press, 1926.

ANDREWS, WAYNE, *Battle for Chicago*. New York, Harcourt, 1946.

ASBURY, HERBERT, *The Gangs of New York*. New York, Knopf, 1927.

AUSTIN, ALEINE, *The Labor Story: A Popular History of American Labor*. New York, Coward-McCann, 1949.

BACON, EDWIN M., *Walks and Rides in the Country Round About Boston*. Boston, Houghton Mifflin, 1897.

BARNARD, HARRY, *"Eagle Forgotten": The Life of John Peter Altgeld*. New York, Bobbs-Merrill, 1962.

BATEMAN, NEWTON, ed., *Historical Encyclopedia of Illinois and Biographical Memoirs*, Vol. 2. Chicago, Munsell, 1903.

BEARD, CHARLES A., *The American Party Battle*, Vol. 12. New York, The Worker's Bookshelf, 1928.

BEER, THOMAS, *Hanna*. New York, Knopf, 1929.

———, *The Mauve Decade*. New York, Random House, 1961.

Biographical Encyclopedia of Illinois of the 19th Century. Philadelphia, Galaxy, 1875.

BLACKMORE, R. D., *Lorna Doone*. New York, Washington Square Press, 1960.

Boston Directory, 1843, 1845.

Boston Illustrated. Boston, Houghton Mifflin, 1886.

BRAYLEY, ARTHUR W., *Bakers and Baking in Massachusetts, Including the Flour, Baking Supply and Kindred Interests from 1620 to 1909*. Boston, Master Bakers' Association of Massachusetts, 1909.

BROUN, HEYWOOD, and LEECH, MARGARET, *Anthony Comstock*. New York, Albert and Charles Boni, 1927.

BROWN, HENRY COLLINS, *In The Golden Nineties*. Hastings-on-Hudson, Valentine's, 1928.

BROWN, MILTON P., ENGLAND, WILBUR B., MATTHEWS, JOHN B., JR., *Problems of Marketing*. New York, McGraw-Hill, 1961.

BULLIS, HARRY A., *Buffalo: Its Flour Milling Heritage*. New York, The Newcomen Society of England, American Branch, 1948.

BURLINGAME, ROGER, *March of the Iron Men*. New York, Grosset & Dunlap, 1938.

BUSH-BROWN, ALBERT, *Masters of World Architecture: Louis Sullivan*. New York, George Braziller, 1960.

The Business History Review, Vol. 29, Nos. 1, 3 and 4; Vol. 30, Nos. 1, 2 and 4; Vol. 34, No. 4; Vol. 33, No. 3.

CABOT, PHILIP, *Addresses, 1935–41*. Cambridge, Mass., Riverside Press, 1942.

CAMPBELL, HANNAH, *Why Did They Name It?* New York, Fleet Publishing Co., 1964.

CARLISLE, NORMAN, "From Cracker Barrel to Cracker Empire," *Coronet*, September 1953.

CARSE, ROBERT, *The Moonrakers: The Story of the Clipper Ship Men*. New York, Harper, 1961.

CARSON, GERALD, *Cornflake Crusade*. New York, Rinehart, 1957.

———, *Country Stores in Early New England*. Sturbridge, Mass., Old Sturbridge Village Booklet Series, 1955.

———, *The Old Country Store*. New York, Oxford, 1954.

CATTON, BRUCE, *Mr. Lincoln's Army*. New York, Doubleday, 1951.

Chain Store Age, Equipment and Construction Guide, March 15, 1964.

CHAMBERLAIN, JOHN, *The Enterprising Americans: A Business History of the United States*. New York, Harper, 1963.

CHAMBERLAIN, JOSEPH EDWARD, *John Brown*. Boston, Small, Maynard, 1899.

CHARVAT, FRANK J., *Supermarketing*. New York, MacMillan, 1961.

CHASE, STUART, *The Economy of Abundance*. New York, MacMillan, 1934.

CHILD, L. MARIA, *Letters From New York*. New York, 1849.

CHRYSLER CORPORATION, *The Story of an American Company*. Detroit, 1955.

COCHRAN, THOMAS C., *Basic History of American Business*. New York, Van Nostrand, 1959.

COCHRAN, THOMAS, and MILLER, WILLIAM, *The Age of Enterprise*. New York, Harper, 1961.

COMMAGER, HENRY STEELE, *The American Mind*. New Haven, Conn., Yale University Press, 1957.

———, *Theodore Parker, Yankee Crusader*. Boston, Beacon Press, 1957.

COPELAND, MELVIN T., *And Mark an Era: The Story of the Harvard Business School*. Boston, Little, Brown, 1958.

The Cosmopolitan, an illustrated monthly magazine, Vol. 15, No. 5, September 1893.

CROLY, MRS. J. C. (JENNIE JUNE), *Jennie June's American Cookery Book*. New York, The American News Company, 1867.

CULLEN, JAMES B., *The Irish in Boston*. Boston, James B. Cullen & Co., 1889.

CUMMINGS, RICHARD OSBORN, *The American and His Food*. Chicago, University of Chicago Press, 1940.

CUTTER, BENJAMIN and WILLIAM R., *History of the Town of Arlington, Massachusetts, 1635–1879.* Boston, David Clapp & Son, 1880.

DANA, RICHARD HENRY, *Two Years before the Mast.* New York, Bantam, 1959.

DARROW, CLARENCE, *The Story of My Life.* New York, Grosset & Dunlap, 1932.

DEDMON, EMMETT, *Fabulous Chicago.* New York, Random House, 1953.

DEFOREST, L. EFFINGHAM, and DEFOREST, ANNE LAWRENCE, *William Henry Moore and His Ancestry, With Accounts of the Moore Families in the American Colonies, 1620–1730.* New York, DeForest, 1934.

Official Proceedings of the National Democratic Convention, held in Chicago, Ill., June 21st, 22nd and 23rd, 1892. Reported for the convention by Edward B. Dickinson, official stenographer. Chicago, Cameron, Amberg, 1892.

DICKINSON, S. N., *Boston Almanac for 1846.* Boston, 1846.

DODDS, JOHN W., *American Memoir.* New York, Popular Library, 1961.

DREISER, THEODORE, *The Financier.* New York, Dell, 1961.

———, *The Titan.* New York, Dell, 1942.

DRUCKER, PETER F., *The Concept of the Corporation.* New York, New American Library, 1964.

EHRLICH, LEONARD, *God's Angry Man.* New York, Modern Age Books, 1938.

ELLIOTT, OSBORN, *Men at the Top.* New York, Harper, 1959.

Encyclopedia of Biography of Illinois, Vol. 1. Chicago, Century, 1892.

Federal Writers Project, Vardis Fisher, Director, *Idaho Encyclopedia.* Caldwell, Ohio, 1938.

Fifty Photographic Views of Chicago. Chicago, Rand McNally, 1899.

FILLER, LOUIS, *Crusaders for American Liberalism.* New York, Collier, 1961.

FIRST NATIONAL CITY BANK, *Working Together.* New York, December 1961.

FLADAGER, VERNON L., *The Selling Power of Packaging.* New York, McGraw-Hill, 1956.

FLANNAGAN, ROY C., *The Story of Lucky Strike.* New York World's Fair Edition, 1939.

EDITORS OF *Fortune, Markets of the Sixties.* New York, Harper, 1960.

———, *Understanding the Big Corporation.* New York, McBride, 1934.

———, *Why Do People Buy?* New York, McGraw-Hill, 1953.

FRANKLIN, BENJAMIN, *The Autobiography of Benjamin Franklin.* Selected and arranged by Carl Van Doren. New York, 1948.

FURNAS, C. C., and S. M., *Man, Bread and Destiny.* Baltimore, Waverly Press, 1937.

GAGE, LYMAN J., *Memoirs of Lyman J. Gage.* New York, House of Field, 1937.

GINGER, RAY, ed., *American Social Thought.* New York, Hill and Wang, 1961.

Godey's Lady's Book, 1852.

GRAY, MILNER, *Package Design.* New York, Studio Publications, 1955.

GREELEY, HORACE, *The Autobiography of Horace Greeley,* New York, E. B. Treat, 1872.

———, et al., *The Great Industries of the United States.* Hartford & Chicago, 1872.

HALE, WILLIAM HARLAN, *Horace Greeley, Voice of the People.* New York, Harper, 1950.

HALES, JOHN G., *A Survey of Boston and Its Vicinity.* Boston, Erza Lincoln, 1821.

HAMPE, EDWARD C., JR., and WITTENBERG, MERLE, *The Lifeline of America.* New York, McGraw-Hill, 1964.

HAMPSON, JOHN, *The English at Table.* London, Collins, 1944.

HANDLIN, OSCAR, *Boston's Immigrants.* Cambridge, Mass., Belknap Press, 1959.

HARPER, WILLIAM HUDSON, and RAVELL, CHARLES H., *Fifty Years of Banking in Chicago: 1857–1907.* Chicago, Merchant's Loan & Trust Company, 1907.

Harper's Encyclopedia of United States History, Vol. 9. New York, Harper, 1905.

CLASS OF 1863 OF HARVARD COLLEGE, *Memoirs,* April 1916 to April 1917. Cambridge, Mass., Harvard University Press, 1917.

HARVARD UNIVERSITY, *Official Register of Harvard University: Harvard University Graduate School of Business Administration, 1963–64.*

Harvard University, 1963–1964, Graduate School of Business Administration. Published by Harvard University.

HAYS, SAMUEL P., *The Response to Industrialism, 1885–1914.* Chicago, University of Chicago Press, 1957.

HERLIHY, ELIZABETH M., et al., *Fifty Years of Boston.* Boston, 1932.

HEROLD, DON, *Humor in Advertising and How To Make It Pay.* New York, McGraw-Hill, 1963.

HIBBEN, PAXTON, *Henry Ward Beecher, An American Portrait.* New York, George H. Doran, 1927.

HOFSTADTER, RICHARD, *The Progressive Movement.* Englewood Cliffs, N. J., Prentice-Hall, 1963.

HOHMAN, ELMO P., *The American Whaleman.* New York, Longmans Green, 1928.

HOLBROOK, STEWART H., *The Age of the Moguls.* New York, Doubleday, 1953.

HOMANS, J. SMITH, *History of Boston from 1630 to 1856.* Boston, F. C. Moore, 1856.

HOWER, RALPH M., *The History of an Advertising Agency: N. W. Ayer & Son at Work, 1869–1939.* Cambridge, Mass., Harvard University Press, 1939.

HULBERT, ARCHER BUTLER, *Forty-Niners.* Boston, Little, Brown, 1931.

JACKSON & CURTIS, Investment Bankers, *Fifty Years of Finance.* Boston, 1929.

JENSEN, OLIVER, *Revolt of American Women,* New York, Harcourt, 1952.

JOHNSON, LAURENCE A., *Over the Counter and on the Shelf: Country Store-keeping in America 1620–1920.* Rutland, Vt., C. E. Tuttle, 1961.

JONES, MALDWYN ALLEN, *American Immigration.* Chicago, University of Chicago Press, 1960.

JOSEPHSON, MATTHEW, *The Robber Barons.* New York, Harcourt, 1934, 1962.

KENNER, S. A., *Utah As It Is.* Salt Lake City, Deseret News, 1904.

KING, MOSES, *Notable New Yorkers 1896–1899.* New York, Bartlett, 1899.

KNOX GELATINE, *Family Album,* Diamond Jubilee Knox Gelatine, Inc.

KYRK, HAZEL AND DAVIS, JOSEPH S., *The American Baking Industry, 1849–1923, As Shown in the Census Reports*. Palo Alto, Calif., Stanford University, 1925.

LAUCK, W. JETT, and SYDENSTRICKER, EDGAR, *Conditions of Labor in American Industries*. New York, Funk & Wagnalls, 1917.

LEBHAR, GODFREY M., *Chain Stores in America, 1859–1962*. New York, Chain Store Publishing Co., 1962.

LEECH, HARPER, and CARROLL, JOHN CHARLES, *Armour and His Times*. New York, Appleton-Century, 1938.

LESCOHIER, DON D., *History of Labor in the United States 1896–1932*. New York, MacMillan, 1935.

LEUCHTENBURG, WILLIAM E., *Perils of Prosperity, 1914–1932*. Chicago, University of Chicago Press, 1958.

LITWACK, LEON, *The American Labor Movement*. Englewood Cliffs, N. J., Prentice-Hall, 1962.

Local Loiterings and Visits in the Vicinity of Boston. Boston, Redding, 1846.

LONGFELLOW, HENRY WADSWORTH, *Longfellow*, in the Laurel Poetry Series. New York, Dell, 1959.

LORD, WALTER, *The Good Years*. New York, Bantam, 1962.

LOVE, ALBERT, and CHILDERS, JAMES SAXON, eds., *Listen to Leaders In Business*. New York, Holt, 1962.

LUNDBERG, FERDINAND, *America's Sixty Families*. New York, Citadel, 1960.

LYON, PETER, *Success Story: The Life and Times of S. S. McClure*. New York, Scribners, 1963.

MAHER, WILLIAM H., *On The Road to Riches, or How to Succeed in Life*. Chicago, F. C. Smedley, 1894.

MARTIN, FREDERICK TOWNSEND, *The Passing of the Idle Rich*. New York, Doubleday, 1911.

MASON, EDWARD S., ed., *The Corporation in Modern Society*. Cambridge, Mass., Harvard University Press, 1961.

McGuffey's Fifth Eclectic Reader. New York, New American Library, 1962.

MEEKER, ARTHUR, *Prairie Avenue*. New York, Knopf, 1949.

MEGOWEN, ROBERT LEE, " 'Educator' in the Cracker and Biscuit Industry in U.S.A. and in Great Britain." New York, Newcomen Society, 1950.

Investor's Reader, "Production Personalities," November 7, 1945.

METRAUX, GUY S., and CROUZET, FRANCOIS, eds., *The Nineteenth Century World*. New York, New American Library, 1963.

Metropolitan Culture Series, *Home-making and House-keeping*. New York, Butterick, 1889.

MILLER, WILLIAM, ed., *Men in Business*. Cambridge, Mass., Harvard University Press, 1952.

MONTAGU, ASHLEY, *Man: His First Million Years*. Cleveland, World, 1957.

MOODY, RICHARD, *The Astor Place Riot*. Bloomington, Ind., Indiana University Press, 1958.

MORISON, SAMUEL ELIOT, ed., *The Development of Harvard University Since the Inauguration of President Eliot, 1869–1929*. Cambridge, Mass., Harvard University Press, 1930.

MORISON, SAMUEL ELIOT, *The Maritime History of Massachusetts 1783–1860.* Boston, Houghton Mifflin, 1961.

MUMFORD, LEWIS, *Sticks and Stones: A Study of American Architecture and Civilization.* New York, Dover, 1961.

Nabisco, March-April issue, 1948, "A Short History of National Biscuit Company." Golden Anniversary Issue.

Nabisco Magazine—1914 to 1945. *Nabisco*—1946 to 1969, publication National Biscuit Co., New York.

NATIONAL BISCUIT COMPANY, "History of the Biscuit," *Nabisco* magazine, 1940–41.

NATIONAL BISCUIT COMPANY, Kansas City, Luncheon and Reception.

NATIONAL BISCUIT COMPANY, Trademark litigation, opinions, orders, injunctions and decrees relating to unfair competition and infringement of trade marks. 1915.

NEWCOMER, MABEL, *The Big Business Executive: The Factors that Made Him, 1900–1950.* New York, Columbia University Press, 1957.

NORRIS, FRANK, *The Pit, A Story of Chicago.* Philadelphia, Curtis Publishing Co., 1902.

NORTHROP, H. D., *The World's Fair as Seen in One Hundred Days.* Philadelphia, Ariel, 1893.

PANSCHAR, WILLIAM G., *Baking in America, Economic Development,* Vol. 1. Evanston, Ill., Northwestern University Press, 1956.

PARRINGTON, VERNON, *Main Currents in American Thought.* New York, Harcourt, 1927–30.

PHILLIPS, WENDELL, *Speeches, Lectures and Addresses.* Boston, Lee & Shepard, 1894.

PIERCE, BESSIE LOUISE, *History of Chicago,* 3 vols. New York, Knopf, 1940.

POUND, ARTHUR, *Industrial America,* Boston, Little, Brown, 1936.

PRESBREY, FRANK, *The History and Development of Advertising.* New York, Doubleday, Doran, 1929.

Printers' Ink, Fifty Years 1888–1938. Printers' Ink Pub. Co., 1938.

Printers' Ink, June 14, 1963. Issue devoted to "Advertising, Today, Yesterday, Tomorrow."

RANDALL, FRANK A., *History of Chicago Buildings.* Urbana, Ill., University of Illinois Press, 1949.

RAUCH, BASIL, *The History of the New Deal.* New York, Capricorn, 1963.

REDMOND, GEORGE F., *Financial Giants of America.* Boston, Stratford, 1922.

RECK, FRANKLIN M., *The Romance of American Transportation.* New York, Thomas Y. Crowell, 1938.

REDLICH, FRITZ, *History of American Business Leaders,* Vol. 1. Ann Arbor, Mich., Edwards Bros., 1940.

REED, EDWARD, ed., *Challenges to Democracy: The Next Ten Years.* New York, Praeger, 1962.

RICKS, JOEL EDWARD, *The Utah State Agricultural College: A History of Fifty Years.* Salt Lake City, Deseret News, 1938.

RIPLEY, WILLIAM Z., *Main Street and Wall Street.* Boston, Little, Brown, 1927.

ROCKEFELLER, JOHN D., Jr., *The Personal Relation in Industry.* New York, Boni and Liveright, 1923.

ROSSITER, WILLIAM S., ed., *Days and Ways in Old Boston.* Boston, R. H. Stearns, 1915.

SANDBURG, CARL, *Chicago Poems.* New York, Henry Holt, 1916.

SHANNON, DAVID A., *The Great Depression.* Englewood Cliffs, N. J., Prentice-Hall, 1960.

SCHIFF, MICHAEL, and MELLMAN, MARTIN, *Financial Management of the Marketing Function.* New York, Financial Executives Research Foundation, 1962.

SCHLESINGER, ARTHUR M., Jr., *The Age of Roosevelt,* Vol. 1, *The Crisis of the Old Order 1919–1933.* Boston, Houghton Mifflin, 1957.

SCHRIFTGIESSER, KARL, *Business Comes of Age: The Story of the Committee for Economic Development and Its Impact upon the Economic Policies of the United States, 1942–1960.* New York, Harper, 1960.

SCHROETER, HARRY F., "Trademarks and Marketing," *The Trademark Reporter,* July 1958.

SEARS, MARIAN V., "The American Businessman," *Business History Review,* Vol. 30, 12/56, No. 4.

SHACKLETON, ROBERT, *The Book of Chicago.* Philadelphia, Penn Publishing, 1920.

SHEAHAN, JAMES W., and UPTON, GEORGE P., *History of the Great Conflagration: Chicago, Its Past, Present and Future.* Chicago, 1871.

SHEEHAN, DONALD H., ed., *This Is America, My Country.* New York, Wise, 1952.

SHEPPARD, RONALD, and NEWTON, EDWARD, *The Story of Bread.* London, Routledge & Kegan Paul, 1957.

SHUMWAY, HARRY IRVING, *Famous Leaders of Industry.* Boston, L. C. Page, 1936.

SLATER, CHARLES C., *Baking in America,* Vol. 2, Evanston, Ill., Northwestern University Press, 1956.

——, *Economic Changes in the Baking Industry,* Evanston, Ill., Northwestern University Press, 1958.

SMALLZRIED, KATHLEEN ANN, *The Everlasting Pleasure.* New York, Appleton-Century-Crofts, 1956.

SMITH, ARTHUR D. HOWDEN, *Men Who Run America.* New York, Bobbs-Merrill, 1935, 1936.

SMITH, EDWARD, *Foods.* London, Henry S. King, 1873.

SMITH, MRS. E. VALE, *History of Newburyport, From the Earliest Settlement of the Country to the Present Time.* Newburyport, 1854.

SMITH, H. ALLEN, *Robert Gair, a Study.* New York, Dial, 1939.

SMITH, RICHARD AUSTIN, *Corporations in Crisis.* New York, Doubleday, 1961.

SMITH, WILSON, ed., *Cities of Our Past and Present.* New York, John Wiley, 1964.

Sketches and Business Directory of Boston and Its Vicinity for 1860 and 1861. Boston, 1860.

Sketches of Somerset. Somerset, Pa., Somerset Sesquicentennial Association, Historical Data Committee, 1954.

Souvenir of the Centennial Exhibition. Hartford, Conn., George D. Curtis, 1877.

STATE STREET TRUST Co., *Old Shipping Days in Boston.* Boston, Yale, 1918.

STEGNER, WALLACE, *Mormon Country.* New York, Duell, Sloan & Pearce, 1942.

STEWART, GEORGE R., *Ordeal by Hunger.* New York, Henry Holt, 1936.

SULLIVAN, MARK, *Our Times: The United States 1900–1925,* Vols. 1, 2, and 3. New York, Scribner's, 1926.

SULLIVAN, MAY KELLOGG, *The Trail of a Sourdough.* Boston, Gorham Press, 1910.

The Sunset Club, Chicago, *Year Books* 1892–93, and 1893–94.

SWANSON, W. W., and ARMSTRONG, P. C., *Wheat.* Toronto, Macmillan, 1930.

WARNER, W. LLOYD, and ABEGGLEN, JAMES, *Big Business Leaders In America.* New York, Atheneum, 1963.

WARSHOW, ROBERT IRVING, *Alexander Hamilton, First American Businessman.* New York, Greenberg, 1931.

WATSON, ALICE, *Food Packaging.* New York, McGraw-Hill.

A Week at the Fair. Chicago, Rand McNally, 1893.

WEISS, EDWARD B., *Merchandising for Tomorrow.* New York, McGraw-Hill, 1961.

———, *The Vanishing Salesman.* New York, McGraw-Hill, 1962.

WHYTE, WILLIAM H., JR., *The Organization Man.* New York, Doubleday, 1957.

WHYTE, WILLIAM H., JR., and the Editors of *Fortune, Is Anybody Listening? How and Why U.S. Business Fumbles When It Talks with Human Beings.* New York, Simon and Schuster, 1952.

WILEY, BELL IRVIN, *The Life of Billy Yank.* New York, Bobbs-Merrill, 1952.

WILSON, EVERETT B., *Vanishing Americana.* New York, Barnes, 1961.

WINKLER, JOHN K., *Incredible Carnegie: The Life of Andrew Carnegie (1835–1919).* New York, Vanguard, 1931.

———, *Morgan the Magnificent.* New York, Vanguard, 1930.

WITTKE, CARL F., *Irish in America.* Baton Rouge, Louisiana State University Press, 1956.

WOLFF, JANET, *What Makes Women Buy.* New York, McGraw-Hill.

WOODHAM-SMITH, CECIL, *The Great Hunger.* New York, New American Library, 1964.

Joint Committee on Ceremonies of the World's Columbian Commission and the World's Columbian Exposition, *Dedicatory and Opening Ceremonies of the World's Columbian Exposition.* Chicago, Stone, Kastler & Painter, 1893.

Utah: A Guide to the State, Compiled by Workers of the Writers' Program of the Work Projects Administration for the State of Utah. New York, Hastings House, 1931.

World's Columbian Exposition, 1893, *Official Catalogue,* Part 14, Woman's Building. Chicago, W. B. Conkey, 1893.

Yale Law Journal, January 1951.

ZIMMERMAN, MAX M., *The Super Market: A Revolution in Distribution.* New York, McGraw-Hill, 1955.

Index

NOTE: Figures in *italics* indicate illustrations.

357

341; education of, 16-17; establishment of NBC, 54-60; last years of, 151-59, 161-65; law practice in Chicago, 19-23, 25-26, 30-33, 39, 112-13, 121, 172; law student in New York City, 18-19; management of NBC by, 66-75, 82, 83, 84-87, 90, 96-98, 103, 104, 108, 109, 112, 125-26, 128, 131-32, 151-58, 161-65, 195, 227, 228, 238-39, 341; marriage of, 20; national advertising initiated by, 89-93; photographs of, *14, 122, 135, 151;* president of the American Biscuit Company, 45; president of NBC, 128; reputation of NBC protected by, 111-12, 113-14, 116, 117, 118; success of, secret of, 134, 151
Green, Esther, 151, 164
Green, Esther Walsh, 20, 36
Green, Honore & Peters (law firm), 33, 53, 79, 112, 173
Green, Jane Ryan, 15, 16
Green, John Henry, 15, 16
Green, Minnie, 20
Green, Nellie, 20
Green, Peters & Babst (law firm), 113, 164
Green Company, Thomas L., 198
Greenwich, Connecticut, 151, 166
Griffin & Sons, Ltd., 320
Gristede Brothers, 140
Groton, Massachusetts, 17

Hale, Barbara, 142
Hanks, B. G., 157
Hanna, Howard M., Sr., 185
Hanna, Mark A., 185, 215
Hardtack, 27, 30
Harpers Ferry, West Virginia, 16
Harriman, Joseph, 182
Harrison, Carter, 21
Harvard College, 16, 17
Harvard Graduate School of Business Administration, 263-66, 330
Hazen, James W., 54, 56, 102, 164
Health fads, 207-08

Hetfield & Ducker, 43
Hills Brothers, 298
Hine, Francis L., 165, 185, 196
Hippodromes, 144
Holbrook, Stewart H., 38, 39, 183
Holland Rusk Company, 201
Holmes & Coutts Company, 43, 106
Holt, C. L., 96, 156
Home Insurance Company Building, Chicago, 58, 173
Honore, Lockwood, 33, 112, 121
Hoover, Herbert C., 190
Horse-drawn delivery vehicles, 228-29
Howe, W. B., 74
Howe & Davidson Company, 74, 80-81, 84
Hunter, Robert, 157-58

Ice cream cones, 203-04
Illinois Trust & Savings Bank, Chicago, 54
Immigrants, 30, 127, 326
Ince, Thomas H., 142
Industrial organization, 41-42
Industrial revolution, 30, 152
Industries Nabisco Cristal, S. A., 320
Inflation, 191
Inter-Ocean Publishing Company, 37
International Workers of the World (IWW), 161
Interstate Bakery Corporation, 295 n.
Interstate Commerce Commission, 232
Investor's Reader, 251, 278, 305
Isselhardt, Louis, 154
Iten Biscuit Company, 271

Jaeger-Schmidt, André, 123
Jeritza, Mme. Maria, 226
Jenney, William LeBaron, 58
Jinjer Wayfer, 103
Johnson, Andrew, 18
Jones Brothers Tea Company, 140
Jonnies, 116
Josephson, Matthew, 181

Kansas City, Missouri, 129-31